THE W ELEANOR GILLEN STORY

AS TOLD BY THEIR CHILDREN

Virginia Gillen Poole and
Sherry Gillen Butcher Belmonte

outskirts
press

Sylvia.
So fun to know you. Enjoy our family story!
Love, Cathy

Sylvia,
I hope you will
enjoy our family story.
I treasure our friendship.
♡ Sherry

To Walter and Eleanor, our beloved parents,
who raised us and are missed beyond measure.

cover story:
   Our parents loved to dance
   mom was raised in Toledo,
      thus, the Toledo skyline.
   Dad was raised on a farm
      20 mi. west of Toledo.

Hey Sylvia,
Our HS activities were
memorable enough to include
you in my story (p.171)! they
were great times. Glad to know
things are going well for you.
      Mom

TABLE OF CONTENTS

Part Four: Memories

Part Five: Our Heritage
1719 – 1946

FOREWORD

"I liked the book especially because it didn't try to make everyone into a saint. You pointed out the human flaws as well as the virtues.

This is a slice of Americana that no longer exists. This is a real gift for future generations, who will read this and laugh and really get to know their forebearers."

Anne Smith

PREFACE

By Virginia "Ginger" Gillen Poole

LITTLE DID I know how challenging writing our family story would be. This effort began as a seemingly easy project with our brother and sisters all providing input and encouragement.

As I began discussing the project with friends, it expanded into a much larger project. Upon review of the initial draft in May 2020, I was asked to expand on the stories and include more details of our family life. I was also encouraged to self-publish our story. I incorporated both recommendations and have been following Outskirts Press publishing guidelines.

I spent 36 years as a civilian with the U.S. Navy, primarily as a budget and program analyst that required writing technical documents in government lingo. Luckily, I was able to enlist the assistance of Sherry Belmonte, my youngest sister, as a co-author. Readers will witness Sherry's writing talent throughout the book. It is interesting to note that I am the youngest of the four oldest children, and Sherry is the youngest of the four youngest children. This became very helpful in piecing together the story.

Sherry and I are two of eight children born within 10 years of each other and raised together in the same house with the same parents. Even being born this closely together, the four oldest girls had a very different childhood than the youngest four children. Our annual family gatherings since 2018 allowed most everyone to attend. The stories told by the oldest and youngest children seemed like we were from two different families. This revelation encouraged us to collect our family memories and records and write the story of our family while most of us are still living. Our youngest brother Gary died in 1975 from complications associated with muscular dystrophy.

We had a wealth of information from our mother's records that helped us clarify dates and events when we had questions. Eleanor our "Mom" was the family historian and maintained meticulous records of both sides of the family throughout her life. My oldest sister Irene made an album of our father's side of the family. My second oldest sister Cathy made an album of our mother's side of the family. My third oldest sister Noreen and her husband used Family Tree Maker to compile the information they had from archives and notes from Eleanor to create a family tree that provided the first detailed ancestry records of our family. Noreen also interviewed our aunt Sister Lorenzo and cousins for further insight into our family history. Brother Norm reviewed and edited our final book drafts and maintained our backup files.

All siblings contributed family memories, wrote individual family stories, reviewed, and consolidated family records, researched missing military and ancestry records, and provided photographs.

Several unexpected problems were encountered, the first being how to write a book with seven people. I didn't have a problem with conflicting information as much as I had a problem with the different writing styles, vernacular, and changing people's wording. When we all decided the book had to be from the author's perspective, we decided, the author could recommend and make changes. Sherry and I had good communication with our brother and sisters throughout the process, and this became a non-problem. Another problem was deciding the focus of the story we wanted to tell – our ancestors, our parents, or the children. We decided it would be our parents' story since we could include both our ancestors and children.

The book title and heritage research were also challenging. We changed the title of the book at least six times to try and depict our family story. We have the Gillen family ancestry dating back to 1719. All our great-grandparents immigrated to America from Germany. It was also extremely challenging to present our ancestry and their stories to make the book interesting to the reader.

Several friends were instrumental in urging me to continue and publish the book:

Lisa Coberly is a longtime friend of Sherry's and the family and an avid genealogist and historian in her spare time. She researched specific family homes and ancestors for the book. Lisa introduced Sherry and me to the Lenawee Historical Society Museum Archives, the County Register of Deeds Office, and the Historical Archives, where the curators educated and assisted us in our research. Sherry used this indoctrination to continue research of our ancestors for the book.

Anne Smith is a longtime "Navy wife" friend and a professional journalist who also was the founding editor of *CUA Magazine* at The Catholic University of America.

Linda Ely is a longtime neighbor who once wrote copy for a national mail order catalog. She is currently a proofreader for the John Wasowicz legal mystery book series.

The late Susan Weaver was a bridge partner who suggested self-publishing.

The book provides a biographical and autobiographical narrative of past and present family members that future generations can enjoy and build upon.

PART ONE
OUR PARENTS
1916 – 1946
Their Early Years

Walter in Chicago 1943

Chapter 1

❧

WALTER'S EARLY LIFE

By Virginia "Ginger" Gillen Poole and Norman "Norm" Gillen

Walter Andrew Gillen
Our Father

WALTER'S FATHER, PETER John Gillen, Jr., was born in Rhinebrice, Germany, on October 1, 1872. Peter Jr. was the second oldest of nine children: Magdalina (Lena), Peter, Jr., Mary Ann (Maria), Catherine (Kate), John, Anthony (Tone), Mariam Elizabeth, Francis (Frank), and Rose Anna.

Walter's mother, Margaretha Malburg, was born in Ogden Township, now Blissfield, Michigan, on July 1, 1877, and was the oldest of six children: Margaretha, Robert, Ann, Joseph, Rose, and Frederick. Many of these 15 aunts and uncles lived within five miles.

Peter Jr. and Margaretha, often called Maggie or Mag, were married on February 1, 1898, in Caraghar, now Assumption, Ohio. They had nine children born and raised on the family farm in Assumption: Cecilia (Celee), Edward (Eddie), Louis (Louie, later McGrory), Martin, Arnold (Spike), Leslie (Poodle), Marcella (Sally), Cletus (Charlie), and **Walter**

(Walt). His oldest sister, Cecilia, was 17 when Walter was born on June 28, 1916. She left home the next year to become a Dominican nun. When Walter was born, his father was 44 and his mother was two days shy of her 39th birthday.

The 120-acre farm was 20 miles west of Toledo, Ohio, and one mile east of Assumption on Central Avenue, U.S. Route 20. Walter's Grandfather Peter Sr. established the farm in 1876 that passed onto Peter Jr. Walter's father continued farming and concerned himself with the chores to be done about the barn. He fed and cared for horses, cows, and pigs. He and the older boys milked the cows each morning and night. In the spring they readied the fields for planting corn, wheat, and oats by plowing and disking. In the fall the crops were harvested and stored or sold. Since there wasn't weed killer in those days, busy work for the kids in the summer was to hoe the rows of corn to keep the weeds out.

Walter grew up in a happy family. The family always ate breakfast, dinner, and supper together. They had plenty of everything to eat and were never concerned about being wasteful because the table scraps were used to feed the dog, "Shep," and the cats.

The family worked hard, and they also took time to relax. Walter's father went into Metamora to have a beer daily during the week after the farm chores were done, a practice Walter continued when he was old enough to drink. The family attended St. Mary's of the Assumption, in Assumption. After Sunday morning mass, the day was set aside for visiting and relaxing, whether in summer or winter.

Walter's aunts and uncles lived in many neighboring areas around northern Ohio and just over the Michigan border. He had 56 first cousins and many playmates. They hooked up their sleigh to go for rides with sleigh bells tied to the horses. They often visited this way, even traveling as far as their Grandma Malburg's house five miles away in Ogden Township. Grandma Malburg was Walter's only living grandparent and died when he was 10.

Walter's Family 1942

Walter watched parades, and went to county fairs, the local corn festival, and church festivities. In the summer, the family and company played croquet, ran races, and played long ball, hide-and-seek, tag, and other games.

Wintertime fun was playing in the snow, giving each other snow rides, and making snowmen. They cracked hickory nuts, popped popping corn, and made ice cream. The special feature of a Sunday afternoon was the "family project" of making homemade ice cream with ice cakes cut and hauled in a gunny sack from Koelch's Pond near Metamora. Their father pounded the ice fine until the pieces fit around the container in the freezer while their mother made the mixture poured into the container. After the mixture was poured into the outer bucket packed with ice, it was time for all the kids to take turns turning the freezer. When it became too hard to turn, their father took over until the mixture was stiff and ready to eat, and their mother brought out the sauce dishes. They would all say, "Nothing is quite so good as homemade ice cream."

Walter was 5 years old when his father bought his first car - a 1921 Willy's Overland Aster, most likely built in Toledo. Toledo was second only to Detroit, Michigan, in car manufacturing at the time. His father learned how to drive and took the family for rides, which they all loved except their mother. She was hesitant to go for a ride but said she would if he didn't exceed 20 miles per hour. The speed limit at the time was 30 miles per hour.

Walter attended Assumption School and received good grades. With only one sister at home and being the youngest child, Walter had to help his mother with housework. He had daily chores outside but was not allowed to help with farming. When he completed 10th grade, he rebelled against having to do housework and he was allowed to begin helping with the farm work. Like the older boys in the family, his father bought him his first car in 1934 when he was 18.

Walter worked at Magnesium Fabricators in Adrian, Michigan, from January 1941 to April 1942. On March 19, 1942, he enlisted in the U.S. Navy and entered active service on April 13, 1942. The United States entered World War II in the European Theater on December 11, 1941, after the attack on Pearl Harbor on December 7, 1941. Walter likely went to the Great Lakes Naval Training Station outside Chicago, Illinois, for boot camp after enlisting at the Naval Recruiting Station in Detroit.

Walter was 25 when he began his military service. He started with the rating of Seaman Apprentice (AS) and completed boot camp as Fireman 3rd Class (F3c). After he was trained to repair and maintain aircraft engines, he became an Aviation Machinist's Mate (AMM). He began as an Aviation Machinist's Mate, 3rd Class (AMM3c), became an Aviation Machinist's Mate, 2nd Class (AMM2c), and achieved the highest rank, Aviation Machinist's Mate, 1st Class (AMM1c).

One of Walter's photographs places him in Chicago in late 1943. Chicago is an hour south of Great Lakes Naval Training Station. Another photo shows Walter in Key West in early 1945. Son Norm places Walter's duty stations in chronological order based on the limited information available and guesswork found on Walter's discharge paper, a DD-214 equivalent.

ComFLAIR - Commander, Fleet Air Wing, Naval Air Station (NAS), Quonset Point, Rhode Island. Note: Fleet Air Wing 9 (FAW-9) relocated from Quonset Point to NAS, New York, on August 24, 1943.

Hedron 7 - Headquarters Squadron 7, Naval Air Facility (NAF), Argentia, Newfoundland Fleet Air Wing 7 (FAW-7) relocated to Plymouth, England, on August 21, 1943.

FLAIRWING 12 - Hedron 12 Detachment, Fleet Air Wing 12 (FAW-12), Headquarters Squadron 12 Detachment NAS, Key West, Boca Chica, Florida. FAW-12 relocated to NAS Miami, Florida, on September 15, 1943. FAW-12 returned to Key West in 1945 and was disestablished on July 14, 1945.

NTS, NAS - Naval Training School (NTS), Naval Air Station (NAS), Astoria, Oregon, (postcard dated May 31, 1945). Note: One course taught at NTS was "Line Maintenance."

RecBks - Receiving Barracks, Naval Air Facility (NAF) or Naval Air Auxiliary Facility (NAAF), Treasure Island, San Francisco, California.

FLAIRWING 8 TADCEN - Hedron Fleet Air Wing 8 (FAW-8), U.S. Naval Training and Distribution Center (TADCEN), Shoemaker, California (postcard dated August 31, 1945). Camp Shoemaker is outside Pleasanton, California, and was designed to handle naval personnel on their way to, or returning from, the Pacific Theater.

Walter completed his service on January 4, 1946, eight months after the Victory in Europe (VE Day) on May 8, 1945, and four months after Victory in Japan (VJ Day) on August 15, 1945. He was a Navy World War II veteran and became a charter member and lifelong member of

Catholic War Veterans of Assumption, Ohio Post Number 306.

Walter, "Walt" to his friends, returned to Assumption, Ohio, after his navy enlistment to help run the family farm. After finishing a day of farming, and supper was over, he washed up, changed into clean clothes, and went out for the evening. When he went into town for a drink, he picked up friends and cousins along the way to share the evening. He could also be found frequently stopping at a brother or sister's home for a visit and was often seen with a niece or nephew in his arms. He also made trips to Detroit to visit his oldest sister, Dominican Sister Lorenzo, or to spend time at one of the many lakes in southern Michigan.

Walter and his best friend Bernard "Dudley" Lumbrezer also drove the 20 miles into Toledo to dance halls for the evening where there was square dancing or round dances. On Saturday, April 6, 1946, Walter went alone to the Odd Fellows Hall in Toledo where Eleanor Bucklew immediately caught his attention. Walter asked Eleanor for the next round dance before he had to leave, and they agreed to meet again the next Saturday at the Odd Fellows Hall.

On the next Saturday Dudley went with Walter to the Odd Fellows Hall and met Eleanor. He continued to see Eleanor, and Dudley often joined them in the evening, with or without a date.

Walter proposed to Eleanor on July 6, 1946, and she said, "Yes." Walter took her to the 7 a.m. mass with him the next day at St. Mary's of the Assumption. They also began attending marriage instructions at the Blessed Sacrament Church in Toledo where they planned to be married on November 23, 1946. Walter was 30 when he married Eleanor and won a longtime bet with Dudley that he wouldn't marry before age 30. Eleanor was 27. In October, Walter found a farm for them to rent near Metamora, Ohio, after the wedding not far from his parent's home.

Chapter 2

ELEANOR'S EARLY LIFE

By Sherry Gillen Butcher Belmonte

Eleanor Ruth Gutzmer Bucklew
Our Mother

Eleanor Gutzmer 1945

Harold Gutzmer 1946

ELEANOR'S FATHER GUSTAVE Charles Gutzmer was born in Rochester, New York, on January 8, 1884, and was the oldest of seven children. His siblings were Bertha, Alma, Eleanor (stillborn), Lillian (Lil), William (Will), and Della. He also had four older half-brothers and sisters: Mary, Henry, Charles, and Emma.

Eleanor's mother, Martha Marguerite Henrietta (Beneke) was born in Bremen, Germany, on March 17, 1881, and was the third oldest of six children. Her siblings were Herman (Tom), Reinhardt (Reinie), Alexander (Alex), Catherine (Bep), and Marguerite, who lived only for three months.

As this family grew, Eleanor had 18 aunts and uncles and 20 cousins in the Toledo area, and aunts, uncles, and cousins living in New York.

Gustave and Martha were married on January 18, 1916, in Pasadena, California, and had two children: **Eleanor,** and Harold, 18 months younger. Eleanor was born on November 24, 1918, two weeks after the Armistice, now celebrated as Veteran's Day, was signed on November 11, 1918, to end World War I. When Eleanor was born her father was 34 years old and an acetylene welder at Willys-Overland Motor Company in Toledo. Her mother, 37, was a seamstress and fashion designer of women's clothes.

Eleanor's parents owned a duplex at 3001-3003 Albion Street in west Toledo, Ohio, during most of Eleanor's childhood years. The family lived downstairs and ran a boarding house upstairs. Their home had a combination gas and wood-burning kitchen stove, a gas heater in the dining room, and a coal-burning stove in the living room. Around 1930 they excavated a room under the house and installed a furnace. The home always had electricity and an electric wringer washing machine.

The family liked to travel. They went to New York every summer to visit Martha's family. They went on the New York Central Railway from Union Depot and boarded the train with a berth for the overnight trip.

The longest trip they took by train was to the home of Uncle Tom and Aunt Catherine "Bep" in Greenwood Lake, New York, 38 miles from New York City.

The year 1929 was a big one for Eleanor. Every summer the family went to Put-In-Bay Island on Lake Erie for the Fourth of July. Eleanor was 10 years old when her mother took a job at the hotel there for the entire summer. Their father alternated taking Eleanor and Harold to the hotel so they could take turns spending two weeks at a time on the island with her. This was the year when the family also bought their first radio. Her favorite items in the house were the piano and the dining room buffet. This buffet is still in the family today. Later in the year, her father fell from a 15-foot scaffold at work smashing every bone in his left ankle and splitting the femur in his right leg. When he couldn't return to his job, her parents opened a store at their home.

Eleanor attended Glenwood Elementary School and walked one mile to get there. When she attended Scott High School four miles away, she walked and roller-skated to school with her friends and classmates. She had a busy, fun-loving childhood. She and her brother Harold were very close. They played dominoes, jacks, and chess. They went swimming, roller-skating, ice skating, sledding, bicycling, and fishing. They loved going to the movies for 5 cents. When Eleanor was older, she played tennis and was on a bowling team.

Eleanor's family owned a Hupmobile, however, most of their travel was done by public transportation. When she went fishing with her father, they rented a rowboat and took it to Maumee Bay. She swam at Willy's Park and Walbridge Park. Walbridge Park also had an amusement park and a zoo. The amusement park burned down in the 1940s. The parks were close enough that Eleanor and Harold often rode their bikes to get there.

Eleanor's Grandpa and Grandma Gutzmer lived in south Toledo. The family took a streetcar to the Long Belt station on the Toledo "belt" line and then transferred to the Nebraska Line to visit them. Her Grandma Johanna died when she was 2-years old, and her grandpa August died when she was 16.

Eleanor's mother was involved in spiritualism and was the medium for weekly seances. When Eleanor and Harold were little, they were afraid of these meetings. One time when they were in a bed together, huddling under the blankets, Eleanor saw a hazy, ghostly form materialize on the staircase. She also told stories of seeing a trumpet, a prop of sorts, floating in the air. During that time, writing was done on slates with chalk. There is a slate in our family possessions with very tiny writing on it foretelling someone's good fortune that is soon to come to them. This message was written during one of the seances.

As a child, Eleanor began attending the neighborhood Central Methodist Episcopal church. One day when she was 4 years old, she told her mother that she wanted to go to a church. Her mother walked her down the street to the local church and left her there, assuming she would come home immediately. Eleanor apparently loved it and continued attending for years, staying active at the church throughout her 20s. She taught Sunday school classes and was the secretary for the primary department during her teens.

Eleanor was a senior in high school when she met Arnold Bucklew at a church picnic. They began dating and Arnold taught her how to drive a car. Eleanor graduated from Scott High School on June 5, 1936, and was hired by Owens-Illinois Glass Company soon after as a stenographer, file clerk, and secretary. Eleanor bought her first car, a Ford, in 1937. That same year, Harold graduated from Scott High School and enlisted in the U.S. Navy Reserve.

Eleanor and Arnold's relationship flourished, and they were married by the justice of the peace on February 2, 1938. She was 19. Arnold was 29, a chauffeur with the Red Cab Company, and a divorcee. Arnold was raised in Toledo and was the youngest of five children. He had three brothers and one sister and attended Central Methodist Episcopal Church. He graduated from Scott High School in 1928. Throughout high school, he was a tenor in the Glee Club and then in the Orpheus Club of Toledo throughout his adult life. During their first summer together, Eleanor and Arnold traveled to Cedar Point Amusement Park in Sandusky, Ohio, with family and friends; Marblehead Lighthouse in Port Clinton, Ohio; Clearwater Lake, Indiana; and Detroit to visit Arnold's family.

On February 3, 1939, Eleanor's father died of a heart attack. Later that summer, she and Arnold traveled to Gettysburg, Pennsylvania; Washington D.C.; Ocean City, New Jersey; Valley Forge, Pennsylvania; and Niagara Falls, New York. During this year Eleanor was pregnant and they were in a car accident. She lost the baby and broke her pelvic bone. She had a life-long ache in her hips from this injury.

The following February, Arnold became ill. He was diabetic and contracted pneumonia and convalesced at his mother's home in Toledo. At the same time, Eleanor was staying at her mother's home in Toledo recovering from a miscarriage. Arnold never recovered and died at age 31 on February 18, 1940.

During the summer of 1940, Eleanor had a house built at 1815 Brame Place in Toledo and continued to work at Owens-Illinois Glass Company. She joined a bowling team and took art classes. Late in the summer, she went on a road trip with her mother and a couple of their close family friends. They went to West Virginia; Virginia Beach; Roanoke, Virginia; North Carolina, and Kentucky. Eleanor and her mother and friends continued to go to Cedar Point, Ohio, in the summers. Eleanor lived in her house and enjoyed her classes, activities, and friends for the next six years before her mother encouraged her to start dating again.

After bowling on Tuesday, March 19, 1946, Eleanor went square dancing with several friends for the first time at the Trianon Dance Hall in Toledo. Eleanor and one of her girlfriends had a date for the next night with two sailors from Pennsylvania. The two couples went to Valentine's Theater to see *Sailor Takes a Wife* and then went dancing in the Rainbow Room. Eleanor and her girlfriends continued going to the Trianon on Tuesday evenings. On Saturday, April 6, 1946, Eleanor went with her mother to the Odd Fellows Hall on Sylvania Avenue where her uncle Will worked as a ticket taker. Eleanor met Walt Gillen after the intermission, and he asked her for the next round dance.

Eleanor and her girlfriends continued going to the Trianon on Tuesdays, and Walt and his friend, Dudley, started going to the Trianon after the intermission. Eleanor began dating only Walt by the end of the month and continued to see him on Tuesdays and weekends. During the week Walt always arrived late in the evening because he was a farmer. After Walt and Dudley put in a full day's work at the farm and ate supper, they had to get cleaned up and drive the 20 miles into Toledo. On April 28, Eleanor's mother told Walt about Eleanor being a widow. The next weekend they told each other their life histories.

Eleanor wrote a diary during their courtship that is filled with nothing but fun times – dancing, going for a drink, eating out, visiting with family and friends, swimming, going to a movie, and taking short trips. On Memorial Day, Walt took Eleanor to the family farm. She met his mother and father and had a tour of the farm and the daisy field in the woods. They continued to travel back and forth between the city and the country, and she enjoyed the many new experiences. In June, Eleanor saw the beet field and picked daisies in the woods. She had her first lesson in milking a cow. She watched the men, mostly Walt, Dudley, and Leslie, working in the field loading hay onto the wagon. Eleanor rode with them on the wagon for two loads and drove the horses.

On July 1st Eleanor's mother and Harold met Walt's family at the farm. Eleanor also began helping on the farm in July. While watching the wheat harvest, she rode on the tractor with Walt and Leslie pulling the binder to cut the wheat. After the wheat was cut, she helped bundle up the wheat shocks. This kept the grain heads off the ground to allow the seeds to dry before they were threshed. Corn was harvested in a similar manner before shucking the kernels. Soybeans and beets were harvested by pulling up the whole plant.

On another day she rode with Leslie to Richfield Center to have grain ground for feed. In September she watched the silo being filled with corn silage using the grain elevator. In October she went hickory nutting with Walt. They were thrilled to get a full bushel of shucked nuts from trees in the woods.

Eleanor continued to help on the farm. She helped Walt's mother plant a garden. She painted the sign for the barn and a couple of barn windows. Later she painted the name on the mailbox. She helped mend and wash clothes, and feed and water the chickens. She learned how to can fruits and vegetables and make soap. She also took fresh water to the men working in the field.

After Walt proposed on July 6, 1946, they drove to Metamora to celebrate and began making wedding plans and preparations for their new life together. At 7 a.m. they attended mass together at St. Mary's of the Assumption. Eleanor was raised Methodist and normally attended Central Methodist Episcopal Church in Toledo. She took instructions to convert to Catholicism at the Blessed Sacrament Church in Toledo where she and Walt planned to marry. Eleanor was Baptized on September 7, 1946, and made her First Communion the next day. For her first communion, Walt gave Eleanor a statue of the Virgin Mary, and his family gave her a sick call set in the shape of a crucifix that Ginger has today. Eleanor's mother gave her a rosary, Mr. and Mrs. McMahon gave her a leather-bound Roman Missal, and Joyce and Ray gave her a linen handkerchief.

Eleanor's last day of work at Owens-Illinois was October 31. Her co-workers had a party for her and gave her a 30-inch mirror and a 22-carat, gold-edge cake set. On November 18, she received her 10-year pin at the Owens-Illinois Service Awards Dinner at the Commodore Perry Hotel in Toledo. November continued to be a busy time for final wedding preparations.

Eleanor was given a bridal shower by her mother in Toledo at Mrs. Braun's house. All their relatives were invited plus four close friends, Walt's mother, and Aunt Rose Malburg. The relatives came for the lunch, the friends came for dinner, and Harold and Walt's family came later in the evening.

Eleanor's Aunt Ethel Gutzmer and family friend Beulah Trautwein gave them some furniture that Walt and Eleanor picked up before they went into Metamora to buy a bedroom set and look for a topcoat for Walt. Eleanor and her mother visited the reception hall at St. Mary's of the Assumption and ordered flowers on their way home to Toledo. Finally, their big day arrived.

Walt and Eleanor were married on November 23, 1946, at Blessed Sacrament Church in Toledo. After the wedding, they spent the afternoon at Eleanor's mother's home, where her mother made the groom and best man take naps separate from the bride and maid of honor. The reception was held later in the day at the Gillen family church, St. Mary's of the Assumption in Assumption.

Walt and Eleanor began their honeymoon with a visit to his oldest sister, Sister Lorenzo, in Grosse Pointe, Michigan, and spent the night in a hotel in Detroit. They continued their honeymoon trip to Sault Saint Marie, Michigan; Green Bay, Wisconsin; and Chicago, Illinois, before returning to Assumption to begin their new lives.

PART TWO
WALTER AND ELEANOR'S MARRIAGE

1946 – 1976

The growing family and
family life
in Ohio and Michigan

Walter and Eleanor Gillen 1946

Chapter 3

FARM LIFE IN OHIO

By Irene Gillen Snider, Catherine "Cathy" Gillen Osborn,
Noreen Gillen Litchard, and Virginia "Ginger" Gillen Poole

1946 – 1959

WALTER AND ELEANOR'S early married life continues as noted in Eleanor's journals and records, and memories of the four oldest girls.

Soon after Walter (later Dad) and Eleanor (later Mom) were married in November 1946, Walter left to attend agriculture school and learn the latest farming techniques. While Eleanor's new husband was away at school, she stayed on the Gillen farm in Assumption, Ohio, to learn about being a farmer's wife from her new in-laws and the Gillen relatives that lived nearby. Eleanor was eager to learn, and everyone was very helpful in teaching her.

The next year was filled with many events. Walter completed agriculture school and the newlyweds began their new life together. Walter and Eleanor moved into their first home near Metamora, Ohio. Walter's brother Arnold or "Spike" lived just down the road with his wife Rose and their children Kenny and Harvey. As a new couple, Walter and Eleanor spent much of their free time visiting Spike and Rose. They also made a couple of trips to Grosse Point, Michigan, to visit Sister Lorenzo.

This same year, Walter and Eleanor's family began with the birth of Irene Martha on August 3, 1947. Eleanor's mother married George Wood on July 27. Eleanor's brother Harold married George Wood's daughter Pearl on August 22. Eleanor was very close to her brother and gave Harold her diamond ring from Arnold, her first husband, for Pearl's engagement ring. When she married Walter, she gave Harold her house and car.

Walter and Eleanor's family grew with three more children born while they were living in their first home. Catherine "Cathy" Ann was born on January 20, 1949. Velma Jean was born at home on November 14, 1949. She died on November 15. Walter and Eleanor went to the hospital when Eleanor was in labor with Velma and was sent home by the hospital the same day, saying they were too early. Velma was born that night at home. They returned to the hospital soon after the baby was born, but she didn't survive. Eleanor always said she believed if she could have stayed overnight in the hospital, Velma would have survived. Noreen Margaret was born the following year on November 24, 1950, Eleanor's birthday.

Grandma Gillen passed away from bladder cancer on April 27, 1950, and Grandpa Gillen passed away as the result of a car accident on August 15 of the same year. Soon after, Walter and Eleanor moved to the P. J. Gillen and Sons family farm. Walter and his brother, Leslie "Poodle", bought the farm in 1951 where their remaining five children were born: Virginia "Ginger" Ruth on December 13, 1951, Linda Marie on September 12, 1953, Norman Paul on October 3, 1956, and twins Gary Martin and Sherry Jean on December 21, 1957.

When Linda was born, Mom had a black eye from the oil stove heater door hitting her. Mom was huge when she was pregnant with Norman, the long-awaited boy in the family. The five older girls remember when her water broke with Norman and again when the twins were on the way. Mom didn't know she was having twins and wondered how one baby could kick so much at one time. After Gary was born, the doctors told her there was another one coming. They didn't see Sherry hidden behind Gary earlier in the sonograms. Mom suggested some names for the twins and asked the girls what names they liked. None of the names rhymed, and Ginger thought that they should. When Mom had a new baby, either cousin Wilma or cousin Jeanette Gedert came from Toledo, Ohio, to help her at the house. They loved playing with the babies. Wilma said, "There were always one or two around, they were so cute. With the older kids, we played a lot of croquet outside at both our homes. We all had big yards. We also played red light and green light. Inside, we played cards – Old Maid, rummy, and Button Button."

Dad went to work every day at Blissfield Products in Blissfield, Michigan. Cathy thought he drove miles and miles to far-away Michigan. Many years later, she learned that Blissfield was just the other side of Metamora, about five miles to the north - an amazing discovery. Dad also worked on the farm with his brother Leslie, who went by his nickname "Poodle," who lived in the farmhouse with our family.

Life on the farm was busy. By the time we woke up, Dad and Poodle were at work. We were awakened, mostly by Mom singing "Good morning Merry sunshine! How do you wake so soon?" Mom had the table set for breakfast and was cooking meals on the stove for the day when we were dressed and ready for breakfast.

Front of Ohio Farmhouse

Back of Ohio Farmhouse

THE WALTER AND ELEANOR GILLEN STORY

The farmhouse was about 50 feet from Central Avenue, U.S. 20, a major highway, and the property crossed the highway. The rooms in the farmhouse were big and included the washroom inside the kitchen door, kitchen, pantry, bathroom, dining room, living room, bedrooms, and basement. Old rugs and newspapers were used as padding under the large area rugs. We listened to the semi-trucks going by the house at night. Cathy, Noreen, and Ginger slept three across in the bedroom at the top of the stairs. There were two more bedrooms upstairs and one downstairs off the living room or parlor. The twin's cribs were in Mom's and Dad's bedroom on the main floor. We had a large playroom off the living room filled with toys. Ginger remembers spending many hours playing there.

In 1953 three or four of the girls were being rowdy on a bed while Mom was wallpapering the room. She told them to settle down, but they didn't. She threw the wallpaper brush and it hit 4-year-old Cathy in the face. She ended up with a black eye. Mom gave her many hugs, and they napped together that day. They had a close relationship with each other after that day. Noreen remembers Mom cleaning wallpaper in the playroom using putty. Now it's called "Silly Putty."

We had indoor plumbing, but we had to use a hand pump outside the kitchen door for drinking water. The water in the house was pumped in from the cistern in the basement. After it was heated on the stove it was used for washing dishes, bathing, the toilet, and cleaning. There was also a functional outhouse by the chicken coop. The coal room in the basement is where Grandpa Gillen kept the batteries charged for the electricity in the house. A furnace in the basement near the fold-out cellar doors was used to heat the house.

The telephone was on a party line with several houses in the area being on the same phone line. Anyone on the line could pick up the headset and listen to a neighbor's conversation. At one time our phone number was two long rings and one short ring. After that, there was a four-digit number. Ours was 2634.

Our family was the last one in the area to get a black and white television in 1958. We could get two channels out of Toledo, ABC 11, and CBS 13. Noreen and Ginger stood in the kitchen door and looked diagonally through the dining room to watch the television in the living room. Mom tied them to the cupboards in the pantry just off the kitchen so they would finish the dishes. The rope was very long but just short enough so they couldn't get to the dining room doorway where they would be able to watch television.

We had a stove and refrigerator. Mom and Dad usually shopped for groceries in nearby Metamora at Kroger's. Eggs and milk were produced on the farm, and we churned butter. Dad had hogs and steers slaughtered when they were needed. The butcher shop cut, packaged, and stored the meat at the Locker in Assumption which we could easily access. Popcorn was stored in the granary on corn cobs ready to be shelled and popped.

We all helped with the chores. Mom made a large chore chart and changed the chores each week for each child. At the end of the week, she put colored stars on the chart to show how well we did. Gold was the best. We had fun playing together, but we had to finish our chores first.

We had a large fruit and vegetable garden with a row of raspberry bushes at the edge to screen the garden from the house. The older girls picked the baby carrots, washed them at the hand pump, and ate them until they got caught. There was also a huge grape vine on the front porch with purple grapes.

The four oldest girls learned how to can fruits and vegetables and took turns helping make butter. Mom made ice cream, which we loved. Many years later, we learned the ice cream was really a "Betty Crocker" Bavarian cream-type dessert made in ice cube trays.

Mom did laundry with a wash tub, a wringer, and a rinse tub. In the summer she hung the laundry outside on a clothesline to dry. In the winter Dad strung clotheslines in the living room, and we played hide-and-seek among the clothes until we got caught.

Mealtime chores included learning to cook, setting and clearing the table, and doing the dishes. Washing, drying, and putting the dishes away were all separate tasks, as was sweeping the floor after every meal. Irene asked for her own broom and mop for Christmas one year. The water for dishes was heated on the kitchen stove and carried into the pantry and poured into dish pans. On occasion one of us would spill or drop the full dish pan of water either going in or out of the pantry.

On Saturday afternoon, Dad and Poodle caught three chickens, cut off their heads, and let them flop around in the yard until they were dead. Mom then dipped the chickens into a pail of hot water and then plucked out the feathers. Sometimes we would help pull out the feathers. Then she lit a kerosene lamp to burn off the "pin" feathers. Mom made home-made noodles every Saturday. She rolled the dough into rounds and laid them out on the kitchen table to dry before she cut them into small noodles, like "Campbell's Soup" noodles.

We went to church at St. Mary's of Assumption on Sundays and Holy Days when mass was still said in Latin. We used Spoolies button curlers and flexible rubber pin curl rollers in our hair the night before church and special occasions. For church Dad wore a suit, Mom wore a dress and hat or veil, and the girls wore their best dresses and a Sunday hat. The boys were too little to go to church when we lived in Ohio. In 1954 Grandma Wood made matching Easter dresses for the five oldest girls. We colored Easter eggs on Saturday. Dad hid our Easter baskets after we went to bed for us to find in the morning, and Mom hid a small gift in our slippers for us to find in the morning.

We celebrated other holidays and events as well. We all played April Fool's Day tricks. We had fancy dresses for the May Pole dance and celebration on May Day, May 1st. Dad, a charter member of the Catholic War Veterans (CWV) of Assumption, wore his Navy uniform and carried one of the flags in the Memorial Day parades, the Fourth of July Parade, and church festivals. We all loved the parades and festivals. In the summer we went to the annual CWV picnic that was often in Michigan at Wamplers Lake. One year the picnic was at Posey Lake in Hudson. We loved going to the picnic and the lake, even though none of us could swim at that time.

Sunday afternoons were often spent at a different aunt or uncle's home. Mostly, we visited Uncle Norbert and Aunt Sally Gedert in Toledo who had nine children, or Uncle Cletus and Aunt Grace Gillen in Swanton who had 11 children, or they came to our home in Assumption. We all lived on farms. Uncle McGrory, "Uncle Louie"- no one ever called him Louie, and Aunt Mary Gillen's kids, Anne Marie and Jimmy from Assumption were always in the mix. The men played cards, usually Pinochle and Euchre, and the women talked about the men and kids. The cousins played a lot of croquet, which Anne Marie always brought, along with her camera.

Cathy was always happy to tell her friends there were 30 first cousins - Anne Marie and Jimmy Gillen; Jeannette, Wilma, Jimmy, Bernard, Margie, Louella, Roseanne, Ronnie, and Carl Gedert; Barbara, Danny, Roger, Joe, Gene, Tom, Roy, Tim, Sue, Mark, and Jeff Gillen; Irene, Cathy, Noreen, Ginger, Linda, Norman, Gary, and Sherry Gillen. There were many more cousins that we didn't see often. With Dad being the youngest in the family, there was quite an age difference between the oldest (1925) and youngest (1957) cousins. Many of the second cousins were closer to our ages.

The sign raising in July 1952 added "GILLEN BROS. - 1951" below Grandpa Gillen's "P. J. GILLEN, A. D. 1917" sign, in time for Sister Lorenzo's homecoming in August. Leslie was 44 and Dad was 34. We all loved Sister's homecoming visits, family reunions, and other family gatherings that were often held on the family farm. In 1952 Dad and his brother Arnold escorted Sister and her companion up to the middle of the grain elevator for a photo. Irene especially liked visiting Sister Lorenzo at St. Augustine's Convent in Detroit, Michigan.

THE WALTER AND ELEANOR GILLEN STORY

Walter's 37th Birthday

Homecoming 1952

We visited Grandma and Grandpa Wood in Toledo regularly with all eight kids and Mom and Dad in the same car. Mom couldn't take a nap on the way home because we were usually giggling in the back seat. Mom would fuss at us to hush, but that only made us giggle more.

The older girls took turns staying with Grandma and Grandpa Wood. Linda tried spending the night, but Grandma sent her home because she was afraid of the cats. Grandma, Grandpa, Irene, Cathy, and Noreen walked several blocks to the theater to see the *Wizard of Oz*. When Irene was scared by the tornado and Cathy was afraid of the wicked witch, Grandma and Grandpa Wood never took us to the movies again. The younger kids were never old enough to stay overnight before grandma passed away.

Irene remembers Grandma Wood's kitchen in Toledo. The kitchen had a big black Hirsch Vogel gas and wood-burning stove. The cupboards had glass doors that held every color of Fiesta pottery such as dinnerware and serving pieces including bowls, platters, pitchers, and casseroles. There was also a big baking cupboard with a counter. The back stairs, from upstairs, came down to the kitchen by the table and a big window. Every morning Grandma sat at the table and smoked a Salem cigarette to clear her sinuses. The back door off the kitchen had a small porch that led out to the small, enclosed backyard with a path, shed, flower and herb gardens, and a bird bath.

In addition to our visits to aunts and uncles and Grandma and Grandpa Wood, we loved visits from Mom's friends in Toledo - Ernie and Beulah Trautwein, Eileen and George Balfe, and Molly Nugent. They brought us coloring books and crayons on every visit. We also loved going to the annual Fulton County Fair. Mom always packed us a picnic lunch. Cathy loved the ground-up bologna sandwiches on a bun. She doesn't remember much about the fair, only the picnic lunch. She says it was the only time we ever had those sandwiches.

In addition to gifts on our birthdays, we always had a white cake with maraschino cherries in the cake and icing. When we were 10 years old, we could have a birthday party. One of the games we played was Pin the Tail on the Donkey or Pin the Waddle on the Turkey, Mom's creation. Linda started Kindergarten in September 1957, two weeks before her fifth birthday. Mom kept her home on the first day of school. The bus went off the road and into a ditch that day. Kindergarten was held at a different location than the elementary school. Luckily, the older sisters rode another bus to school.

There were also childhood diseases and health issues. In January 1955 Cathy, Noreen, Ginger, and Linda all had chickenpox at the same time. We slept in Mom's and Dad's bedroom downstairs with all the curtains closed to keep the room dark. The same year Ginger was hospitalized with an asthma attack at age 3, and Linda was hospitalized with pneumonia when she was 19-months old. Linda had to re-learn to walk after she came home. The next year, the five older girls all had the hard measles at the same time.

Ginger had earaches very often and had her tonsils and adenoids out at age six to see if it would help. During her recovery, she slept on the couch in the living room and had ice cream and ginger ale – an extra special treat. Noreen recalls having a severe earache and the doctor coming to the house to look at her.

We raised cattle, hogs, and chickens. Poodle took care of the livestock. He fed and watered the cattle and hogs and milked the cow. We only had one at a time. On occasion, Poodle let Noreen and Ginger help with the milking. A heater hung from a rafter in the barn to heat milk for the calves. Irene was age 4 in 1951 when she saved the barn from burning down. When she went into the barn, she saw the rafter on fire and told Dad. The fire was found before it caused any damage. The milk heater had overheated.

Barn in Ohio 1952

Barn in Ohio 1959

THE WALTER AND ELEANOR GILLEN STORY

Dad bought new baby chicks each year. They stayed in the brooder house with the light on to keep them warm until they were old enough to move to the chicken coop. Mom and the girls fed the chickens and collected and cleaned the eggs. We gathered eggs every day in the chicken coop. Cathy often threw a corncob at the chickens to get them to scatter. Our neighbor, Maria, sometimes helped. She walked in the chicken coop with her bare feet and didn't mind getting chicken poop on her feet and between her toes.

After we gathered the eggs in a basket, we took them to the basement to clean and weigh for size to get them ready to sell. To clean the eggs, we held them against a cleaning wheel under the stairwell. If we held onto the eggs too tightly the egg would shoot out and hit the wall behind the table. Mom taped a grocery bag to the wall so the eggs would *splat* onto the paper and make it easier to clean up.

The fields were planted with corn, wheat, soybeans, and alfalfa to use as feed and bedding for the livestock. We had a red Farmall tractor and the equipment to plant and harvest the crops – plow, disk, planter, corn picker, cutter, binder, mower, cultivator, rake, baler, flat wagons, grain wagon, elevator, corn sheller, and manure spreader. After the crops were harvested, the stalks and shucks were cut and baled. Hay and straw were baled and stored in the barn, and grain was taken to the feed mill for grinding and returned in feed bags stored in the granary. Mom used the feed bags to make pillowcases and play clothes. During the harvest, the farmers worked together helping each other on their respective farms. Many of the farmers were related in some way.

Mom often drove the car out to the fields to take lunches to Dad and Poodle. The four oldest girls went with her in the car and sometimes were allowed to walk to the fields and carry their lunch. It was quite a long walk to go through the ditches and ravines. Noreen loved the picnics at the stream. When Ginger was 3, she climbed on a large dirt mound that turned out to be a very large ant hill. She started screaming when the ants crawled up her legs. Mom took off all of Ginger's clothes to get the ants off her.

Farm Buildings 1959

Gary & Laddie in Yard 1959

THE WALTER AND ELEANOR GILLEN STORY

We loved playing in the farm buildings. There was a double barn, silo, granary, tool shed for the farm equipment, chicken coop, garage, corn crib, and an old stone smokehouse filled with sand. We liked the barn the best. The barn had upper and lower levels, trap doors, grain chutes, lofts, and other openings between the floors. The older girls were often on the upper level playing or watching the men work below. They had to

Cathy in Barn 1953

be careful when they played on the hay bales, so they didn't fall into a crevasse or get a leg stuck in between the bales.

Mom and Dad had a few scares with the four oldest girls. In 1953 the men were loading steers in a cattle truck and 4-year-old Cathy grabbed onto a swinging barn door above the cattle. Dad was afraid she would fall and get trampled. Dad hit her with a cane, grabbed her off the door, and threw her over the fence to Mom. Cathy remembers having to apologize to him later that day.

In 1954, Cathy was age 5 and Noreen was 4. They were playing around with the corn planter in the tool shed. Cathy pulled one of the pulley ropes "playing horsey" and it released a blade. The blade cut through Noreen's tennis shoes and between her second and third toe on her right foot. Had it landed across her foot she would have had some toes amputated. Poodle carried Noreen to the house and Mom took her to the doctor where she had six stitches. Mom also made Cathy go to the doctor with her. Ginger was 2 or 3 when she climbed to the top of a windmill. Dad saw her from the field and came up to the house to talk her down before Mom saw her. He eventually had to carry her down. Another time, Cathy and Noreen were playing near the windmill. There were very large burdock bushes underneath. Cathy had her hair caught in the burrs and Mom had to cut her hair to free her.

Once when playing on the barn's second floor on the corn chute, Poodle opened the chute and Ginger fell through. She wasn't hurt, but we couldn't play there again.

Cathy and Noreen were riding in the back seat of Poodle's car in the summer of 1955. Cathy put her foot on the door handle and the door swung open, throwing her out of the car. She rolled down the berm for quite a way before Noreen could get Poodle to stop the car. It was a hot day, so she was only wearing panties. Cathy had sores all over her body, from head to toe. Mom and Dad set up a cot with mosquito netting in the backyard so she could go outside and keep the bugs off her sores.

Later in the year, Cathy climbed a pear tree. She was reaching for a leather strap attached to the tree, missed it, and fell out of the tree. She was scraped up and remembers telling all her friends at school that a cat scratched her because she was embarrassed to tell them what really happened.

We were allowed to play in the wagon after the soybeans were harvested in October. If we spilled any of the beans out of the wagon, we had to get out of the wagon. We liked riding in the wagon, so we were very careful not to spill the beans. We also played in the silo when it was being filled with silage using the grain elevator. We had to be careful not to get buried.

When Poodle drove the grain wagon into the tool shed, we stood on the back of the wagon and tried to touch the top of the door. One day, Poodle popped the clutch on the tractor and Noreen fell out of the wagon and was knocked unconscious. Noreen woke up in the dining room in the house when Mom was calling the doctor and said, "No, don't call

Loading Steers 1952

New Corn Picker 1942

Ginger, Cathy, and Noreen 1953

Memorial Day 1956

THE WALTER AND ELEANOR GILLEN STORY

the doctor." Noreen has had problems with her neck ever since. When she rides in a car and falls asleep, her head doesn't fall forward. Her neck remains straight and upright.

Another time, Poodle was driving the grain wagon through the field and the girls were riding in the back. Noreen had put her foot on the bracket on the back of the wagon. When Poodle hit a bump, she was thrown out of the wagon with her foot caught in the bracket. The other girls couldn't get Poodle's attention while Noreen was hanging onto the back of the wagon through the field. No one thought she was hurt, but as she has grown older, she has had more problems with her back (Deteriorating Disc Disease).

Irene and Cathy were above the pig pen in 1957 when they saw a rat. They ran and Irene fell through the trap door and landed on a pig and sprained her little finger. Cathy was so scared she jumped from the second-floor door to the ground, rather than use the ladder, and sprained her ankle. Noreen was outside on the ground and ran to get Mom, even though Irene and Cathy begged her not to. Mom and Dad carried Cathy around for a couple of weeks.

Of all our neighbors in Assumption, Minnie and Harold Dowling were one of the nearest families on our side of Central Avenue and had two children, Patrick, and Maria. Maria was adopted from Germany and was a few years older than Irene. She didn't know English, and we didn't know German. Kids being kids, this was not a barrier. Mom said the girls and Maria played together for hours on end. Maria often walked in her sleep and rearranged all the furniture in the living room at night. Her doctors and parents tried different techniques to get her to stop. Finally, someone recommended that her parents fill a large pan with water and slide it under her bed until she fell asleep. After she was asleep, her parents were to pull the pan of water out from under the bed so Maria would step in the water getting out of bed at night. This was supposed to wake up her. It worked. Maria never walked into her sleep again.

The girls were not allowed to have bikes in Ohio living so close to Central Avenue with heavy semi-trailer truck and farm equipment traffic. Our neighbor Maria brought her bike over to the house one day for us to ride. Irene scraped all the knuckles on her hand riding too close to the garage. While we had the bike, Ginger taught herself to ride on the stone driveway.

In April 1959, Dad and Leslie sold the family farm at auction to Fred Lumbrezer for $52,000. Dad and Mom were given the use of the house, chicken coop, and garden plot until October 31, 1959.

In August 1959 Walter and Eleanor purchased a 180-acre farm at 859 Knapp Road in Brooklyn, Michigan, 40 miles north of the Ohio border in Cambridge Township, Lenawee County. The farm was on Stony Lake at the front of the property and Vineyard Lake at the back of the property. It was a wonderful location for the family, particularly Walter, who spent many days visiting and working in Michigan before he was married. We moved to Brooklyn on Labor Day, 1959, the day before school started.

Poodle moved to Wauseon, Ohio, and the two brothers remained close through the rest of their lives.

12th Anniversary 1958

Chapter 4

Growing up in Michigan

*By Irene Gillen Snider, Catherine "Cathy" Gillen Osborn,
Noreen Gillen Litchard, Virginia "Ginger" Gillen Poole,
Linda Gillen Thompson, Norman Gillen,
and Sherry Gillen Butcher Belmonte*

1959 – 1972

LEAVING OHIO AND moving to Brooklyn, Michigan, was memorable for everyone. There was a going-away party in Ohio on August 29, 1959. Dad moved most of our furnishings in the big cattle truck to Knapp Road on Labor Day. Noreen was so excited she ran and got into the truck before anyone else had a chance. Norman was almost 3 years old and remembers riding in the "huge" truck.

The five older girls started school the next day. Irene was in 7th grade and Linda, the youngest of school age, was repeating kindergarten. Linda started school when she was 4 and was lagging her classmates at the half-year mark in Ohio. Her teacher recommended that she start kindergarten again since she would be a year older and in a new school system. The girls rode the school bus five miles to the Brooklyn public school.

Irene couldn't sleep at night for a while in the new house because it was so quiet. In Ohio, we were used to semi-trucks traveling U.S. 20 day and night, 50 feet from the house. Our 180-acre farm was a half mile from U.S. 12 on a quiet lake. U.S. 12 was also the dividing line between two school districts. Brooklyn was North of U.S. 12, and Onsted was south of U.S. 12.

Poodle or Uncle Leslie, who lived with us in Ohio, didn't initially join us in Michigan. He moved from Wauseon, Ohio, to Cement City, Michigan, early in the 1960s and worked on the Wittenberg's dairy farm. In the mid-1960s he bought a trailer and moved it to our farm on the old garage slab.

Our new house was much smaller than the big farmhouse we were used to. Dad and Mom did a lot of work to get us settled. Mom put a second mirror in the bathroom on the back of the door. This was in addition to the one on the medicine cabinet above the sink. Two girls used the full-length mirror, one stood up, one squatted down, and two girls shared the mirror over the sink. There was only one bathroom with a shower and no bathtub, so we tried to be quick because there was often a waiting line. We alternated taking showers on different days and in the morning and evening so the hot water wouldn't run out. Often one of the older girls had the younger sisters shower with them. Everyone used the same two or three bath towels for the week. We brushed our teeth in the morning before school and in the evening at bedtime, and we all used the same rinse cup.

We had a septic tank and drain field for the bathroom. There was also an overflow pipe on the outside of the house near the bathroom window. It often overflowed and the ground was soft and smelly in that area, so we didn't play there.

Dad and Mom hung curtains, and Mom replaced the wallpaper

throughout the house. Everyone old enough helped remove and replace the six or seven layers of wallpaper on the walls and ceilings. Dad and Mom put in floor-to-ceiling shelving across the entire wall at the top of the stairs for our linens, board games, toys, Sunday hats, and other items.

The house had four bedrooms. Mom and Dad's room was downstairs. The other three were upstairs. Sleeping arrangements varied over the years as ages changed and when the older girls left after high school. While the twins were still in cribs they slept in the room with Mom and Dad and later in Irene's room. When the twins were older, there were three double beds in the large room that ran the full length of the house. Norman and Gary slept in one bed, Noreen and Ginger slept in one bed, and Linda and Sherry slept in the third bed. Irene and Cathy slept in the medium size bedroom. There was a connecting closet between these two bedrooms. Another small room started out as Mom's sewing room and changed over time into the toy room, Ginger's bedroom, Poodle's bedroom, and then Sherry's bedroom. Ginger took the time to convert the sewing room to a bedroom and was only able to use it one or two months before it was needed for Poodle.

A furnace in the basement provided heat in the house. The heat register in the large bedroom was the only one for the entire upstairs. There was an open grate between the living room ceiling and the floor in Irene and Cathy's bedroom that allowed more heat to come upstairs. The house was hot in the summers and cold in the winters.

An old brass double-bed frame we found in the barn was set up in the house for Noreen and Ginger. One summer day Noreen noticed the cap on one of the bed posts was loose and it fell off. She found $310 in Union greenbacks wrapped in newspaper. Dad was able to cash them at the bank.

We had to kiss Mom and Dad good night on our way to bed and say our prayers. We knelt by our beds and prayed, "Now I lay me down to sleep, I pray the Lord my soul to keep. And if I die before I wake, I pray the Lord my soul to take." Bedtime was consistent during the school year. During the summer, we were allowed to stay up an extra half hour. We had to take naps until we completed kindergarten. It was so hard to go to bed when it was still light out during the summer. Mom was always up early. She went to bed late because she liked to watch television after everyone had gone off to bed. Dad worked the second shift at a factory, so he was sleeping when we left for school in the morning and was gone before we got home from school. When we woke up, we got dressed for the day. We were not allowed to go to the breakfast table in our pajamas. We were all required to make our beds in the morning.

Dad bought a record player along with 78 and 45 RPM records from a friend of his in Onsted. We played the records over and over. We used the 78 records we didn't like, or the ones that got scratched, as Frisbees until they were all broken. They were wonderful. They wouldn't break. We had to make a special effort to hit them against a post or tree to get them to break.

Ginger has the four-record album *On Wings of Song* which cost $2.50 plus tax, and seven records recorded by Columbia, Tops, Dana, Capital, and Victor. These are not the records that came with the album, but we liked them: *Charlie was a Boxer* (polka), *Blue Skirt Waltz, The Doggie in the Window, Side by Side, Oh Boy!* (polka), *Where Are You Blue Eyes* (waltz), *Every Little Thing Rolled into One, One-Woman Man, An Old-Fashioned Tree, Here Comes Santa Claus* by Gene Autry, *Serenade, Indian Love Call, Take Me Back to Little Rock,* and *Huggin' And A Chalkin'*.

We could get three television channels: ABC -11, CBS -13, and some-times 50 out of Detroit. We watched *I Love Lucy, Gun Smoke, Bonanza, the Adventurers, Red Skelton, Mickey Mouse, Lawrence Welk;* soap operas: *Secret Storm, General Hospital, Edge of Night, and Dark Shadow;* cartoons: *Casper the Friendly Ghost, Scooby Dooby Doo;* game shows: *Supermarket Sweep and Treasure Island.* We saw *Wonderful World of Disney* on Sunday nights and *Captain Kangaroo* and *Mr. Green Jeans* on weekday mornings. *The Wizard of Oz* was shown once a year, around Easter.

Mom and Dad liked listening to the radio in the kitchen. As teenagers, we listened to the CKLW radio station in Detroit. Mom didn't like this station and changed it as soon as we left the room. When we returned to the kitchen, we tuned the radio back to CKLW as soon as Mom left the room. Norm remembers the older girls playing Elvis records on the record player in the living room and dragging him into the kitchen when Sue Thompson sang *Norman* on the radio.

Mom joined the Mother of Twins Club. The whole family loved to attend the meetings, picnics, and gatherings at the house.

There was a three-minute time limit for talking on the phone. One time Linda slammed the phone down so hard that the buttons got stuck down. Another time Noreen slammed the phone down so hard that the headset broke in half.

Mom cut everyone's hair at home until the girls were in high school. On special occasions, the girls went to a beauty shop. Noreen and Ginger had their first permanent at age 8 for their First Communion. On Friday or Saturday nights the girls sat on the floor in the living room in front of Mom and Dad watching television getting their long and thick hair done by someone. When Sherry was 10, she had a pixie haircut at the beauty shop that she hated after customers in the Coffee Shop called her a boy and hurt her feelings. After those comments she kept her hair long well into her college years.

The daily routine around the house focused on raising eight kids. Inside the house was always a busy place with a lot of people. We had sibling rivalries, but no major fights. If one of us got a little out-of-line, or moody, another sister usually corrected us. Whenever someone was mad at you, you always had someone who wasn't mad at you. We could always find a friend. Sherry went through a stage where she hit Linda on the back for no real reason. Norman and Sherry picked on Linda during outdoor games, too, because they could move faster than she could.

We were disciplined but never hurt, and it wasn't necessary very often. When we were young, Dad spanked us. Mom never used her hand. She used a wooden paddle. Norman and Sherry recall most of the spankings happening at bedtime when they were supposed to be settling down. The big bedroom was right above Mom's and Dad's bedroom. The noise carried easily in the house, so we didn't get away with much talking into the night. When we were older Dad talked to us harshly and made us cry. Then we toughened up and didn't let him make us cry. He didn't like that. For the most part, we were all thoughtful, helpful, and courteous to everyone in the family.

A few tenets were framed and hung on the kitchen wall so we wouldn't forget them: "When idle moments mount, hustle up and make them count." "If you can't say anything nice, don't say anything at all." "When in a flurry, don't be in a hurry."

We went to the doctor when there was a health scare, or someone was hurt. We had typical childhood health issues and injuries. Linda was 6 in 1959 when she ate a bottle of St. Joseph Baby Aspirin. Mom had to make sure she didn't fall asleep during the night. When Gary and Sherry had chickenpox at the same time in 1963 at age 6, they slept on the couch for a week, each with their head at the opposite end. Sherry says there were plenty of footsies. Sherry had pneumonia in 1964 when she was in 1st grade and was able to stay at home. Linda sprained her ankle in school one year and didn't tell anyone. When the bus driver, Vic Wells, stopped at our house after school, Linda couldn't walk. He carried her into the house. Another time Linda jumped out of the boxelder tree in the side yard and sprained her ankle again.

We all had scrapes and bruises from playing, and climbing trees, fences, and buildings. There was a large 4 x 4-foot box hay dryer on a platform in the barn. It was great for pretending to play ship/boat. Norman and Sherry turned the blades with a corncob and turned the floor motor with their foot. One time Sherry's hand slipped into the blades, and she cut three fingers. Mom had to call a neighbor on Pink Street to get a ride to the doctor. Linda fell and was knocked out when climbing over a board fence next to the barn. She remembers sitting on a bale of straw after her fall, but not going to the house, where she woke up on the couch.

We always had a lot of cavities to fill when we went to the dentist. We brushed our teeth every day and the school offered fluoride treatments, that we couldn't afford. We ate candy every week after Mom bought groceries and it was eaten within a day or two. The four youngest kids didn't go to the dentist until age 12 or 13. They went to the dentist when Linda had been complaining about a sore tooth. She had several cavities. At that point, Norman, Gary, and Sherry were also taken to see the dentist. Our eyes were tested in school. We saw an optometrist if a problem was noticed. Irene, Norman, and Gary needed glasses in high school. No one else needed glasses until their college years, or later.

Gary's nickname was "Tubby." When the twins were about to start kindergarten, Mom said we should call him Gary, because kids would make fun of him if they knew his nickname. Gary was a little heavier than Sherry. Not sure of the timeline, but the family noticed that when Gary happened to fall, he didn't bounce right back up. When he did fall, he had a certain way of getting up. It was kind of hands to knees, then standing. His kindergarten teacher, Mrs. Goings, noticed, too. She had seen the same actions with another student, the Hudson boy. She alerted Mom and Dad to the fact, and they took Gary to the doctor. Gary was diagnosed with Duchene muscular dystrophy in 1963.

When the twins began kindergarten, all the kids were in school together for two school years, 1963-1964 and 1964-1965. If there was a snow day, none of the kids had to go to school if the bus couldn't pick them up. Knapp Road was a hilly and curvy gravel lake road prone to snow drifts, and on the county line that was often plowed last.

As time went on Gary began to fall more. He was fitted for braces on his lower legs to help keep his toes from turning under so he wouldn't trip as often. He often walked with his hand in his pocket and against his thigh to help him balance. Gary continued to struggle more, but the doctors and Dad wanted Gary to do as much as he could before getting him more support equipment. Eventually, Gary needed more support. Dad had someone fashion a small walker for Gary, and it made life easier for him when he could support himself. Norm remembers Dad using a two-wheeled hand truck or dolly to move Gary around. It was great fun for Gary, and Sherry to play with, too. The Muscular Dystrophy Association and Crippled Children's Association eventually provided medical support and equipment to help manage his mobility.

Mom had a car accident with our blue and white Buick on Knapp Road. The kids on the school bus told us about it. When we tried to get off the bus, the bus driver, Mr. Stack, made us stay on the bus and go to school. Mom was not hurt badly, but we had to sit through a full day of school before we knew how she was. Mom had stepped on the accelerator instead of the brake. The car was totaled. They said if she had hit the tree one inch to the right, the engine would have been in her lap.

Noreen and Ginger joined the beginning band and played the kazoo. Irene, Noreen, and Norman were in the band throughout their school years. Irene played the bells, Noreen played the clarinet, and Norman played percussion instruments. Ginger, and neighbor Laura Klassen alternated between first- and second-chair clarinetists. Ginger quit the band when she had to march in formations at football games. She couldn't manage to play music and march in changing formations at the same time.

The new farm was a part-time job for Dad. He supplemented the farm income as a tool and die maker working on the second shift at Tecumseh

Products about 30 miles from home. Dad only held his manufacturing job for a couple of years because of his drinking and health issues.

In addition to the house, there was a barn with a silo and milk house, a Quonset hut, a chicken coop, a small building, a corn crib, and a small shed close to the house. Next to the garage and workshop was a large gas tank used to fuel the farm vehicles that sat on an elevated structure built with railroad ties.

Dad didn't bring the farm animals from Ohio. There were free-range fighting chickens on the property when we moved to the farm, and Dad bought new hogs, sheep, and chickens. We fed and watered the animals and chickens and gathered eggs daily. We used the meat and eggs we needed and sold the excess.

At one time we had a Shetland pony named Trigger. When Noreen and Linda tried to ride Trigger, they were bucked off halfway down the lane and had to walk home. Eventually, they were able to ride him. We had goats one year and let them graze around the house to keep the grass "mowed." Linda was afraid of them and stayed on the front porch if they were around. They were gone as soon as they started eating in Mom's flower beds.

For several years we boarded horses for our neighbor, the Swifts, and learned to groom and tack them. We weren't allowed to ride them too often. The pigs got out sometimes and rooted in the yard, and occasionally we had to corral the horses. We liked the new piglets, puppies, and baby rabbits and kittens we found. We watched the sheep lambing and being sheared. Natural animal behavior taught us about "the birds and the bees."

We had the red Farmall tractor from Ohio and the equipment to plant and harvest the crops. While we had farm animals, crops were rotated in the fields with corn, wheat, oats, alfalfa, hay, or soybeans. Excess grain was sold. The first summer in Michigan, our cousin, Gene Gillen, number six of the 11 children in his family, came for a couple of weeks to help Dad fit and plant the fields. Gene recalled how different the soil was in Michigan. The soil turned over very easily compared to the clumpy clay soil in Ohio. The kids loved playing card games at night after supper.

One year we had to hoe the cornfield next to the house. Everyone old enough had a hoe and a row to weed. When we finished one row, we all went on to the next one until the field was done. The older girls also helped in the field with baling, but Dad generally had men to help him. For some years Dad was required to put the fields in the Federal Land Bank and was paid for leaving the fields to lie fallow. When Dad's health worsened in 1963, he rented out the fields to local farmers. They planted and harvested the crops and paid him a fee for the use of the land.

We had many pets over the years. Our first dog was a collie named Laddie. All our pets stayed outdoors, and we fed them table scraps. Cathy had a hunting dog named Prince. He was white with black ears and killed all the fighting chickens on the farm. Dad made her give Prince back to the people who gave him to her. She didn't know anything about training a dog but wished she had because he was a nice dog. In the mid-1960s we had an Eskimo huskie dog named Butterscotch. Dad had to get rid of him when he chased kids walking along the road. Norman and Linda remember "Heinz's 57" dogs named Gizmo and Angus. When a sales-man came to our house and got out of the car, Angus chased after him. As he was running back away from the dog, he tumbled backward over the stone wall that edged our driveway. The salesman went on his way quickly without making it to the door. Noreen named the cat Tippy because of the white on the end of his tail, and he ran away. There were many other feral cats around in the yard because of the farm buildings. The younger kids tamed the kittens and dressed them in doll clothes. Indoors, Mom had an aquarium and canaries for many years. We had hamsters that survived a much shorter time.

First Day of School 1963

When Gary and Sherry were home from kindergarten one day Sherry took a hammer and ice pick that Mom was using and coerced Gary into tapping a hole in the glass aquarium, which he did. She then ran upstairs and tattled on him. We never had an aquarium after that, and Mom never knew the true story until the twins were much older.

The kitchen was a busy place. We had an electric GE stove and a Frigidaire refrigerator. The freezer had to be defrosted often from frost buildup. The table was in the middle of the kitchen and large enough to seat 11 people around. We all had assigned seats. The tabletop was yellow linoleum and had small gaps between the leaves where food and spilled milk fell or dripped through onto the floor.

For breakfast, we usually had cereal or toast. On occasion, we had leftover pie, cake, or stale popcorn. For lunch, during the school year, the older girls made their own tuna fish salad, bologna, or peanut butter and jelly sandwich on store-bought bread. Mom made the younger kid's lunches until they complained when she got the wrong condiment on the wrong sandwich. Then they made their own lunches. In grade school and middle school, we carried lunch pails. In high school, we used brown paper lunch bags. Lunch in the summer was pretty much the same - lunch meat, tuna, and peanut butter and jelly sandwiches.

One of Cathy's favorite meals was hamburger hash. Noreen did not like hamburger hash or beef stew, perhaps because we had it quite a bit. We also had tuna and noodle casserole, goulash, pot roast, and liver and onions. Mom modified the liver and onion meal by cooking the bacon first and then the liver, but we still didn't like it very well. We liked the steak well done. For a vegetable, we sometimes had to make a quick cucumber salad or pick dandelion greens for a salad. Sherry remembers carrots and celery always being on the table. We had to eat all our dinner to have dessert. We often had cooked rice with cinnamon and milk for dessert.

When Poodle ate with us, he loved to spread bread with a thick layer of butter. Many of the kids tried it and loved it. Sherry hated to have him butter her bread. The teenagers didn't eat bread like this very often because they struggled to keep their weight under control. Dad always wanted Mom and the kids to be on the heavier side of the scale. Otherwise, it would appear to others that we weren't being fed enough.

We ate meals at the kitchen table and always said "grace," a traditional prayer, before eating supper: "Bless us, O Lord, for these Thy gifts for which we are about to receive from Thy bounty, through Christ our Lord. Amen." We ate supper together until our teens when some of the girls were working at the Coffee Shop. Food was served family style and passed from left to right ending with Mom and Dad.

We had to eat what was on our plates. Ginger was sneaky about this rule. Since there were so many people seated at the table for supper, she would throw pieces of her meal she didn't like under the table near someone else's feet. This is one of the reasons we had a sweeper chore after supper. Sherry was often still sitting at the table after all the dishes were done, attempting to finish a meal. We don't remember having second helpings very often. If there were leftovers, they were most likely on Sundays and consumed by the adults. Small leftover portions were given to the dogs.

We shared the kitchen chores. Two of the older girls helped Mom cook the meal. The other two had dish washing duty. The younger kids helped set the table, clear the table, or put the clean dishes away in the cupboards. If we were putting the dishes away, they went outside to play for the 20 minutes or so that it took the girls to wash, dry, and stack the clean dishes on the kitchen table. The floor was swept every night after supper and the trash was taken out. Trash was collected behind a shed and emptied by Dad in a ravine near the fence line in one of the back fields. We used a 55-gallon drum for a burn barrel in the backyard near the garden to burn paper waste. It needed to be replaced periodically as it filled with ash and debris and burned through the side of the drum due to the heat. It was fun to watch the fire burn at night and emit glowing embers into the sky.

We were in the government surplus program from 1961 to 1963. Dad could pick up food once a month. We received 5-pound blocks of cheese, powdered milk, powdered eggs, SPAM, flour, rice, butter, and peanut butter. We used powdered milk to stretch out the whole milk from the store. We mixed the two together and called it "made milk." We didn't like it, but we got used to it. We got very tired of eating SPAM, a pork canned meat. Sometimes it was the only meat we had, so we tried fixing it in different ways. It tasted best when fried. It didn't help that Dad didn't like it because he had eaten it often while on duty during the war.

The main garden was in the far backyard near the corn crib. Everyone helped with the weeding and harvesting - shelling peas on the porch, picking strawberries, hulling sweet corn, and even selling the vegetables at a roadside stand at the corner of Pink Street and Wamplers Lake Road.

Another large garden with potatoes and turnips and a strawberry patch next to the sour cherry orchard was across the road from the house by the lake. When the cherry blossoms came on the trees, we hung shiny pie plates in the branches to keep the birds from eating the cherries. Dad hung the plates on the higher branches. We liked climbing the trees to pick the cherries. Later we pitted and canned the cherries. One time Noreen was cleaning cherries outside and fell into the window well. She was scratched up a little, but not hurt badly.

Dad, Poodle, and everyone liked to eat the ripe fruits and vegetables directly from the garden, dirt, and all. We picked dandelion greens on the lawn for salad and black and red raspberries from vines along the fence lines. At the back of the property, Dad showed us how to identify huckleberry trees, hickory nut trees, walnut trees, and sassafras trees. We loved picking the huckleberries, gathering, and shelling hickory nuts, and drinking sassafras tea. Dad also knew how to find edible wild mushrooms.

Along with what we grew, Mom and Dad bought tomatoes, peaches, corn, apples, and beans by the bushel for canning. Canning was a big job and everyone old enough could help clean and prepare the vegetables. The ends could be snapped off the beans. The tomatoes and peaches were skinned by dipping them in boiling water and then cold water. The skins slid right off. One vegetable or fruit variety was canned at a time and usually took one day. Mom made homemade applesauce by steaming the apples, peeling, and coring them, and putting them through a hand-turned food mill. One time Mom made sauerkraut that spoiled down in the basement. The older girls had to scoop it out of the crock pot and carry it outside one pan at a time. It was very smelly. The canned jars of food were kept on a shelf in the basement and used throughout the winter months.

We shopped for groceries in Brooklyn at Kroger's on Saturdays and received S&H Green Stamps equal to the amount of money we spent. Mom mostly used them to purchase free dinnerware. We also selected soap boxes with drinking glasses, and cereal boxes with toys. For other family needs we shopped in Brooklyn at Van's Five and Dime, Arksey's Hardware, Cole's Jewelers, Cooper's Department Store, and Weatherwax Drug Store. As we got into our teens, we went to department stores and Paka Plaza in Jackson, about 20 miles away.

There were always store-bought bread and saltine crackers in the cupboard. If we couldn't find anything else to snack on after school, we made a tray of cinnamon toast. We buttered the bread, sprinkled on a mixture of sugar and cinnamon, and put the bread under the broiler in the oven until it bubbled. If we were still hungry, we made another tray. Buttered crackers were another favorite snack we learned to make from the Ackley kids across the lake. We buttered white crackers and put them on a baking sheet under the broiler until they browned and bubbled. We also made saltine cracker sandwiches with a marshmallow in between two squares. Graham crackers sandwiches with frosting in the center were a favorite. These were all delicious.

We made ice cubes in metal ice cube trays. We had homemade popsicles made with Tupperware forms and Kool-Aid, always a refreshing treat! It was always a trick not to spill them when you were the one remaking them. Dessert was rationed. We were allowed to have two cookies, two scoops of ice cream, one piece of candy, and two ice cubes in our drink glasses.

Mom could cook, but she especially loved baking and making sweets. After she took a cake decorating lesson in 1962, she sold tiered graduation and wedding cakes, lovely doll cakes, and sugar Easter eggs. She liked making fudge and peanut brittle for home and taught us how to make cookies - always a triple batch. During the Easter season when she made sugar eggs, she used molds and baked them. The sugar eggs were scooped out, baked, and then a decorative scene was put inside the egg. These were usually Easter grass, jellybeans, and little chicks or ducks. Then two halves of the egg were 'glued' together with frosting and Mom lavishly decorated the outside with borders and flowers. The doll cakes that she made started with a Bundt pan cake. After they were baked, a plastic Barbie doll was placed into the center hole and posed. She then decorated the doll's bodice and the cake to look like a princess.

Many of the family traditions that started in Ohio and continued at our new house on the farm in Michigan. Everyone got a cake and ice cream for their birthday. Linda's 6th birthday was the first birthday celebrated with a maraschino cherry cake. We all had one birthday party with friends for our 10th birthday. The family threw a surprise party for Cathy when she turned 18. She was so surprised she cried. Cathy was not a crybaby but so surprised that she cried happy tears.

Mom loved flowers and established several flower beds along the front of the house and on both sides of the driveway. She planted a trumpet vine against the shed, inside the circular driveway that she was proud of. She tried to grow daylilies in the ditch along the road, but they never took. She had rose bushes along the front edge of the yard along the road and covered them with large jars to keep them from freezing in the winter. We all learned the art of pulling weeds and planting flowers with Mom. Dad planted a row of cedar trees about 50 feet behind the house as a wind break. We transplanted the trees from the woods. When we dug up trees, Mom tied a marker on the north side of each tree, so they could be re-planted in the ground in the direction in which they already grew.

We all continued to help with the chores, and we still had to finish our chores before we could play. We cleaned on Saturday mornings. The house didn't stay clean for long. It was ideal to clean when no one else was around, and that was infrequent. Books and clutter generally landed on the dining room table. The younger kids could see Mom's car driving home around the curvy road from the living room windows. Often that is when they jumped up and started dusting and vacuuming. Our annual spring house cleaning included the windows, curtains, rugs, and blankets. The rugs and blankets were hung on the clothesline, batted, and left in the fresh air for a day.

Laundry and clothing for this large family was another huge task. Mom and the oldest girls color coded all the clothing with thread for each child. When we were younger, laundry was done every Monday. After we bought the Coffee Shop, laundry was done on Saturdays. The clothes were put into a wringer washing machine and two rinse tubs. There were two or three kids on each job – sorting, washing, running the clothes twice through the wringer into the rinse tubs, filling the laundry baskets and carrying them upstairs from the basement to the clothesline in the back yard, and hanging the laundry to dry.

In the summer, everything was hung outside to dry. In the winter, heavy pants, sheets, and towels were hung on clotheslines in the basement. After the clothes dried, two or three of us took the clothes down and carried the laundry baskets into the living room to be folded. After the twins were born, we had an electric clothes dryer, but it wasn't used for heavier clothing. A small basket of odd socks was kept by the dryer. Mom created a divided sorting box and used this to hold the folded clothes. The older girls were responsible for putting the clothes away until the younger kids were old enough to put away their piles of clothes in their dresser drawers. The younger kids climbed into the sorting box, rode it down the stairs, and got in trouble for it. The ironing went into a separate basket.

In later years, the laundry was taken to the laundromat in Brooklyn every Monday and washed and dried there. Cathy had this task for several years and then the younger kids helped Mom do it weekly. Norman and Sherry played outdoors in the creek behind the laundromat in between loads of laundry.

The ironing board was almost like a piece of the dining room furniture and set up with a clear view into the living room and TV. There was a perpetual basket full of ironing and we all learned how to iron on Dad's handkerchiefs. The clothes were sprinkled with water, rolled up, and put back into the ironing basket. We had a spray bottle of water if we needed more steam while we were ironing, and many of the clothes were sprayed with starch. It was always important to keep the iron moving to avoid scorching the clothes. There was a specific order to ironing shirts and blouses. The collar first, then the sleeves, and then the body. When ironing skirts and dresses with pleats, we laid the skirt across the ironing board, used straight pins to pin seven or eight pleats into place, and ironed those. Then we rotated the garment to the next six-or seven-inch pleats until it was done. When we got older, we tried to be scarce on Saturday afternoons. The one Dad could capture had to iron his Sunday shirt. Norman learned to iron Dad's shirts at an early age.

We all learned how to take care of our clothing. Mom was a wonderful seamstress and altered our school clothes to fit us as we grew. Aunt Sally had four girls older than Irene and gave us her girls' clothes as they outgrew them. The older girls especially loved their "new" dresses from Aunt Sally. Other people also gave us clothes that Mom altered as needed.

The girls started to sew by darning socks and sewing on buttons in the evening. Ginger was good at darning but not at sewing on buttons. She was told she sewed with a hot needle, meaning the button would not stay on very well. Most of us learned to sew in home economics class and from Mom. All the girls made an occasional skirt or dress they could wear to school. Cathy made a beautiful, blue, reversible wrap-around skirt that she wore for several years. Mom taught us how to knit and crochet during the summer.

Most of us are good seamstresses today. Irene made her prom dress and a Christmas party dress. She alters her own clothes and sews duffle bags to hold homeless mats. Cathy does alterations as a side business. Noreen made an apron in school and does a lot of sewing today

- pillowcase dresses for orphanages in Honduras and Nicaragua, bags for The Christmas Child boxes that are given out around the world through The Billy Graham Foundation, face masks for family members and nursing homes during the COVID-19 scare, backpacks for the homeless, and alterations.

Ginger made some of her own clothes and curtains for her apartment before she was married. Linda sewed in school and made a skirt in class and curtains for their first truck camper. Norman took one semester of home economics and had an introduction to sewing but remembers more about the cooking lessons. Sherry sewed some of her own clothes over the years, made one of her prom dresses, and continues to sew as a hobby.

We stored clothes and shoes in the attic in boxes at the end of the summer and winter. At the beginning of the next season, we retrieved the boxes and tried on the clothes and shoes to see what fit or had to be altered. There was one closet between the two upstairs bedrooms. Irene, Cathy, Noreen, and Ginger shared clothes. On one occasion Cathy spilled tuna on Irene's skirt and had to buy Irene a new skirt. We all got a new pair of shoes at the beginning of each school year.

Holidays were always made special. On Easter, when we were little, we had our slippers laid out next to our beds the evening before. In the morning we found a small gift in them. For Sunday church, women and girls wore nice dresses and had to wear a hat or veil to cover their heads. Men wore suits and boys wore white shirts and ties. We colored eggs the day before, and each of us had an Easter basket. Easter was one of Dad's favorite holidays. When we were older, we helped him hide the Easter baskets after the younger kids were in bed. The first thing we did in the morning was look for our Easter basket. One of the girls' baskets was hidden inside a cooking pot that hung on a peg board on the wall. It took more than an hour for that one to be found. Other small items we found throughout the day, like an Easter egg in the grass or on an upper windowsill.

In the summer, it was a big deal for us when we had a barbecue. Lighting up the grill with charcoal and cooking hot dogs, probably for holidays, is a fond memory of the family being together and playing outdoors, with everyone happy and smiling.

We always watched the Fourth of July fireworks displays. From our property, we could see fireworks from many of the local lake communities. Some of us climbed up onto the corn crib roof with our popcorn and watched the fireworks. One year, on the Fourth of July, a fire started on the neighbor's property behind the barn. Dad got the tractor and plow and created a fire break while the fire department was on its way. Another time Dad was burning the brush across the road from the house so that it wouldn't catch fire later in summer. It was under control, but the neighbors called the fire department.

We loved making Jack-o-Lanterns at Halloween and Dad loved candy corn and peanuts. We had a large box of dress-up clothes we retrieved from the attic every year and everyone chose the costume they wanted to wear. There was a serape, Mexican hat, gypsy, clowns, and more. When we were younger, we wore our costumes to school. Once we went to Grandma's and Grandpa Wood's in Toledo to trick-or-treat. It was a long way to go just for Halloween. Dad wouldn't let us trick-or-treat in town. Instead, he drove us around the lake to the neighboring houses. One year a neighbor invited us into the house to fill our bags. He had his entire kitchen table filled with treats for us to take home.

We had a large traditional turkey dinner on Thanksgiving. This was one of the few meals that we ate in the dining room and not in the kitchen. One year Mom's cousin Meredith and her girls came from Toledo to have dinner with us, but it was generally just our family.

Christmas was Dad's other favorite holiday. It was also Norman's favorite holiday. We put a Christmas tree up the weekend before Christmas. Sometimes we went into the woods and cut our tree. Other times we bought a tree in town in front of the Kroger store. Later, we went to a tree lot for our tree. We kept the Christmas decorations in boxes in the attic, mainly ornaments, garland, an angel for the top, and light strings.

Dad and Poodle were both playful. On Christmas Eve, Dad or Poodle often made boot tracks in the snow and then rang some harness bells, making us believe the reindeer and Santa had come and gone. We always found a bag of gifts on the porch by the front door. The older girls also played pranks on the younger kids. One of the most fun things about being one of the older kids was making Santa magic for the little ones.

One particular year Cathy and Ginger got to be Santa's helpers. Just before supper, Ginger claimed she couldn't find her missing shoe. Cathy asked Mom if she could go help her find it. Mom said, "Yes, but hurry up, so your supper won't get cold." On Christmas Eve, Mom made chili for supper so we could have something quick to eat for supper, open presents, take a nap, and go to midnight mass. Before Ginger and Cathy sat down for supper, they ran and hung up the stockings with care on the stairway rails and ran to the shed to retrieve Santa's bag they had hidden there earlier and put it on the porch. Then they came back into the kitchen through Mom's and Dad's room and sat down to eat supper. We took our time eating so Norman, Gary, and Sherry would go into the living room first and make the Santa discovery on their own. It worked like a charm.

Norman, Gary, and Sherry were the first ones done with supper and went into the living room. They started yelling "Santa was here! Santa was here!" Mom and Dad and the rest of us raced into the living room to see what all the yelling was about. Sure enough, Santa Claus had indeed been there while we ate supper. The stockings were hung from the stairway rails, and Santa's bag full of gifts. Toys were found on the front porch right by the door. The excitement and the happy looks on their faces were priceless. Years later they learned how we made that magic happen for them on Christmas Eve. Making magic for the little kids is a favorite memory.

There were a lot of weekend visits to and from family and friends. We especially liked the big family reunions every three years when Sister Lorenzo was allowed a home visit. This is when we were able to visit with all our aunts, uncles, and cousins. We also liked pop to drink – something we never had at home. Dad and his brothers drank beer and played cards. The cousins talked and had fun, and Mom worked on the family history. She was the collector of family photos. When she received new photos, she made sure to identify the place, occasion, and people in the pictures. The entire family was invited to our cousin Bernard Gedert's wedding. Adults and kids of every age danced all night long, mostly square dances.

Most of our relatives and friends lived close by in Ohio and Michigan. Grandma (Mom's mama) and Grandpa Wood lived the farthest from us in Toledo, about 60 miles away. Before we left for Toledo, Dad took the car to the gas station to fill the gas tank and check the tires, battery, and hoses under the hood. All 10 of us in the family rode together in the Buick or Oldsmobile prior to seat belts. The twins sat between Dad and Mom in the front seat. The girls and Norman sat in the back seat, alternating one sitting forward and another sitting back. We usually sang and played the "license plate game."

Grandma (Martha Marguerite Henrietta Beneke Perrine Gutzmer) Wood passed away in February 1965, just shy of her 84th birthday. Eleanor was very close to her mother she called "Mama." The funeral was during a major blizzard with 10 inches of snow which required the Coffee Shop to close for two days. When an ambulance came down the street in Toledo. Dad pulled over and got the car stuck in a snowbank. He had all the older girls get out to push the car out and it wasn't long before he had help from other travelers. We headed back to Michigan the same afternoon and couldn't make it to our house because of snow drifts on our road. Dad tried a second route and the car got stuck again. We ended up spending the night at two of the neighbors' houses who lived across the lake from our farm. The next morning Dad walked to our house to get the tractor and pulled the car out of the snowbank.

When a car pulled into the driveway it was usually relatives visiting. We all scrambled in the house to clear off the dining room table and pick up the clothes, toys, and papers in the living room. We hid the items wherever we could find room – Mom's and Dad's bedroom downstairs, the landing leading to the basement, and upstairs in our bedrooms. The Gedert cousins spent time at Wampler's Lake on Sundays and visited afterward. Cousin Wilma said Mom always fixed a nice supper for everyone. They also liked visiting the Coffee Shop and enjoying the fresh donuts.

Mom and Dad went out on Saturday nights when we were older. They went to one of the area bars where they could dance. Sherry enjoyed watching Mom put on her make-up and get dressed up to go out. They usually went to the Twin Gables Bar, Sand Lake Inn, or Pike's Inn. Sometimes the older girls went with them.

When the older girls wanted to go on a date, they had to tell Dad the details of where they would be. They had to be home by midnight. Neither Mom nor Dad provided advice on dating, and none of us had problems with smoking or drinking or behavioral issues. We all loved when neighbors, schoolmates, and boyfriends visited, and they loved playing with us. We played outside every day and had lots of fun and games. Neighbors and friends say how much fun they had coming over to the Gillen's because there were so many kids and such fun things to do.

As Catholics, we attended Saint Joseph's Shrine in the Irish Hills in Brooklyn. We went to mass on Sundays and holy days and took catechism lessons on Saturdays. Mom began playing the organ and singing in the choir in the early 1960s. When we entered the church from the back entrance on Sundays, Mom went directly up the stairs to the choir loft. For a couple of years, Dad took all eight of us with him down the aisle and got us seated in one or two pews where he could keep an eye on us. If we misbehaved, he took us outside to give us a spanking and brought us back into the church. One spanking was usually enough. We often started to giggle, but we weren't punished for it. We didn't know until years later that many parishioners thought Dad was widowed. They felt sorry for him for having to raise us alone and thought he did a wonderful job. Mom also earned money playing the organ for weddings and funerals.

When we were older Mom drove to church separately so she could play the organ for all the morning masses. She started Sunday dinner in the oven before she left for church and left instructions on the blackboard for what we needed to do to finish cooking the meal while she was away. When Irene began driving, she went to an early mass and took whoever was ready with her. Dad always attended 11:30 a.m. mass. On the way home, he stopped for a beer at the Twin Gables bar at the end of Knapp Road. The kids who went to church with Dad got to have a Coke at the bar. In later years many of us went to mass on Saturday evenings.

Sunday dinner was ready when everyone was home from church. We often had chicken noodle soup with homemade noodles and fried or baked chicken on the side. At other times we had barbecued pork spareribs with mashed potatoes or pot roast, meatloaf, and all the fixings. Like Sunday meals in Ohio, Mom made the noodles on Saturday and laid them out to dry on the kitchen and dining room tables and then cut them into small strips. Dad killed the chickens on Saturday that we had for Sunday dinner. Chicken noodle soup is still one of our favorite meals.

We observed Lent by abstaining from meat on Fridays and praying the rosary together every night in the living room with the family. Everyone knelt by the sofa or a chair in the living room, and Dad led the family in prayers. We ate tuna and noodle casserole, tuna salad, grilled cheese sandwiches, and tomato soup, fish, and fish sticks. We liked our Friday meals.

Mom often played the piano after Sunday dinners. Irene played her accordion, and we all sang along from old songbooks and many classics on sheet music. Mom tried her heart out to teach all of us to play the piano. Mom even made a template of the keyboard for us to refer to while we learned. Cathy and Ginger just couldn't get it, and Mom finally gave up. Irene is the only one who learned well, and Noreen learned one hand. Ginger has the songbooks now.

We often played cards with Dad on the weekends, usually hearts or euchre at the round dining room table. The table and chairs were lovely and made by Uncle Andrew Laux, Grandma Gillen's brother-in-law. On rainy days we spent many hours playing card games: solitaire, double solitaire, Go Fish, and Rummy; board games; working puzzles; and building card houses. Norm remembers playing marathon Easy Money, like Monopoly, and Pick-Up Sticks games during the summer. Gary could do these things with us. He couldn't do the agility games Norman and Sherry created. One of the agility games was trying to navigate the living room by walking across the furniture to avoid the "alligators" on the floor. Gary spent many hours building and painting model cars and designing homes and floor plans. During summer break during junior high, Gary and Sherry played the Risk game every day. Not sure who had the final tally of wins.

On other Sundays, Dad took us for a drive somewhere in the Irish Hills. One of our favorite places was Hidden Lake Gardens. Another ride we liked was the steep hill going into Onsted. Dad would step on the brake, or the gas, at the bottom of the hill to make the car lurch and we had to "push" from inside the car to make it up the hill. He also took us to tourist sites when they had specials. We liked Mystery Hill, Frontier City, and the Prehistoric Forest.

We also enjoyed bowling on Sunday afternoons. After Irene got her driver's license, Mom made her, and the older girls take the younger kids with them. They were so mad, but the younger kids learned how to bowl at a young age. Irene would also drive some of the kids to the movie theatre in Brooklyn. We could take bags of popcorn with us and buy candy.

Dad taught the older girls to drive the tractor and one-ton farm truck in their early teens. He then went with them in the car on the road when they had their learner's permits. After the truck quit working, the younger kids spent hours playing in the truck and pretending to drive it.

We all took driver's education through high school. Mr. Kidder was Cathy's driving instructor. She learned to drive a manual transmission, a stick-shift car and loved it. Our car at home was a blue station wagon with a stick shift. Irene learned to drive an automatic-transmission car, so Cathy got to drive Irene to her accordion lessons on Saturdays. Cathy later taught Irene how to drive a stick-shift car. Noreen learned to drive an automatic-transmission car. At the time our car had a manual transmission and Mom taught her how to drive it. Ginger learned to drive both automatic- and manual-transmission cars in driver's education. As a part of Dad's driver's education, we had to learn how to change a tire, read the gauges on the dashboard, and track mileage.

Dad taught Linda how to drive an automatic, and Dexter Layman taught her how to drive a manual-transmission car. Norm remembers driving the Ford Falcon down the lane to the fields at age 13 or 14. He learned to drive an automatic-transmission car at driver's education. Years later he was taught to drive a manual-transmission car by the dealer who sold him a 1975 Toyota Celica. Sherry learned to drive an automatic-transmission car. She learned to drive a stick shift from Mom after she bought Tim and Noreen's Ford Mustang when she was in high school.

Linda earned $3 babysitting at home. Most of us earned money at home by mowing the two acres of lawn every week in the summer, a continuing and hot chore. The yard was divided into six sections with each section given a dollar amount we could earn for mowing. The smallest section in the middle of the circular driveway paid 25 cents. The larger areas paid up to $1.25 each. The more areas we mowed, the more we earned. Long before we had a self-propelled lawn mower, we had a power-lawn mower that had to be pushed. The key to keeping the speed higher was the throttle. At one time the throttle wouldn't stay in place and Cathy wedged a popsicle stick next to the throttle, and it worked. We took turns mowing the yard until it was done.

Mom recorded our earnings in her "Earnings Booklet" and paid us week-ly. Many of our allowances and wages were paid on account. This was money Mom considered borrowed. She kept meticulous records and paid the money back as soon as she could.

We had frequent thunderstorms. Dad would have us go out to the cov-ered porch during some of the storms to watch so we wouldn't be afraid of them. One time we watched a tornado form over the barn. We opened windows a little on two sides of the house so air pressure wouldn't build inside the house. The tornado missed us but touched down nearby. There was another time when a tornado touched down about 15 miles away near Manitou Beach on Palm Sunday in 1964. There was a lot of debris in our fields that we all cleaned up. We found an orange life preserver from Maine. Noreen recalls being in the shower when all the power went out. We drove around the next day to see the destruction. The front of one house was completely gone but all the rooms were intact. It looked like a doll house. A camper truck was split in half with one half being on each side of the street. There was a stove in a tree, a boat in a tree, trees down and debris everywhere.

We often walked around our property. In addition to the fields and roll-ing hills, we had 30 or 40 acres of woodland. It was a great afternoon walk. There were walnut and hickory nut trees. There was an old junk dumping area where we often found special treasures, like Norman's red tractor. There were the remnants of a burned-down house. When we saw squirrels and snakes and heard other critters running in the underbrush, we quickly went the other way. The woods were especially beautiful in the autumn.

Outdoor play included simple things like climbing trees, and tag games. Free tag was an all-time favorite. After all the players hid, the "It" person would call "All Ye, All Ye, Outs In For Free." Sherry always thought these words were "Ollie, Ollie, in for Free." Others thought it was "Ollie, Ollie, Olson Free." We threw a rubber ball over the roof of the house from the back yard to the front yard calling "Eeny-Einy-Over." Dad put an end to this game because it damaged the shingles. Croquet was a family favorite. However, several of the mallets got broken when Dad hit them against the ground to try to tighten up the handles. King of the Hill was played on a pile of lumber stacked against the barn. One person was at the top and all the other players tried to get to the top of the pile without being tagged. The first new person up was the new king. We had an empty 55-gallon drum that we turned on its side and walked on to make it roll across the yard. Dad built many pairs of stilts and puddle jumpers, which were coffee cans with ropes attached, for us to walk on. While Gary couldn't participate in most of the outdoor activities, he was often nearby with us.

Linda, Norman, and Sherry spent many hours playing "ghost" softball. One person batted, one pitched and one played outfield. Whenever the batter made it to base, they put a ghost on first base and then went back up to bat. The ghost ran as many bases as the batter. If you made it to second base the next batter, your ghosts, were on second and third base.

Bikes were particularly dangerous on the stones in the yard and on the hilly dirt road. Noreen was riding to a neighbor's home on a bike that had hand brakes. While riding down the hill on the dirt road, she flipped herself head over heels because she used the wrong hand brake. Many of us fell off our bikes or ran downhill too fast. We slipped on the stones and got bad abrasions on our hands, arms, and legs. Norman almost ripped the nail off on his index finger from the bottom to the top. Mom bandaged and splinted his finger. It was a bit more difficult for him to serve coffee.

Linda and Sherry often walked two-and-a-half miles around the lake. They started along Knapp Road to the east, and turned right to go down Pink Street, and right onto U.S. 12 gathering bottles along the way.

When they reached Twin Gables Bar at the south end of Knapp Road, they cashed in the bottles for the deposit and bought ice cream or candy.

Playing in the barn and out-buildings continued to be a huge pastime. Ginger walked around the ledges in the barn looking for pigeon eggs to break. We loved the barn swallows that built mud nests on the outside of the corn crib, but not the pigeons and crows that sat on the electric and power wires.

There were several ways to get from the upper-level barn to the lower level in the barn. We could drop down through the trap door, go through a grain closet and climb the rock wall foundation there, or go through a side storage room and climb the silo ladder. On the outside of the barn, we got good at climbing the slanted tin milk house roof and sitting on the roof.

There was a small shed behind the corn crib that the older girls turned into a little playhouse with curtains and dishes from the burned-down house in the woods.

The Quonset, where the hay was stored was next to the barn. Norman spent hours and hours building rooms and tunnels in the hay. He supported the bales with boards to avoid collapses. He brought out flashlights and radios so Linda, Gary, and Sherry could eat snacks out there. He created a monorail from the top of the haystack to the end of the Quonset. It ended at a concrete pole, so we had to be prepared to stop early.

There was a water pump in a "well pit" down the hill behind the Quonset hut to supply water to the house. The water well pit was a small 6-foot by 6-foot concrete room, 7-feet deep that was accessed by a hatch in the roof. Norm remembers helping Dad replace and repair the pump. The pump didn't work on occasion when the younger kids were still home. They had to carry pails of water from the lake up to the house. It was quite a trek to cross the dirt road, go down the hill, and then back up to the house. Sherry can't remember how many trips they made and how much water was left in the buckets at the end. Thankfully this did not happen often.

It was quite easy to climb the corn crib walls and ladders. Ginger was adept at climbing the walls and then crossing the expanse of the building by going across the beams to the other side wall. Linda, Norman, and Sherry climbed up onto the corn crib roof and took popcorn up there on the Fourth of July. They could see fireworks from multiple neighboring communities. Also in the corn crib was a corn sheller and an old bin of soybeans that we would drop into from several feet up. We always had dirty powder on us afterward. We wonder now how many mice lived in that pile of soybeans.

We were allowed to be in the corn crib when it was being filled from the top using the combine and grain elevator. We played in the corn crib and silo when they were being filled. We jumped off the top of the corn crib down into a wagon of shelled corn. When we didn't farm anymore, Linda, Norman, and Sherry used the elevator as a "Teeter Totter."

Brooklyn, being in the Irish Hills, is lake country. We were told we could see 50 lakes within a 15-minute drive. Our new farm was between two lakes. Stony Lake was across the road and Vineyard Lake abutted our property at the back. It was a big lake. We could also access it on the other side of a neighbor's property. Approximately two acres of our property across Knapp Road was waterfront property.

The lake was not usable for swimming in this area because of lily pads, reeds, and muck. We had a right-of-way a couple of houses down the road next to the Blatchford's. Dad and the older girls spent a lot of time cleaning out lily pads to make the area good for swimming. The girls were pulling lily pad roots out of the lake yelling, "pull, pull, help." Dad heard this from the house. He thought someone was drowning and came running. The lake bottom was still mucky. We could sink up to our knees

Sunrise over Stony Lake 1970

in some places. Afterward, we had to check for bloodsuckers on our legs and between our toes.

Dad taught us how to fish and clam, and he taught Mom how to cook them. We mostly caught sunfish, bluegill, bass, perch, and an occasional catfish. As soon as we got home, whoever helped Dad catch the fish had to clean the fish and open the clams, even if it was raining. We scaled, cut the fins out, and gutted the fish. Catfish were much harder. The head had to be nailed to a board, the skin cut all around behind the head, and then the skin pulled off with pliers. We learned to like eating fish, but not catfish. They tasted like mud.

Dad allowed friends to hunt on the farm. In return, he was often given quail, rabbit, squirrel, and foxes. Norman recalls helping to skin a rabbit and the pelt peeling off like removing a jacket. Luckily, we didn't have to clean these animals, but we had to eat them. We didn't like to eat wild game. Mom didn't know how to cook the meat, so it was tough, not tasty, and we often found buckshot in the meat.

One time Noreen found a huge snapping turtle in the backyard by the burning barrel. Dad decided that it would make good turtle soup. He put a stick in its mouth and used a hatchet to chop off its head. The hatchet bounced off the turtle's neck and cut Dad's wrist down to the bone. It was a deep cut, and he needed a trip to the emergency room to get stitches. Before he left for the doctor, he hung the turtle by the tail on the clothesline to die and let the blood drain out. We had turtle soup for dinner and liked it. We thought it tasted like chicken.

Mom and Dad knew all the neighbors. Stony Lake provided swimming in the summer and skating and sledding in the winter. The small lake was 40-foot-deep with approximately 25 properties around it in the 1960s. Our farm was on the west side of the lake next to the Randall's. They lived at the top of a hill. The mother, Maybelle, lived there full time, and Irene and Cathy took turns caring for her during the week. They went in the evenings, fixed her dinner, and stayed overnight. Maybelle had two sons who came on the weekends. Jack had male friends. Harry lived in Homer, Michigan, with his son Chuck. His wife had passed away. Chuck was around Irene's age.

The closest neighbors had a cottage on the water across the road and down the hill. Tom and Pepper Cavanaugh came from Detroit on weekends during the summer. Tom's Dad, Grandpa Cavanaugh to us, spent the entire summer. They had a dock and a raft that the older girls could swim out to and play on. The younger kids often played on the dock with a net and caught tiny sunfish. Dad and Mom ran errands for Grandpa and took him to the store with us in town on weekends. When we carried his groceries or just visited, he always had a candy dish out for us. They also had an outhouse on the side yard. Pepper hired Norman to keep the steep hillside cut.

The Blatchford's lived next door to them and had a pontoon boat on which they gave us rides. They had a Chihuahua which nipped at the kids all the time. It was not a favorite pet of ours. We had lake rights at the edge of their property. We had an old rowboat that someone had given Dad, and this is where we kept it. It never got repaired and had leaks in the bottom. We took it out on the lake and learned how to row, but we didn't take the boat out alone. One person had to row while another person had to bail the water out.

The Randall's had a dock, boat, and raft. We were allowed to use their raft and often swam the 50-foot distance between the Randall and Cavanaugh rafts. It was easiest to get out to the raft with the rowboat. Linda would only play around the shore. One summer the older girls decided Linda should learn to swim. She did not want to. They dragged her kicking and screaming into the boat, rowed out to the raft, and got her up onto it. As she calmed down, they got her to get into an inner tube and taught her how to float around in the water, and then how to swim from corner to corner around the raft. The following summer she was able to swim from the shore out to the raft.

Another time some of the older girls told Linda her cat couldn't swim. Linda threw Buffy in the lake anyway. The girls were yelling at her when Buffy swam to the shore.

Past the Randall's was a small cottage on a hill and next to that was Sonny Bauer's property. They were very private people, but they had dogs that barked non-stop and scared us when we walked or pedaled our bikes by their property. Sonny's face was deformed. He was in a fire when he was young and was thrown into a huge bucket of water to save him. His face ended up with huge blisters that formed into his skin.

The Herrmann's lived across the road and down the hill on the south side of the lake. Their family owned most of the south side of the lake. Mom visited Mrs. Herrmann (Betty) occasionally and we mostly saw the kids (Lyndell, Shelly, and David) when we waited for the school bus.

The Stark's lived up on the hill on the north side next to the Whitfield's. Jim and Judy Stark learned to swim across the lake with their dad rowing his boat alongside them. The Whitfield girls (Kathy and Nancy) lived next door and came to their cottage during the summer from Detroit.

Darwin Fisher lived at the other end of Knapp Road on the lake. Before he married Diane, Dad enlisted him to give the girls dance lessons. Dad and Mom taught us how to slow dance at home and at Twin Gables, but they couldn't teach us the current dances of the 1960s. Irene, Cathy, Noreen, Ginger, and maybe some of the younger kids – it seemed like a lot of us, lined up across the living room while Darwin faced us and showed us dance moves. Around this time, Noreen went to the junior prom with Alan Snider, Benny Snider's cousin.

The Klassen's and Ackley's lived across the lake on the east side. The Klassen's had five kids and their father owned and flew a small airplane. Laura was Ginger's classmate and a good friend. Next to them were the Ackley's. Cathy remembers sliding down their grass hill on sheets of cardboard toward the street. They used to start little grass fires and put them out. One of them got out of control and everyone available grabbed brooms from their homes to beat the flames out. Marlene was Ginger's classmate and had fun sleepovers. After the older girls left home or worked summer jobs, Linda, Norman, and Sherry walked further around the lake and swam at friends' houses

Noreen and Ginger learned to water ski on Vineyard Lake, a much larger lake, from co-workers at Elliott's Bait Shop when they were teenagers. Vineyard Lake was behind Randall's property and abutted the back of our farm. There was a strip of summer homes in that area called Knapp's

Landing. It was one area where Linda, Norman, and Sherry swam because the lake was sandier than Stony Lake. That lake seemed to have tons of clams, and we often cut our feet on them. One of the summer residents was always opening and cleaning a bucket full of them.

Living near water brought many critters around the house in the summer months. We found and caught frogs, toads, salamanders, and turtles. Some of these made it into our basement through the window wells. After a huge thunderstorm, one of the window wells was teeming with frogs. Ginger didn't mind getting down in there. As she caught them, she put them in a gallon glass jar to move them away from the house. The jar was filled to the top.

A culvert ran under the road from the lake and came out on our farm near the swamp. Norman and Sherry crawled through the smelly thing a time or two among the empty turtle shells and other critters. It was very yucky.

Winter on the lake was fun. It brought out almost all the neighbors at the same time. None of the kids were allowed on the lake until the ice was four inches thick. Mr. Stark and Mr. Herrmann were the dads that usually kept a close watch over the neighborhood kids until the ice was safe and reported to the parents about the curious kids. Almost every year, Ginger was the first one to test the ice when it first started to freeze and after it started to thaw. She often fell through the ice near the shore and Mom and Dad always heard about it. When the older girls were in and out of the house a lot, Linda, Norman, and Sherry went down to the frozen lake alone. If it wasn't quite frozen solid yet or if it was starting to melt in the spring, Mr. Herrmann, would call Mom at the restaurant and tattle on us. She would send whoever might be home down to the lake to get us. We used to get so upset at Mr. Herrmann, but he kept us safe.

Norman and Sherry both fell through the ice on the swamp at different times. Norman was able to keep breaking away the ice and walk all the way to the shore. Sherry saw an open spot in the ice with tadpoles swimming. When she went to look, one leg fell through the ice. She climbed along the ice to get back to shore and the house. In 1968 when Tim and Noreen were dating, Tim was pulling Norman around in a circle on the swamp. The toboggan wrapped around Tim's legs causing him to hit his face on the ice. He broke his nose.

We all skated and usually had to shovel paths in the snow to skate. We cleared areas to play hockey using something for hockey sticks. We used the hockey pucks to play shuffleboard, and we made long fox and geese game tracks. On days when we stayed at the lake late in the day Mom or Dad flashed the house porch light. We saw it from the lake, and it was a signal for all of us to come home. By the time Norman and Sherry were old enough to skate, they had to share a pair of skates. One played in their boots while the other one skated, and then they switched.

One extremely cold winter day Cathy skated too long. When she got to the house her feet were numb and swollen with frostbite. Mom and Dad wrapped each foot in a towel and got her under the covers. She healed but her feet have been super sensitive to cold her whole life. Cathy also recalls a time when she fell on the ice hitting the back of her head. She didn't remember walking home or getting out of her winter clothes. She started getting more aware when her friends' parents came to pick them up. Thinking back, she probably had a slight concussion.

There were many hills behind the barns that we used for sledding. Some of them allowed us to continue our run onto our frozen swamp. When we used the saucer or sledded on the sand hill, we could get airborne after we pushed off from the top until we hit the bottom of the hill.

We tobogganed down the sand hill and down to the lake from the Randall's driveway. We would go down their driveway, across the road, and down the hill to the lake, dodging trees, and rocks along the way. It was fun, but not very safe. Chuck and one of his friends hit a fence post sticking out of the ground and broke the front end of the toboggan.

Those with more energy took the toboggan into the woods and sledded in what we called "the bowl." Often, we only had two people at the bowl, which made the toboggan too light. The person on the back had to jump off before they got whip lash or thrown off at the bottom of the hill. Sherry was often afraid of the hill and jumped off the toboggan partway down the hill. Norman crashed into a tree one time and hurt his leg.

There was always so much to do on the farms and lake that childhood memories are endless. There were some injuries and illnesses, but it is truly amazing that none of the eight kids ever had a broken bone.

In the summer of 1964, Mom and Dad bought a restaurant and named it Eleanor's Coffee Shop. This business adjusted family living quite a bit. There was much work to be done and everyone in the family had a part in helping.

Two bad years for Dad were 1968 and 1969. In 1968, he was in the Veterans Administration Hospital in Ann Arbor from January 22 to February 20. Aunt Annie Malburg died on February 22. Dad had a car accident on August 3. His sister Sally died on October 19 and Dad went to the Mercy Hospital emergency room when he collapsed on November 11 and was hospitalized for three days.

Money problems led to verbal arguments at night between Mom and Dad. They stayed together for the kids. We could hear their loud voices when we were in bed. One argument was loud enough for some of us to hear Dad planning to shoot himself in the backyard. Several of us ran downstairs and convinced him to put down his gun.

Dad was picked up for drunk driving on December 25 and taken to jail. On New Year's Eve, he was picked up by the state police at 10 p.m. Mom posted the $200 bond on January 1, 1969, and drove him home at 1:30 p.m. He was tried in District Court on January 2, fined $75, and had to pay $25 for court costs. His license was revoked for three months, and he had to spend one day in jail from 8 p.m. on January 4, Saturday, to 8 p.m. on January 5, Sunday. He also had to attend monthly Alcoholics Anonymous meetings as part of a program called ABWA. On April 13, 1969, Dad wrecked the Buick and was jailed for driving on a revoked license. He had a three-day, mandatory jail time, without visitors for the first three days, and $75 in court costs, or an additional 15 days in jail. He was released on April 30. In May, Dad was diagnosed with right lung upper lobe Bullous disease, pneumonia, and chronic bronchitis. As a result, he was unable to work in a factory or where there was dust. On May 22 Dad wrecked the Ford Falcon and had a friend repair the car.

The highlights of 1969 were Gary and Sherry's Confirmation on May 3, Noreen and Tim's wedding on June 6, and Mom and Dad's 25th wedding anniversary celebration one month early in October 1971. Mom and Dad lost Eleanor's Coffee Shop on May 22, 1970. Poodle died in June 1970 at age 61.

In April 1972, the family was required to vacate the farm. They had sold the farm for $42,500 in June 1966, and were renting the property, which they could no longer afford. Mom and Dad found a house to rent on Springville Highway in Onsted about five miles south of the farm. The four younger kids were still at home. Dad drove Linda and Norman to Columbia Central High School, and Gary and Sherry to Columbia Central Junior high until school was out for the year.

These were very trying times for the family and drove Dad and Mom further apart. So much so, that the four younger kids still at home had to relay messages between Dad and Mom. Through all these trials, every one of us learned to be hardworking, ethical, responsible adults. The bonds formed in our growing years remain strong.

Farm in Brooklyn, Mich. 1970

Chapter 5

ELEANOR'S COFFEE SHOP

By Virginia "Ginger" Gillen Poole, Irene Gillen Snider,
Catherine "Cathy" Gillen Osborn, Noreen Gillen Litchard,
Linda Gillen Thompson, Norman Gillen,
and Sherry Gillen Butcher Belmonte

1964 -1970

MOM AND DAD bought Vinnies Grill & Donut Hut at 208 S. Main Street in Brooklyn, Michigan, on August 14, 1964, from Vincent Comstock for $2,000. The terms of the agreement were $1,000 for the business and $1,000 for the equipment and supplies. A $200 down payment was required with the balance of $1,800 paid monthly in installments of $125 within two years, or until paid in full. Other costs were $1,650 for prepaid Consumers Power and Michigan taxes, and fire and theft insurance. No interest was charged. If they defaulted on any payments, Mr. Comstock had the right to repossess the property and consider all payments made to date as rental payments; or he could accelerate the payments and require the entire remaining principal to be paid.

Eleanor's Coffee Shop 1969

Mom and Dad named the new restaurant Eleanor's Coffee Shop. It was 15 minutes from our home on Knapp Road and on the edge of town between L.J. Beal and Son, Inc., a cement trucking company, and the Party Shoppe. Neely's lumber company was across the street. These were three thriving businesses among many others in the village of 800.

The Coffee Shop was an endeavor Mom and Dad thought they could manage with the help of eight children and hired help. It changed life for every member of the family – work, school, and play. Dad's health and alcohol problems worsened throughout his life and at this time in 1964 he was not working as a mechanic or farmer. Mom ran the Coffee Shop, and Dad worked smaller jobs and made money from the farm so he could be at home with the four youngest children. He was especially worried about Gary, who was diagnosed with Duchenne Muscular Dystrophy disease in 1963. Dad helped Gary with his exercises and worked with his doctors to keep Gary as mobile as possible for as long as possible.

The family cleaned and painted the Coffee Shop to get it ready for opening day on August 17, 1964. Linda was age 10 and painting shelves in the kitchen when someone painting the ceiling above her tipped their paint can over and dumped oil-based paint on Linda's head.

The Coffee Shop opened at 6:30 a.m. and closed at 8 p.m., six days a week except for major holidays and family events. The Coffee Shop was also open on Sundays after school was out for the year. The first time the Coffee Shop closed for a major family event was for Grandma Wood's funeral in 1965. The next closings were for Irene's wedding in 1968 - the first wedding of the six girls in the family, and Noreen's wedding in 1969.

The four oldest girls took turns going to work with Mom before school. Two girls worked before school and the other two girls worked after school until closing. When they worked, they had to walk more than a half mile to and from school in Brooklyn. Mom, or sometimes one of the customers, provided a ride to school when it was raining. When the new Columbia Central High School opened on the outskirts of town in 1969, the girls were old enough to drive to school or Dad drove them.

Mom was our first "official" boss and trained us well. We were all extremely nervous at first when we had to wait on customers. We had never dealt a lot with strangers. We had to learn what to say to them. As teenagers and siblings, we all had a complaint of one sort or another, and Mom wouldn't let us leave the kitchen to wait on customers until we smiled. Many of the truckers from Beal's trucking company enjoyed embarrassing us and making us blush. Irene was a senior in high school when the Coffee Shop opened. Ginger was the youngest and shyest worker at age 12. She particularly hated to wait on school-age kids in the dining room. Cathy was very outgoing, and her classmates liked her to wait on them because she fixed their sandwiches the way she liked hers. Mom told her to just slice and stack the roast beef for the sandwich. Cathy cut all the fat off first.

The kitchen had a center island with one shelf, a large steam table, a storage cabinet, two refrigerators, a gas stove with a grill, a deep fat fryer, two large wash tubs for dishes, and a hand sink. We all washed a lot of dishes and liked to cook on the large stove-top grill. The one restroom for employees and customers was off the kitchen.

The Coffee Shop could seat 36 and had a large take-out service, mostly coffee and donuts. The main entrance door opened into what we called the "counter room." Customers could take a seat at the u-shaped counter at one of the 12 bar stools, take a seat in the dining room or request a take-out order.

The counter room was customer and work oriented. Along the front wall was a counter for the cash register, coffee maker and cups, and donut and dessert case. This room also had a Coke machine, cigarette machine, and freezer. Linda and Norman placed the "goods" they were selling for school next to the donut and dessert display case and always had the highest sales of their group. Eleanor's daily *Ripley's Believe it Or Not* quote-of-the-day and the daily specials were posted on the walls.

The dining room had a round table that could seat eight, four tables for four, and a large jukebox. We could play the jukebox anytime we wanted by using the painted quarters in the coin box. We played the jukebox frequently when there weren't any customers.

The donut hut entrance was through the dining room. Mom or Dad bought 25-pound bags of *Dawn* donut mix from the mill in Jackson. In the morning, one of the girls mixed, fried, and frosted or sugar-coated 10 dozen *Dawn* cake donuts. The other girl waited on customers. The girls hated going to school smelling like donuts. They even changed clothes after making donuts and still smelled like donuts because of the odor still in their hair. Kids at school always asked if there were any donuts for them and wanted lockers next to theirs because of the donut smell. Doreen and Rich Turner ran the Party Shoppe next door and lived in the small house behind the donut hut with their two daughters Leann, and Lori. Sherry was often found on the swing set playing with the girls.

Cathy Mixing Donut Dough 1964

When we bought the Coffee Shop, Mom didn't know how to cook "restaurant food" or how to manage a restaurant. She learned by hiring an experienced cook. She also hired wait staff. She was always looking for help outside of the family. In 1965 when we started the school year Mom hired from two-to-five people for the wait staff. In 1969 she hired 10: Karan, Kaye, Norma, Suzie, Peggy, Marcia, Marcia, Marie, Mary, and Blanche. One year, our neighbor Chuck Randall was a waiter. The hired help was paid $1 an hour. The girls were paid weekly based on their ages until they graduated from high school. Irene was paid $10 at age 16, Cathy $8, Noreen $6, and Ginger $4. After high school, they were paid a dollar an hour when they worked.

In July 1967, Linda was old enough to start working at $3 a week. Her jobs were washing and putting the dishes away. The silverware tray was under the counter where customers were seated. She made coffee and refilled coffee cups for customers. She frosted donuts with vanilla or chocolate icing or rolled them in cinnamon or powdered sugar. When she was older, she made donuts, waited on customers, helped Mom in the kitchen, and burned trash in a barrel behind the kitchen.

Cathy, Noreen, Ginger, and Linda continued to work at the Coffee Shop, and Norman and Sherry started to help and earned wages. At this time, Cathy earned $35 a week. Once a week she was given an extra $10 to do the family laundry at the laundromat, and "she could keep the change." Norman's wages or allowance ranged from $8.50 to $9.64. Sherry received 45 cents to $2.30 to buy something or to go to the Star Theater in Brooklyn to see a movie.

Often on Saturday nights, Mom let Linda, Norman, and Sherry take enough money out of the "till" to walk to the theater to see a movie. By the time they walked back to the Coffee Shop Mom had it all cleaned up and it was time to go home. On other Saturday nights, Mom stopped at the Dairy Queen and bought "Dilly" ice cream bars for everyone still at home.

As part of our wages, we were allowed to eat and drink what we wanted in the Coffee Shop. Ginger most often had pop, hamburgers, potato chips, shrimp, donuts, and pie. When she had time, she worked on her homework at the end of the counter near the kitchen. Sherry alternated after-school shifts with Norm and always worked with Ginger. She had French fries on those days and frequently a fish sandwich. Those are both still some of her comfort foods.

Mom had a Coffee Club. If customers had a club card, their coffee was 5 cents a cup, including refills. Menu Specials were $1 to $1.15 and included sandwiches, dinners, and cold or hot plates. Some of the specials noted in Eleanor's ledger are scalloped potatoes and ham, Swiss steak, liver and onions or bacon, pork chops and dressing, beef stew, salmon patties, tuna with homemade noodles, roast beef with vegetables, spaghetti with meat sauce, spareribs, scalloped potatoes and Polish sausage, western omelet, hot meatloaf sandwich, Salisbury steak, roast pork and dressing, stuffed pork chops, creamed chicken, roast chicken and dressing, baked ham and pineapple, short ribs, salmon loaf, corned beef and cabbage, and fish plate. The chicken noodle soup was 35 cents. One year on April Fool's Day Mom cut pieces of cardboard in the shape of a hamburger bun and put the hamburger on top of the cardboard. One customer ate half of his sandwich before he found out. He was so mad he stormed out without paying.

Mom worked a split shift, leaving every day after the noon rush hour to run errands and go home for a break. At the end of the day, after closing, she put the chairs on the tables and swept and mopped the floors. When Linda, Norman, and Sherry were old enough they alternated working days after school and worked with one of the older girls. When Norman was working, customers often told him how he would "make someone a great wife one day." Sherry had a pixie haircut one summer and was frequently called a boy. Because of this, she grew her hair long well into her 20s. Sometimes whoever was working wouldn't get home until 10 p.m. and then would still have to do homework. If it wasn't too busy at the Coffee Shop, we could get our homework done there. This didn't happen very often. Mom got up around 2 a.m. to work on her ledgers, and then went back to bed for a few more hours.

Someone was always cooking and baking at home in the evenings and on weekends. In addition to cooking for home, Mom worked on the specials, pies, and bread for the next day at the Coffee Shop. Noreen was the original bread maker, although we could all make bread and help when it was needed. Noreen baked five loaves of bread twice a week. Norman took over this duty when he was 10. Breadmaking was a three-hour process. When Norman was making the bread, he used a large Tupperware bowl for the dough and placed it on the stove to rise with the oven turned on warm. One time Norman turned the oven higher, and the Tupperware bowl melted into the bread dough and had to be thrown out. Many times, the dough for one loaf was sacrificed for cinnamon rolls, bubble bread, or "frogmen" as a treat for the family. Frogmen were made by deep frying pieces of dough and shaking them in sugar or powdered sugar after they were cool.

Mom and Noreen in Kitchen 1971

The Coffee Shop participated in the annual village "Sidewalk Sales Day" in the summer, selling donuts from a red wagon. Dad would drive back and forth to the Coffee Shop to keep the wagon supplied. Cathy returned to the Coffee Shop on one occasion and was mortified to see 10 dozen donuts on the pavement. She breathed a sigh of relief when she found out Dad was the one at fault. He had set the donut trays on the car and when he opened the car door the trays slid off.

When the Michigan International Speedway (MIS) opened in October 1968, the Coffee Shop opened on race days, regardless of the time of year. MIS was highly successful and so was the Coffee Shop on these days. Irene and Cathy worked part-time at the Coffee Shop, and Ginger worked at the racetrack. At the time, there was one traffic lane through Brooklyn to the racetrack and the cars were at a standstill for quite a while. Mom and Dad came up with a plan to sell coffee and food to the people waiting in traffic. The girls went to the cars stuck in traffic, took orders, ran back into Coffee Shop, and took the orders back to the cars. The cars would have only moved a few spaces. Later, we sold boxed lunches next to the street from a folding table. Pretty innovative.

The Coffee Shop was so successful that Mom was viewed as the bread-winner of the family. This was something Dad always thought of as his job. Gross monthly sales began at $752 and peaked at $2,249 in October 1969. Sometimes Mom ran out of bread, hamburger, or something else at the Coffee Shop and one of us walked one block to Bill's IGA to pick up the items.

Mom paid herself as much as she could afford. At most, it was $65 per week. In 1967 Dad was in the hospital and on unemployment receiving $50 a week. Expenses at home left little money to spare. Dad, not having an eight-hour-a-day job was often at bars throughout the day, sometimes winning money playing pool and shuffleboard. His nickname was "Lucky." He also had the flexibility to run errands for Mom and to be available for any of the kids in need of something, mostly a ride to the Coffee Shop or school. Dad still needed cash from Mom. On most days, he took money out of the till, or the cigar box Mom took home every night with the day's receipts and cash. One time when Mom received a driving citation, customers chipped in to help her pay the fine. All the family income helped to pay the bills and was eventually reimbursed.

There were a few accidents at the Coffee Shop through the years. Mom was standing in the doorway to the kitchen, near the coffee station. When the waitress picked up a pot of boiling water to make more coffee, the coffee pot shattered, and the water poured down Mom's back. She had a girdle on and stripped it off immediately and still ended up with third-degree burns. She was home for a few days healing.

Dad hired someone to change the gas stove from propane to natural gas. The contractor didn't change the connection properly and when Mom opened the oven door to light the pilot light, the flames burst out and burned her face. Her eyebrows were burned off and her hair and eyelashes were singed.

Mom used to freeze hamburgers in a stack. She tried to pry them apart, using a butcher knife, but she didn't lay the meat on the counter first. When she pried the stack apart, the knife went through the palm of her left hand and required a trip to the doctor's office.

Noreen was slicing potatoes on a mandolin slicer which didn't have a cover or guide over the blade. She was trying to slice every bit of the potato. Irene came into the kitchen and said something to Noreen. Noreen looked at her and kept on slicing potatoes. Irene yelled, "Look at your hand." There was blood running from Noreen's middle finger and the skin was hanging down. Noreen had sliced the end of her middle finger across the tip. They bandaged her finger as best as they could, and someone took her to the doctor. The doctor was out, so the nurse bandaged her finger and let it heal. The end of Noreen's finger is now a little crooked, but it works fine.

One Sunday, when Noreen was working with Linda or Norman, there were a couple of guys acting strange. They were checking out the doors and windows. When they went outside and started walking around,

Noreen called Mom and Dad, and they called the police. When the policeman came, the men left. Another time Noreen was 16 when four or five young men in their 20s came into the Coffee Shop. They offered her $100 if she would go to the races with them. She didn't go. It is scary to think what might have happened if she had gone with them.

In 1968, as a senior in high school, Noreen worked at the Coffee Shop in the afternoons three days a week as part of her Community College Program. Irene was attending school to be a legal secretary in Jackson and Cathy was going to beauty school in Jackson. When they were home, they worked at the Coffee Shop. This is how Irene met her future husband, Ben Snider.

Linda at the Coffee Shop 1969

Mom was able to get a few breaks while we owned the Coffee Shop. She was on a Monday evening bowling team with Mildred Tompkin, Wilma Drake, Thelma Thatcher, Jeannette Hicks, and Virginia Dermeyer. She also enjoyed monthly TOPS (Take Off Pounds Sensibly) meetings. Mom and the older girls were always watching their weight. The major high-light was Linda winning a trip to New York in June 1968 for mother and daughter. Customers signed Linda's name on the back of their Bill's IGA receipts and put them in a jar next to the donut case. Linda won the nationwide teen competition.

Mother's Day was not a happy time in 1969. There is a note in Mom's Coffee Shop ledger that says "Failure. Lost the Battle. Do what has to be done, and keep your damn mouth shut." Things must have gotten better between Dad and Mom when Dad "won" a trip to Lake Havasu, Arizona. Mom loved to travel, and this was their first vacation ever without the kids. A real estate company was offering free trips to a planned retirement community in exchange for listening to their promotional pitch. They left on June 28, Dad's birthday, with $30 in their pocket and returned happily to tell us their story.

Working at the Coffee Shop was hard work, but it taught all of us how to talk to people and interact with total strangers. The customers taught us a lot and were mostly friendly. Things Norman learned while working at the Coffee Shop (and doing crossword puzzles):

- Joe Budak "drafted" his little red car behind semi-trucks to save fuel.
- "Shank's mares" means walking.
- Antidisestablishmentarianism is not the longest word in English… Pneumonoultramicroscopicsilicovolcanoconiosis is the winner (45 letters)
- Do not set a battery directly on concrete.
- When "cashing out" the register and making change, the dollar bills should all be face-up and right-side up.

- The U.S. Post Office transitioned to two-letter state abbreviations.

Some of our favorite customers were Ray Balliet, John Neely and his mother Amelia, Jack Elliott and his mother Josie, Fred Snider and his son Benny, Charles Daugherty, the Knutson's (Jim, Jan, and Don), Don Rose, Merlyn Wilson (our music teacher) and Joe Budak (Ginger's math teacher and a good friend of the family), Red Ambler, and Julie Ksiazkiewicz. To pronounce her name, Julie would say, "Say skunk cabbage and slur it or sneeze it." Other favorites were Boots Smith (who was crushed while unloading his cement truck), Clark Griggs, Norman Kope, Don and Peggy Onsted, Joe Munson, Ralph Lehuy, Ross Moore, Jim Knapp, Bob Borchardt, Bill Kerr, and Joe Holland.

The customer's Sherry most remembers are the Munson family. Joe and his three kids ate dinner every night at the Coffee Shop. The kids also came and played with us at the house a few times.

Mr. Comstock sold the property in October 1968 after Mom and Dad did not fulfill their contract. He allowed Mom and Dad to pay a $100 monthly rent to continue the business. At the time Dad was an Amway Home Products distributor but didn't have enough money to make the rental payments. The property was repossessed on May 22, 1970. We were lucky to have had the Coffee Shop for the time we did. It fed the family and paid the family bills for almost six years.

After we owned the Coffee Shop, it became McCabe's, then Ruth's for Ruth May, who bought the property after the restaurant at Cambridge Junction burned down. It is currently Poppa's and still thriving.

20th Anniversary 1966

25ᵗʰ Anniversary 1971

Chapter 6

HOME LIFE AFTER BROOKLYN

*By Virginia "Ginger" Gillen Poole, Sherry Gillen Butcher Belmonte,
Linda Gillen Thompson, and Norman Gillen*

1972 - 1976

First Home in Onsted, Mich. 1973

IN EARLY SPRING the family was notified that they would need to move out of the house. The family received a second notice to vacate the farm property on Knapp Road on April 12, 1972. To avoid paying the $250 rent due, they had seven days to pack their possessions and vacate the property. Mom and Dad rented a house on Springville Highway in Onsted about five miles from Brooklyn. They moved into the new house on May 1st.

The four oldest girls were married or working away from home. The four younger kids were still at home. Linda was a senior and graduating in June, and Norman was a sophomore. Both attended Columbia Central High School in Brooklyn. Sherry was finishing the 8th grade, and Gary was just finishing the 7th grade at Columbia Central Middle School. Gary was a year behind Sherry because he stayed in 5th grade when he missed a lot of school one winter due to colds and ear infections.

Prior to moving into the house on Springville Highway, everyone still at home spent weeks getting the house ready to live in. Every room had old wallpaper to be removed, up to 13 layers in some rooms. One evening Dad was on a ladder and stretched too far with his scraper and fell to the floor gashing his head open. It required a trip to the emergency room for stitches.

The house was awesome. Entering the house from the front formal entry was a parlor on each side of the hallway and the stairwell to the upstairs. One of the parlors became Mom and Dad's bedroom and one was Gary's. Continuing into the house were the dining room and living room side by side. Moving through the dining room was the kitchen at the back of the house with a narrow back staircase. There were four bedrooms upstairs, three of which we used. There was another staircase on the bedroom level that opened onto the flat roof. Sherry liked going up to the roof to read and sunbathe in the summers.

The rooms were huge, and the structure was solid. The ceilings were 10 feet tall on the main level, and the doors and windows were all tall and wide. The walls, doorways, window frames, and sills were four inches deep. The flooring was hardwood. The kitchen and dining room cupboards were floor-to-ceiling. Norman's upstairs bedroom was so big he had his double bed in the middle of the room.

There was a huge tree with weeping branches in the side yard that looked as old as the house. Ginger loved to visit.

The Greek Revival plantation house was built in the mid-1830s by pioneer Sylvanus Kinney. He cleared and developed his heavily wooded 160-acre property into one of the best farms in the county. Prior to the beginning of the Civil War, the property was said to be a stop along the Underground Railroad. The area was well known for its antislavery support from 1830 to 1860. One of the bedrooms had shackles on the wall. In one of the basement rooms there was a large hole in the brick wall and a hidden room behind it. We had to duck down to about waist-high to get into it. We also thought the house was haunted. Often in the living room, upstairs, and at the entrance to the kitchen, we smelled pipe smoke, but no one in our family smoked a pipe.

Mom was hired as the secretary at St. Joseph's Shrine when Dad was very ill the first summer in Onsted. He was in Bixby Hospital in Adrian with pneumonia from July 19 to August 22. He was home until he was admitted to the Veteran's Administration Hospital in Ann Arbor on October 12 with bronchitis and metastasized lung cancer. At that time, no visitors under the age of 16 were allowed in the hospital. Mom finally received special permission for Norman, Gary, and Sherry to visit Dad. He was allowed to come home for a visit the last weekend in October.

When Dad was home, he said he knew he was dying when the entire family gathered at home several weeks before Thanksgiving. He was sicker than ever before. Many times, when he was less sick, he hadn't been allowed to come home. When he was not sleeping, he was able to sit in a wheelchair and visit with us together and individually. He said that if he lived, he was sure he would be admitted to the psychiatric ward because he thought he was going crazy. He didn't know he was on a heavy dose of morphine. We also gave him a shot of whiskey when he asked, which was not often. Norman drove Dad and Mom to the hospital for the last time on October 29, and Sherry rode with them. For the hour it took to drive to the hospital, Mom and Dad reminisced about their life together as they rode in the back seat of the car. It was bittersweet. Dad died the next day on October 30, 1972, about 10 weeks before the twins' 15th birthday in December.

During our first year in Onsted, Norm started 11th grade and Sherry started 9th grade at Onsted High School. Gary was attending 8th grade at the Tecumseh Schools. Tecumseh had facilities for handicapped students and Onsted did not. A school bus with a lift picked him up and dropped him off daily at the house. Mom was still working at St. Joseph's Shrine. Linda continued to live at home while she worked at the D & M Grill. After Dad died, we all worked together to get meals, take care of the home, and make sure Gary's needs were met. The three older girls still living in the area came for the holidays with their families.

In 1974, Mom, Linda, Norman, Gary, and Sherry moved to Main Street in Onsted. Norman had one upstairs bedroom until he graduated and left on July 18 for his Navy enlistment. Linda and Sherry shared the other bedroom. Gary and Mom had the two bedrooms downstairs. Gary spent a lot of time in his room painting, assembling model cars, and sketching homes. Norm and Sherry shared many of the same friends and there was a nice going away party for him.

Mom continued to work at St. Joseph's Shrine, and there was a phone extension at our house that the priests could turn on when they were not available. We generally received calls asking what time the masses were at church. In the spring of 1975 during Sherry's junior year, she was paged to the school office. Mom was on the phone and told her to pick up Carol, a younger student, and take her to the church. Carol's mother Gladys was the church housekeeper. She had phoned Mom at work and told her that she was going to kill herself. Mom tried to keep her on the phone, but she hung up. Mom immediately called one of Gladys' neighbors who also worked at the church, and then 911. The neighbor ran over immediately but was too late to save Gladys. After the incident, Father Fitzgerald was transferred to another parish.

Mom loved her job at the church. Father Bill McKeon replaced Father Fitzgerald. Father McKeon, or "Father Bill" as he was called by our family, had a great personality. He was very social and loved to host dinner parties. He invited our family to eat dinner with him often and was a significant friend for Mom. She laughed often and was finally learning to relax again after many long years of hard living.

Gary was getting weaker at the end of 1975. Sherry remembers his breathing starting to get more exaggerated. He did go to school that fall but also missed many days. There were also some doctor visits to the house. On December 30, Mom helped Gary up during the night to assist him and noticed that his fingernails were turning blue. She phoned the local ambulance to transport him to the hospital. There was an awful ice storm that night, and we followed the ambulance riding with our outside tires on the gravel edge of the street for traction. The next day the whole family visited Gary throughout the day. Mom, Linda, and Sherry returned home around 11:30 p.m. We had slept only a couple of hours when the hospital called and said to come back. We left immediately but Gary died from respiratory distress before we returned. It was New Year's Eve, December 31. Gary had just turned 18 on December 21.

In 1976, Sherry graduated from high school on June 6, and Linda married Bill Thompson on June 26. Mom rented a house on 4th Street in Onsted from Murray Paige, one of Bill Thompson's friends. Mom and

Sherry lived there until Sherry left for Eastern Michigan University in September. Mom was alone for the first time in her life at age 58. It was a major transition for her. She said she came home to an empty house and was sad to have no one to share the news of the day with her.

Family at Home 1973

THE WALTER AND ELEANOR GILLEN STORY

OUR PARENTS

By Sherry Gillen Butcher Belmonte

A family begins, the daily work never ends.
The motion is constant, but oh so still in their beds.
So many words are said and so many forgotten to say.
But the actions are watched, the values set.

The perseverance, the constancy, the challenges,
the struggles, the creativity, the wide-open outdoors,
the sibling rivalry, the sibling cohesiveness, the ups,
the downs, but always...your steadfastness.

One by one they leave, they begin lives of their own –
each with their own strengths and weaknesses, and yet,
so many similarities between them.

We wonder what you think as you watch our lives.
We wonder if you ponder the "what ifs", "if only I"
or "I wish I had" ...   ...DON'T!!

There is no room for what ifs. You did a wonderful job
with the resources you had available at the time.
You loved, you adapted,
you stayed steadfast and strong.

Our quirks are there for us all. They add humor to our
days – they keep us laughing, there's no need to strive
for perfection – We're us – We're our family!

You created a wonderful, healthy set of kids with no regrets
– we hold our memories of you both close to our hearts.

Your legacies will continue in our children too.

Be proud of where you began, who you grew to be, and how you lived your lives. A family is a group unto itself. It's been a job well done!!

PART THREE
THE MATURING FAMILY

1962 – 2022

Our school years
and married life

Hope you enjoy reading my life story. Irene

Chapter 7

———— ✺ ————

IRENE AND BEN SNIDER

By Irene Gillen Snider

Oldest Daughter

IN 1963, CATHY and I went to our first dance at Boysville sponsored by St. Joseph's Shrine church in the Irish Hills in Brooklyn, Michigan. I was 16 and Cathy was 14.

In 1964, I went to the Holly Hop at Christmas time with Sam Armstrong. Sam was my age and from Manchester, Michigan. In the fall, I went with my friend, Pat Griggs and eight classmates, to the Griggs' family cabin for the weekend at South Branch near Grayling, Michigan.

My closest friend in high school was Cheryl Bradley. I spent time at Cheryl's house at Clark Lake, and Cheryl spent time at our house on Stony Lake. Cheryl was an only child, so she liked being with our family, and on the farm.

I went to my senior prom with Sam Armstrong and made my own dress.

Sometimes Sam would come over to see me at our house. He unhooked the speedometer in the car, so his parents didn't know he drove the 12 or 13 miles to Brooklyn. Sam's sister, Virginia, was killed in a car accident in December 1965. After the accident I never saw Sam again.

I attended Brooklyn High School in Brooklyn, Michigan, and graduated in 1965. I was a B student, and my favorite classes were Latin, English, and band. My extra-curricular activities were Latin Club and band. I played the bells, also called glockenspiel, a percussion instrument, in the band at home football games and several concerts during the school year.

I had several jobs during high school. I babysat and helped take care of our neighbor (Maybelle Randall) after school. I was a waitress at Christie's Grill (now Harold's Place) at the end of Knapp Road at the corner of US-12 and Onsted Highway in Brooklyn. Sometimes I walked the half mile to work if I didn't have a ride. I also worked at Eleanor's Coffee Shop in Brooklyn before and after school.

After I graduated, I dated Jim Norton from Homer, Michigan, who was 6 feet 5 inches tall. While I was working at the Coffee Shop, I met Ben Snider, from Snider's Service in Brooklyn. Ben (Benny) worked with his father, Fred Snider, selling and repairing Massey Ferguson farm equipment. In Benny's spare time, he raced his stock car and flew his airplane.

I enrolled in the Lansing Business College Speedwriting and Typing Program in the fall after high school graduation. After completing the program, I worked at Spartan Electronics in Jackson, Michigan, as a secretary until 1968, when I married Benny. I changed jobs and worked at Consumers Power Company in downtown Jackson as a secretary until 1971 when we adopted Mark.

Benny and I were married on September 14, 1968, at St. Joseph Shrine in the Irish Hills by the Reverend James Fitzgerald. We spent our honeymoon driving to the Wisconsin Dells, taking the car ferry to Ludington, Michigan, and driving home through northern Michigan. Our first home was at 2017 Parkwood Court, near Vineyard Lake, about four miles from Brooklyn. Fifty-four years later in 2022, when everyone was home for Dave Osborn's memorial service, Sherry rented a vacation home for their family. The rental turned out to be on the other side of the block from Irene and Benny's first home. It brought back fond memories for everyone in the family.

I was on a bowling team for quite a few years at Brooklyn Lanes. I also spent over 30 years going with Benny to his stock car races at different racetracks in Michigan, Indiana, and Ohio. Benny was racing at Butler Motor Speedway, in Quincy, Michigan, when we met the McFadden's (Eastman, Kathryn, Melanie, Karen and Lisa). The McFadden's have been our life-long friends and extended family ever since. Eastman and Kathryn's three children are now married with children of their own in college.

In February 1969, Benny and I attended the Inaugural Snowmobile Race at Sault Saint Marie with our friends, Doreen, and Rich Turner. Both couples took our snowmobiles, and we camped in the Turner's pickup camper. Later in the year Benny stopped working for his father at Snider's Service in Brooklyn when he started working as a technician at Walker Manufacturing (later Tenneco Automotive) in Grass Lake, Michigan.

In 1970 Benny and I went to Lake Michigan to visit Sleeping Bear Sand Dunes, and to Maine to see the East Coast. Mark was born on January 18, 1971. He was adopted by Benny and me on February 12 when he was 3 1/2 weeks old. The same year, Mark's cousin, Todd Osborn, was born on April 21. Mark's other cousin at the time was Dawn Litchard born on December 16, 1969. Mom and dad celebrated their 25th wedding anniversary on Knapp Road in November 1971. Dad died of lung cancer on October 30, 1972, at age 56.

Brooklyn had a big blizzard in March 1973, and we were snowed in for a week. Our home was on Vineyard Lake at the time, so we used our snowmobile to get around the area.

On a very hot Labor Day in 1973 Benny and I moved into our current home at 11485 Hewitt Road in Brooklyn near Lake Columbia. Our daughter, Kristi, was born shortly after on September 19, 1973, and was adopted by us in November when she was two months old. The same year, Mark and Kristi's cousin, Andy Litchard, was born on September 5, and their cousin, Brian Osborn, was born on September 13. While I was taking care of Mark and Kristi, I babysat for Mike and Pat Williamson, and sometimes watched other children. Sherry often babysat Mark and Kristi when Benny and I went to the stock car races.

In 1974, Norman, graduated from Onsted High School, in Onsted in June. On July 1st he began his 20-year Navy career at Great Lakes Naval Training Center north of Chicago, Illinois. Later in the year on December 23, Benny's father, Fred Snider, died of a stroke at age 61. Fred's death was unexpected and a shock to everyone who knew him.

In December 1974, Benny and I attended the funeral service for his father, Fred Snider, at the Brooklyn Presbyterian Church. I knew a lot of friendly people at the church, and the church seemed very comfortable. I started attending this church and Benny returned to this church that he had attended with his family as a child.

In 1975, we took a family vacation with Helen Snider (Benny's mother). We drove to Washington, D.C. and visited the D. C. sites with Ginger when she lived in an apartment in Alexandria, Virginia. We continued south to North Carolina on our vacation and took the car ferry to Ocracoke Island in the Outer Banks region and continued from there to Cape Hatteras, the southernmost barrier island in North Carolina.

Mark was five years old, and Kristi was three in 1976 when Brooklyn celebrated its Bicentennial the same year Sherry graduated from Onsted High School and began college at Eastern Michigan University in Ypsilanti, Michigan. Our family trip this year, was to Mackinac Island on Lake Huron between Michigan's Upper and Lower Peninsulas where we walked on the porch at the Grand Hotel when it was free.

Benny's racing garage on Hewitt Road caught fire and burned to the ground on March 12, 1977, at 10 p.m. When Benny was working on his race car earlier in the day a spark from his cutting torch landed in the back seat of the race car. The seat smoldered for a while and then exploded into flames. Benny could figure this out having been a volunteer fireman before we were married. The garage was a total loss. Engine blocks and many of Benny's father's tools melted in the fire. Benny was able to get his #3 race car pulled out of the burning garage and unchain our dog Snooper, fastened to the garage. Snooper returned home after a couple days, and Benny was able to continue driving his race car. By the end of April, a new racing garage was built and is still standing.

In January 1978, Brooklyn, Michigan, had another blizzard to deal with. We still had a snowmobile to get around until the roads were cleared.

Over the years, when Mark and Kristi were young, we owned several Recreational Vehicle's (RVs), from pickup campers to motor homes. We usually went on vacation every year in the family RV. In 1980, we traveled to Florida in the RV to camp with other RV friends and to spend time at Disney World. In 2003, we went to Bar Harbor, Maine, camped in our RV, and took a very fast Canadian American Transportation (CAT) Ferry to Nova Scotia on Prince Edward Island in Canada. On our return trip home, we stopped to camp in New Hampshire and Vermont.

I had several jobs through the years while Mark and Kristi were in junior high and high school. I initially worked in the office at Saint Joseph's Shrine to give Mom a break. Then, for a few years, I worked in the office at the Shrine full time. Later, I worked for the Manpower Incorporated Temp Agency and had several jobs. My last job with the Temp Agency lasted five years at Consumers Energy.

Mark graduated from Columbia Central High School in 1989. All through high school he dated Vicki Hansen. Mark lived in Alabama for a few years. In 1995 Mark returned to the local area near Brooklyn and met Angie Weaver. Angie had a 2-year-old son, Jacob, who was born in 1993. Mark and Angie lived together for 11 years and had three children. Joe, their oldest son, was born in November 1999 and was 22 in 2021. Charlie, their second son, was born in April 2002 and is 19. Katie, their daughter, and youngest, was born on St. Patrick's Day, March 17, 2003, and is 18.

Benny and I babysat for the grandkids at our house every week when the grandkids were babies, toddlers, and school age. The grandkids call me "Grandma" and Benny "Papa." I had a dresser drawer for each of the kid's clothes and a lot of toys. Grandma and Papa (Snider) and the grandkids always had a good time together.

Angie moved with her four children, Jacob, Joe, Charlie, and Katie, above the Mackinac Bridge to the Upper Peninsula in Michigan in February 2008. On moving day, they had five feet of snow at their new home. Mark stayed downstate in the Brooklyn area. Angie brought the kids to Grandma and Papa's house to visit Mark, and Angie's parents, Grandpa and Nan Weaver, for a few days every winter, and summer.

Papa and I drove to the Upper Peninsula at least twice a year to visit Angie and the grandkids. Sometimes we picked the grandkids up to camp and tour with us in the RV in the Upper Peninsula. Two of the family's favorite places were Tahquamenon Falls and Pictured Rocks in Munising.

On other occasions, Angie brought the grandkids to the campground where we were staying. The Big Boy in Gaylord, Michigan, was our half-way meeting place to pick up the grandkids or drop off the grandkids with Angie when it was time to go home.

Our last RV was a 38-foot, 1994 Kountry Star, and the nicest RV we owned. The grandkids always had a great time camping with Grandma and Papa in the RV. The last time they camped with us in the RV was in 2005 when their dad was able to go on the trip with us. We camped at Silver Lake in Mears, Michigan, on Lake Michigan. Papa, Grandma, Mark, Joe, Charlie, and Katie all walked to the top of the sand dunes. Joe was five years old at the time and asked Papa to carry him down the sand dune. Sitting around a campfire one night, Charlie forgot the camp stool didn't have a back and fell off backwards. He wasn't hurt. Katie always liked to draw and color, so I had a big activity box in the RV for all the grandkids.

We mostly went to the Upper Peninsula to see Angie and the grandkids when the grandkids played sports. We stayed at the Sandtown Bed & Breakfast about 10 miles from Engadine, Michigan, where Angie and the grandkids lived at the time. Benny and I became friends of the Harpers, the Bed & Breakfast owners. Now that Katie graduated from high school, Benny and I plan to visit at Christmas time.

Angie's oldest child, Jacob, graduated from Whitefish Township School in Paradise, Michigan. Joe, Charlie, and Katie graduated from Engadine High School in Engadine, Michigan. Katie, the youngest grandchild, graduated in 2021. Joe played basketball and football and was a great kicker. Charlie played basketball and football and liked to be on top of the tackle pile. Katie played volleyball and basketball. All the grand-kids worked after graduation. At the close of 2022, Jacob is in between jobs, Joe is working on the pipeline in Wyoming and North Dakota and Charlie works at the Hunt and Fish Shop in Curtis, Michigan, near Big Manistique Lake. Katie works at the Garlyn Zoo on the Animal Care Team in Naubinway, Michigan. Jacob Weaver and Pam Bowler have a son Henry Allan born in April 2017.

Mark spent many years as a cement layer doing flat work and pouring walls. Mark returned to live with us in 2020 to get care for his health is-sues. Mark's most significant issue was cement poisoning (cellulitis) on his legs. Mark's health improved significantly in one year. Mark keeps as busy as he can with yard work, car repair, and handyman projects at home and in the local area.

Kristi graduated in 1991 from Columbia Central High School in Brooklyn. Kristi had a few boyfriends over the years and married three times. Kristi's first marriage was to Jim Lyson on Waikiki Beach in Honolulu, Hawaii, in 2001. Kristi and Jim divorced in 2003. Kristi's next marriage was to Rande Bahnmiller on New Year's Eve in 2007 in Mobile, Alabama. Rande's daughter, Devyn, was eight years old at that time. Benny and I camped at Gulf Shores, Alabama, on this trip. Kristi and Rande divorced in 2012.

Kristi became re-acquainted with Nelson Copeland on June 8, 2013, at his cousin's graduation open house. Nelson is Kathryn and Eastman McFadden's nephew (Benny and my good friends). Kristi and Nelson knew each other from the annual family gatherings and outings the Snider and McFadden families shared together. In 2013, Nelson lived in Pierceton, Indiana, and Kristi lived in Pickney, Michigan. Kristi and Nelson were married the next year on the 4th of July 2014 at Lucerne Park at Pike Lake in Warsaw, Indiana, and bought a small farm in Onsted, Michigan.

Kristi and Nelson took their honeymoon a month before they were married so they could attend a family gathering. The week of June 14, 2014, the Walter and Eleanor Gillen children, and their children, had a family gathering in Kill Devil Hills on the Outer Banks in Kitty Hawk, North Carolina. Twenty-six family members coordinated their visits so they could all stay in the same beach house. The beach house had an elevator, so Linda and Bill could come. Ginger had a broken leg at the time and had to miss all the fun on the beach. We were all thrilled to help celebrate Kristi and Nelson's early honeymoon.

Kristi and Nelson moved to Terrell, Texas, near Dallas, Texas in 2017. Kristi and Nelson named their farm the TX Scratching Post. They don't have children, but they treat their animals as their children. In 2021 they have two horses: Bella and Holly; three donkeys: Momma (Jenni), Rusty, and Daisy; two goats: Henry and Winnie; four ducks: Ricky, Biff, Jeffrey, and Preston; and 19 cats: Mike, Charlie, Tashi, Kevin, Punkie, Sisser, Glenda, Momma, Rosie, Steve, Summer, Sam, Justin, Nick, Tex, Peanut, Willy, Scotty, and Boots. Plus, one critter, rabbit Matt.

Kristi became an author in 2021 and published the novel *Oakdale* by Krisi Copeland and three books in her Texas Summer Nights romance series *Somewhere Outside of Sunset, Home in Paradise,* and the *Art of Loving.*

I retired from Consumers Energy as a Manpower employee in December 1998. Benny retired from Tenneco Automotive in January 1999 as an Automotive Engineer where he worked on exhaust systems for 30 years. After Benny retired, he returned four times to work as a Contract Engineer. Benny and I continue to enjoy our retirement years. I started Memories-type scrapbooking in 1999 and have about 60 scrapbooks so far in our library. I have made another 15 or more scrapbooks for various family members. Ginger and Jim helped me with the *Walter Andrew Gillen Heritage Album* covering Dad's family from 1844 to 1972, ending with the year he passed away. Ginger, Jim, and I worked long hours for several days to complete Dad's *Heritage Album* before the August 2011 annual family reunion in Swanton, Ohio. Benny watched the three of us in action the entire time, shook his head thinking we were crazy, and was successful in keeping from getting involved. The *Album* was a major hit at the reunion. After the reunion I made 15 copies for my five sisters and brother and Dad's remaining brother and sister's families.

We were married on September 14, 1968, and celebrated our 50th Wedding Anniversary on June 19, 2018, with a party and Gillen family reunion at our home on Hewitt Road. Guests were from Idaho, Maryland, Michigan, Tennessee, Texas, Utah, Virginia, and Wyoming. It was a grand success. What I did not know is how well I taught Ginger to scrapbook by working on Dad's *Heritage Album* with me. Our 50th anniversary gift from the family was a 50-page digital scrapbook that

Ginger made for us after our 50th celebration. Ginger had asked relatives and friends for stories and pictures of Benny and me. Unbeknown to us she was collecting the final information on the day of our celebration.

Benny was inducted into the Michigan Motor Sports Hall of Fame on November 7, 2021, to honor his 30-year racing career in red car #3. Benny began racing the local tracks in 1963 as a hobby and retired from racing at the end of the 1993 season posting 125 wins. In the early days I went to the garage to see what Benny was doing and would end up helping him build or fix something. At the races I kept notes on his qualifying times at the time trials and where he finished in his races. Mark helped his dad in the garage growing up and worked for Brian Ruhlman helping build race cars and as part of the pit crew at the races from 2008 -2012 (approximate years). Brian raced in New Mexico in 2012 and Mark was part of the pit crew. Benny's cousin, Don Snider, also raced, and his nephew, Danny Donaldson, is still on the racing circuit in Alabama. Now Benny watches racing on TV and enjoys flying drones and radio-controlled airplanes.

On December 19, 2021, I was recognized as one of the four founding members of the Brooklyn Presbyterian's Handbell Choir in 1975. One of the ringers passed on September 14, 2021. The rest of us received a lovely cross pendent for our 46 years in the handbell choir. Several years earlier I received the Shining Light award at church. Benny also deserved one for all he does there.

Benny's Racing Car 1970

Ben and Irene Snider's Family 1987

Irene and Ben Snider 2008

Chapter 8

CATHY AND DAVE OSBORN

By Cathy Gillen Osborn

Second Daughter

I ATTENDED BROOKLYN High School from 1964 to 1967. I was a B/C student. My favorite classes were English and spelling.

Janice Kohorst and Colleen Seagert were my best friends along with our lake neighbors – Lyndell Herrmann, Judy Stark, and Kathy and Nancy Whitfield. One of the highlights of my high school years was working on floats at homecoming time. Going to movies at the Star Theater in Brooklyn was always a great treat; we went regularly.

I was given $10 a week to do the family laundry at the laundromat and got to keep the change. On one occasion I left two sets of folded twin sheets at the laundromat. They were gone when I went back for them, and I had to buy two new sets of sheets.

Irene, Noreen, and I went on a date with boys from Manchester in 1966.

In the afternoon, we all went swimming. Then we went to dinner. We went to Ann Arbor to the drive-in movie and didn't get home until three a.m. Dad was waiting up for us when we got home. We all got a major lecture, and we never saw those boys again. Dad never liked any of the boys we dated. One exception was Irene's beau, Ben Snider, who she met at the Coffee Shop. We learned what curfew means . . . that is home by nightfall.

When we older girls dated and brought the guy's home, the "little" kids loved it and at times, nearly took over the boyfriends. Of course, the boyfriends loved playing with the "kids" as much as the kids enjoyed playing with them.

At age 16 we became drivers and Dad made us learn to change a tire. Our cars were always at least 10 years old. The gas gauge didn't work in the old green Plymouth. I got in trouble for running out of gas despite no working gas gauge. I was supposed to know how many miles I could drive on the amount of gas I put in the car. I did learn how to calculate that. After that we kept a record book in the car that everyone used to record the amount of gas and mileage.

My senior year was eventful. I became engaged to Larry Wibbeler. Our class went to Cedar Point in Sandusky, Ohio, for our class trip. Not sure why they let us go to a place where it was legal for us to drink and tell us not to do it. It worked out for most of us because we listened and didn't drink. The few who did drink, had a bit of trouble with graduation and getting signed diplomas. Larry and I didn't stay engaged long. He apparently had eyes for Ginger while engaged to me. Poor Mom had to have a serious talk with me and break the news. And I broke up with Larry, needless to say. Ginger was not impressed with him either.

After I graduated from High School, I went to Jackson Beauty School in Jackson, Michigan. Irene worked at Spartan Electronics in Jackson, so she would take me with her and drop me off at beauty school. It was located above the Capital Theater on W. Michigan Avenue. After beauty school, I rode the city bus with a friend to her house on E. Michigan Avenue to wait for Irene to get out of work so she could pick me up on her way home. After a few months, I moved into a rooming house on Wesley Street in Jackson with Bonnie Jett. Once we graduated from beauty school Bonnie and I rented an apartment at Clark Lake a few miles away.

I got my first job in Napoleon at Millie's Beauty Shop. I met Judy Osborn at Millie's, and we became close friends. I would go over to Judy and Greg's home every Sunday afternoon after church. We were not allowed to skip church.

During that time the Catholic Church started having mass on Saturday evenings, which meant I could go to Judy and Greg's earlier on Sunday, since I had fulfilled my "obligation" of attending church. From then on whenever I came to Judy and Greg's, Greg always asked, "Did you "fulfill?"

That statement meant nothing to anyone else. I still chuckle when I think of it. Greg's brother Dave would come over to Judy and Greg's occasionally on Sundays. By and by Dave and I both showed up on Saturday or Sunday, or both days. Soon Dave picked me up and "we" went to Greg's and Judy's together. The rest is history. Dave proposed. I said, "Yes," and we were married in 1970. Dave moved into the apartment and Bonnie moved out. That was 50 years ago. Already! Still in love.

We started our life together in Brooklyn in a rental house. In 1972 we purchased our current home in Napoleon, Michigan. By 1973 we had Todd and Bryan. I had a miscarriage in 1972.

Dave and I were married on November 21, 1970, at St. Rita's Catholic Church in Clark Lake. I quickly realized Dave was not a churchgoer. This fact made it hard for me to go to church every Sunday. Good Catholics do not miss Mass.

I stopped going to the Catholic Church because of Father Dunn at "Our Lady of Fatima" Church in

Michigan Center, Michigan. Father Dunn's reaction to my request, surprised me. He simply waved his hand "poo-pooed" me and said, "Oh you don't need that." When Todd was three years old and Bryan was one year old, I was in the hospital to have my tubes tied. While I was in the hospital Father Dunn came to my room for a visit. It took all the courage I could muster to ask Father Dunn for a pep talk to get me back on track and to go to church on a weekly basis.

I never went back to the Catholic Church again. But I didn't give up on going to church. I began going to Brooklyn, United Brethren Church. The boys and I attended this church until the boys were old enough to say, "None of our friends go to church, so we don't want to go either." At that point, I joined the United Methodist Church in Napoleon, our hometown. As it turns out, many of the boys' friends did go to church, they went to the United Methodist Church in Napoleon.

Ironically, Mom had changed from Methodist to Catholic, and I changed from Catholic to Methodist. The hardest part was telling Mom I quit attending the Catholic Church. Her answer was so easy. She asked me if I was going to church and when I said, "Yes," she was so happy. She claimed that there were many avenues to God, kind of like the spokes of a wheel - they all lead to the center hub - *God*. As long as I was going to church it was okay with her.

Life was busy for many years. I worked three days a week at the Beauty Shop. The boys played summer league baseball. We always had a lot of fun. They learned to ride bicycles (and get them on top of the roof), how to swim, and all the other things little boys do.

Dave worked at Silkworth Tire store. Later it transitioned into Napoleon Lawn & Leisure. Dave was able to follow his dream of being a truck driver. There were many ups and downs along the way with loads, weather, accidents, and long hours. After 15 years Dave quit trucking, not by choice, but because of his eyesight. Sad and happy at the same time though.

After 25 years of marriage, we had a rare opportunity to have a new beginning. Dave retired from trucking and was home again daily, not just on weekends. A nice change.

Todd David, our first son, went into the Army at age 17 after graduating from high school. Three years later he came home a grown man. He was able to leave the Army honorably and receive G.I. bill benefits. He went to California and became an electrician. Todd eventually settled in Idaho and met Kimberly Scheller. They married in 2011 and Dave and I became instant grandparents. Elizabeth was 10 years old, and Aidan was 9. Grayson came along in 2015.

Todd is a brilliant man. He possesses extreme awareness of family, friends, and details. Their activities and accomplishments don't go unnoticed either. He loves his mom and dad. He is a wonderful family man as well. He is a great husband to Kim and stepdad to Elizabeth and Aidan. They turned 21 and 19 in the blink of an eye. Todd is also a wonderful dad to Grayson, who just turned 7. Todd and Kim have a fabulous relationship. They are a great team, and a beautiful couple.

The grandchildren bring great joy into our lives. Elizabeth is a happy young lady and shares her life with her friend Kristin. She works in a restaurant as a cook and chef and loves her job. Aidan is a very kind and driven young man, just starting a job at the Portland, Oregon, airport. He is on track to a lifetime career. He is following in his dad's (Dave Honga's) footsteps. Aidan is also an accomplished Wild Lands Firefighter. Firefighting is also following the footsteps of other Honga family members. Grayson is a happy, fun-loving 7-year-old with exceptional reading skills at such a tender age, He is the top reader in his 1st-grade class. And he loves his Gramma and Grampa!

Todd transitioned into an accountant for Outdoors International, an outfitter for hunters and fishermen that travel around the world for adventures of a lifetime.

Bryan Andrew, our second son, lives in Jackson, Michigan. Bryan gained the name of Ozzie in second grade and is known as Ozzie by friends and family today. Ozzie is a highly talented artist. He loves working with steel and for many years he was a steel sculptor. He was given the title "Man of Steel" by our local newspaper the *Jackson Citizen Patriot* in 2007 because of the fabulous steel sculptures he created. Many of his sculptures are showcased in our yard. Ozzie is a best friend and confidant to all who know him. He is inciteful, kind, and a great mentor. He dearly loves his mom and dad. His endearments to us are Mumsy and Pops. Ozzie currently works for a tool and die company.

I went from working at the Beauty Shop to having an in-home business with the Shaklee Corporation - bringing true wellness to the world. It's a great company. I work when I want, and I make enough extra income to travel to Idaho on a regular basis. I love helping people stay healthy and earn extra income. It's a great life.

Dave works at Napoleon Lawn & Leisure providing John Deere equipment, parts, and services five days a week as a "retired" part-timer. He loves the work and the staff, and the workers love having his expertise available.

For Dave's and my pleasure, we ride our Can-Am motorcycle on weekends and occasionally go on long trips. We have been to the West Coast, Idaho, Arizona, and Canada, just to mention a few.

Retirement is lovely, too.

The happiest day of my life is the day I married Dave, November 21, 1970. The saddest day of my life was the day I lost Dave to cancer, May 31, 2022. We enjoyed 51 years together. I am grateful for those lovely years.

Dave and Cathy Osborn's Family 1999

Cathy and Dave Osborn 2005

Cathy and Dave Osborn

LAST RIDE

By Virginia Gillen Poole

Cathy had a beautiful memorial service for Dave on his 79th birthday.
It was so special.

Todd read the last three stanzas of a Walt Whitman poem
at the tree planting in Cathy's yard to honor his father.

Song of Myself

I bequeath myself to the dirt to grow from the grass I love,
If you want me again look for me under your boot-soles.

You will hardly know who I am or what I mean,
But I shall be good health to you nevertheless,
And filter and fibre your blood.

Failing to fetch me at first keep encouraged,
Missing me one place search another,
I stop somewhere waiting for you.

Bryan planted the memorial tree to honor his father.

Family and friends were all proud to pay their respects
to this kind, quiet, gentle man.

Chapter 9

NOREEN AND TIM LITCHARD

By Noreen Gillen Litchard

Third Daughter

I ATTENDED BROOKLYN High School from 1965 to 1967 and graduated from the newly named Columbia Central High School in 1968. This was the name of the new consolidated school district. The new school was completed two years later. I was a B student. My favorite classes were typing and band. I was in the concert and marching band from the 8th through the 12th grades and went with the band to the Holland Tulip Festival in Holland, Michigan every year. The Brooklyn and Columbia Central High Schools won many band awards. I also marched in the Memorial Day and Fourth of July parades with Dad and Norman.

My close friend in school was Suzette Mannoia. We didn't hang out much after school. Suzette's family owned a restaurant, and she probably worked for them.

Ginger and I worked at Knutson's Bait Shop beginning in 1965 and throughout high school. We worked at the Bait Shop counting worms and night crawlers to get out of work at the Coffee Shop and to earn more money. We both continued to help at the Coffee Shop, but the Bait Shop paid piece rate and was the best paying job in town, if the worm counters wanted to count fast. Ginger and I were the fastest counters at the time.

I babysat for the Ksiazkiewicz's on Vineyard Lake, Bob and Kaye Wheaton, Don and Murphy Knutson, Darwin, and Diana Fisher's baby, our neighbors on Stony Lake, and Don and Suzie Rose. Don and Suzie's daughter, Denise, had both legs pulled out of their sockets during birth and crawled dragging her legs or was carried. I went with the Rose family to the Shriner's clinic in Chicago, Illinois, on a couple of occasions.

I met Tim Litchard in Ann Arbor, Michigan, in the fall of 1967. The schools, at the time, were taking prospective college students on trips to the various universities in the area. The bus left from Paka Plaza, now The Crossing, in Jackson, Michigan, on a Saturday morning. It was a combined trip from Brooklyn High School, now Columbia Central, and Northwest High School in Jackson. When the prospective college students arrived in Ann Arbor there were the usual campus tours and financial meetings. My friend, Suzette, and I didn't want to take the campus tour or attend the meetings, so we left the group and toured the Arboretum with students from Chelsea, Michigan. When we came back to the buses, they were ready to leave. Suzette got on the bus and sat with an underclassman she knew. The only empty seat on the bus for me was next to Tim.

Tim and I started talking about families. I told Tim there were eight children in my family, and Tim said there were 10 children in his family. I didn't believe him until I met them. After Tim and I met, Tim told his best friend that I was the girl he was going to marry. If *God* hadn't set this seating arrangement up, I don't know how we would have met.

About two months later, Tim talked one of his friends, Little Timmy, into calling me. I talked to Little Timmy for about 30 minutes before I talked to Tim. After Tim and I talked on the phone for a while, Tim asked me out on a date, and the rest, as they say, is history. It felt like we had known each other forever, even though we were only 17 years old. If we had been older, we would probably have gotten married within a few weeks. From the first time we dated, both Tim and I knew we wanted to get married but since we were both going to college, we knew we would have to wait.

In the fall of 1968, after graduating in June, I attended Western Michigan University (WMU) in Kalamazoo, Michigan. I enrolled in the Nursing Program and transferred to the Secretarial Program after the first semester. Tim drove to WMU on Friday nights to pick me up and drive back to Jackson to Tim's parent's home for the weekend. Dad was drinking heavily at the time, so I went to Tim's home almost every weekend. Tim's mother welcomed me with open arms and always treated me as a daughter. I left WMU in April 1969, at the end of the semester.

I married Tim on June 7, 1969, at St. Joseph Shrine in Brooklyn, Michigan. We honeymooned at a hotel for the weekend in Jackson so Tim could be at work on Monday. We lived with Tim's parents in Jackson for two years while Tim attended the University of Michigan in Ann Arbor, Michigan. For the next two years, we lived in Ann Arbor during the school year, and with Tim's parents during the summer in Jackson.

I quit going to the Catholic Church in 1969, because birth control was banned. We were young and Tim was going to college. We already had a baby and didn't want another one at that time. Years later we decided to go back to church, and our niece was married in a Baptist Church. We liked the people and continued attending there.

When I found out I was pregnant, Tim and I talked to the doctors about the possibility of the baby having muscular dystrophy. The doctors told us that since muscular dystrophy was a recessive gene and there weren't any genetic issues in Tim's family, there shouldn't be any problems. Our daughter, Dawn Marie Litchard was born on December 16, 1969, and was a healthy baby. We didn't think any more about muscular dystrophy until later after our son Andy was born.

Dawn was Walter and Eleanor's first grandchild. Dawn's brother Andy was born on September 5, 1973. From the time Andy was 3 or 4, he had trouble getting up from the floor, and he always walked on his toes. Andy couldn't run, so he had a hard time keeping up with other kids.

When Tim's parents sold their house in 1976, Tim and I moved with the kids to an apartment in downtown Jackson for one year and moved again to Pheasant Run Apartments in 1977 for another year. In 1978, we bought a double-wide mobile home and moved to Shoreham Drive in Jackson where we lived for 16 years.

In 1978 when Andy was 5-years old, Tim and I took him to the doctor for a preschool physical. The doctor thought Andy was walking on his toes because his Achilles tendons were too short, so the doctor referred us to an orthopedist, Dr. Stolberg, who was also Gary's doctor. When I told Dr. Stolberg that my brother was Gary Gillen, he sent us to the hospital for a CPK-3 enzyme test that would show how much CPK was in Andy's blood. Too much CPK indicates muscular dystrophy. The amount of CPK in Andy's blood was 10 times the normal amount. A muscle biopsy also confirmed that Andy had Duchenne muscular dystrophy, the same type that Gary had. This was the worst day of Tim's and my life. We cried all the way home. Andy started school the next year at age 6.

Andy was accepted into the Muscular Dystrophy Association (MDA) Clinic at Borgess Hospital in Kalamazoo, Michigan. We took Andy every six months to see a physical and occupational therapist, a neurologist, and an orthopedist. Everyone at the clinic was very helpful and compassionate. They showed Tim and I various exercises to continue at home with

Andy. They also told us what to expect through each phase of Duchenne muscular dystrophy.

Andy had several surgeries on his legs to keep him walking as long as possible. His first surgery was at age six to lengthen the Achilles tendon on both feet. After the surgery Andy had casts on for about three months to keep his feet at a 90-degree angle so that he would be able to wear shoes. If he didn't have this surgery, Andy's feet would eventually turn under, making him unable to wear shoes.

The doctors at the clinic watch the kids with muscular dystrophy very closely and know when they are getting too weak to walk. Andy was 8 when he began wearing long leg braces that went from foot to hip to support his leg muscles to keep him walking longer. The braces had a locking mechanism at the knee so that Andy could stand and walk.

In 1983, when Andy was 10, he was no longer able to walk and began using a wheelchair. Andy remained in public school and was very well liked. His teacher assigned one child each day to be Andy's helper, and they all wanted to be his helper. Andy loved being waited on and tried this at home. Tim and I had to make Andy do as much as he could for himself to keep all his muscles working.

At age 11, Andy was beginning to lean too far forward in the chair. The only way to correct this was to have total back surgery. The procedure took approximately eight hours. The doctors inserted a steel rod down Andy's back and wired each vertebra to the rod. If Tim and I hadn't been in his room after surgery, Andy would have died when he began coughing and couldn't breathe. The staff had to use suction to remove the mucus.

On June 12, 1986, Andy had a bad cold. Tim and I took him to the doctor. When we came home, he was very tired, so we put him to bed and kept checking on him every half hour. When I went into Andy's room at 8:30 p.m. I realized that he wasn't breathing. Tim immediately called 911. At the time, we lived about two miles from the state police post. A trooper was at our house within three minutes. He took command of the situation and worked tirelessly from the time he came into the house until Andy was taken to the hospital. Tim and I believe that he was sent by *God* to help us during this time.

It was quite a shock when Andy died at age 12. Most muscular dystrophy patients die from respiratory distress because they can't cough up the mucus that accumulates in the lungs. The doctors had anticipated Andy would live until at least age 18, the same age as Gary when he died. Andy would have been 13 on his birthday in September. Andy was never sick or in pain. His muscles just continued to become weaker as they deteriorated.

Tim and I were shocked by how many classmates and students came to Andy's funeral. We didn't know many of them, but all the kids knew Andy. This was a testament to how much Andy meant to them. After the funeral, the only way I could deal with Andy's death, was knowing that he was in Heaven.

Andy's muscular dystrophy and death brought Tim and I closer together. Something like this can also tear a family apart. For almost two years Tim didn't talk about Andy at all. If Andy's name was mentioned, Tim left the room. We were both so busy trying to deal with our grief, we basically ignored our 16-year-old daughter, Dawn. I thank *God* for watching over Dawn during this time and keeping her from turning to drugs or getting into a bad group.

Dawn graduated from Northwest High School in 1988. After high school Dawn attended the Career Center at Jackson Community College for two years and received a degree in Computer Aided Drafting and Manufacturing (CAD/CAM) and Fixture Design.

Dawn met her boyfriend, and future husband, Todd Ford, "Dragging the Ave" - Michigan Avenue in Jackson. Dawn and Todd were dating when Dawn moved in with Todd and his mother on the Ford family farm.

In 1993, Tim and I purchased 14 acres of land in Michigan Center, Michigan, and spent a lot of time clearing the land and cleaning up the property. We had a Quad Level house built in 1994 and lived in the house for 20 years. In 1997, we purchased horses and saddles, halters, and all the equipment needed for horses. For the next couple of years, we rode the horses around the neighborhood and in the woods behind our house.

Our granddaughter, Kathryn Ann "Katie" was born on April 4, 1997. Dawn and Todd were married in 1999 and built their new house when Katie was 2 years old. The same year Dawn found out she was pregnant again, and they moved into their new house when Dawn was eight-and-a-half months pregnant with Wyatt.

After Dawn learned she was pregnant in 1999, Tim and I began praying that the baby would not be a boy because boys are more susceptible to the Duchenne strain of muscular dystrophy that affected both Gary and Andy, and we did not want to go through another family member having muscular dystrophy. Before Dawn had an ultrasound on the baby, I was driving down the road, praying the baby would not be a boy. I heard a voice out loud, as plain as day, saying, "The baby is a boy." This was later confirmed by the ultrasound. Twice more during Dawn's pregnancy, *God* spoke to me saying, "Everything will be alright," and "The baby is healthy."

Wyatt James was born on February 1, 2000. He had some initial breathing issues, but otherwise he was a healthy baby boy. I still wasn't convinced Wyatt was healthy until after he had DNA testing through University of Michigan and The Johns Hopkins University when he was two months old. The test was repeated when he was 2-years old. All the test's confirmed Wyatt was healthy and did not have muscular dystrophy.

Three days before Easter on Thursday, April 12, 2001, I was kicked by my horse. When Tim and I went to feed the horses, I followed my new horse,

Charley, out of the barn. When I stopped, I was standing only about four feet behind Charley. This is the worst place to stand behind a horse. One needs to stand right next to the horse's butt or at least 15 feet away.

I ended up in the middle of a horse conversation. Charley was telling the other horses to stay away from him. Charley reared up on his two front feet and kicked out his back left foot that was coming directly toward me. I had turned to the left, towards the gate, and was kicked in the ribs on my right side. Four of my ribs were broken in two places. The force of the kick threw me 20 feet away and I broke two more ribs on my back when I hit the ground. I had a total of 10 broken ribs and a collapsed lung. My lung had three holes in it. One was the size of a baseball and there were two smaller holes. If I had not turned toward the gate, I would have been kicked in the heart and would have died instantly.

At the time there were two hospitals in Jackson and Tim told the emergency medical technician to take me to Doctor's Hospital. Tim and I found out later that the trauma surgeon on duty that day was the best surgeon in Jackson County. The trauma surgeon knew they couldn't fix everything that was wrong with me in Jackson, so he prepped me for surgery at the University of Michigan. This was another *God* encounter.

After the accident, Tim made a phone call to a friend of ours, who is a prayer warrior. She made several calls on my behalf. By the time I was transported to the University of Michigan, there were five churches praying for me.

I was air lifted by helicopter to the University of Michigan. During the flight, the helicopter pilot radioed ahead for a fully staffed operating room. I was taken directly from the helicopter into surgery. This never happens, another *God encounter*. I was admitted to the Trauma Burn Unit as a Level 1 patient, which means I was not expected to live more than 24 to 48 hours and one nurse is assigned to the patient 24 hours a day.

After surgery, Tim was told I would be on a respirator for two days to let my good lung rest and I would probably be in the intensive care unit (ICU) for two weeks, then would probably be sent to rehabilitation for a month before coming home.

On Friday night, I was in severe pain and asked *God* to take away the pain. Even though my eyes were closed, I could see a light. I thought it was the nurse coming into the room, but no one came in. I felt a warm light move down my body from head to toe and the pain was gone so that I could sleep. This was another *God* encounter. When Tim saw me on Saturday morning, he told me I looked like a totally different person. The respirator and several tubes had been removed.

I was moved from ICU to a step-down unit on Saturday night. Early Easter Sunday morning around 2 a.m. I was able to get back into bed on my own because the unit was short staffed. On Monday, I started walking around the hospital, and I was released in eight days rather than two weeks.

All the doctors in the trauma unit continually told Tim and I that they were amazed at my quick recovery. One doctor told me that most people with this type of injury would still be in bed and on oxygen for at least a week. It is through "The Power of Prayer" that I was released in only eight days and did not need any rehabilitation. I was able to ride my horse, Charley, on the Fourth of July.

The hostess for the trauma unit told Tim and I she saw the "Power of Prayer" work again and again. Patients who have a strong faith in *God* have a positive attitude and recover faster than those who do not have faith. A friend of ours, who is a nurse, said that one of the reasons I recovered so quickly was because there was no down time. Everything was done for me in perfect timing which was another *God* encounter.

After I was healed, Tim and I traveled with our horse trailer for several years camping and riding in many different areas of the country. From 2006 to 2020, we traveled to Meridzo Ministries in Lynch, Kentucky.

This mission uses horses to share the Gospel of Jesus Christ with children and their parents. During this time, the Meridzo Ministries was also building a youth camp. We helped wherever we were needed. Tim usually worked on a construction or fencing project, and I helped Tim whenever I was not needed elsewhere. I was the receptionist at the mission center and had a sewing room where I made curtains, pillows, baby blankets, and pillowcase dresses to donate to the children in the area. During the COVID-19 scare, I made more than 100 masks that were donated to area assisted living centers.

In 2015, a woman named Patty knocked on our door at home. She said *God* had been telling her to buy our house for about a year. Our house was not for sale at the time. Patty said that every time she drove by our house to visit her son who lived next door, *God* would tell her to come and talk to us. Patty bought our house without a realtor involved. All the transactions were handled by Patty's credit union and the closing was three weeks later. This was another *God* encounter.

For the next five years, Tim and I traveled full-time around the United States in our newly purchased 5th Wheel Recreational Vehicle (RV). In 2016 and 2017 we traveled in the western United States and were gone for 11 months. During this time, we were able to visit with Norm's family in Utah and Sherry's family in Wyoming.

From 2015 to 2020, Tim and I became "snowbirds." We spent the winters in Florida and traveled back to Michigan in the summers. While we were in Florida, I started a Homeless Mats group. The mats were crocheted from plastic bags and distributed to homeless communities. I also made many "pillowcase dresses" for orphanages in Honduras, Costa Rica, and Nicaragua, and I sewed many backpacks for the homeless.

We were able to see a lot of the United States traveling in our RV, which we wouldn't have been able to do if we still owned a house. On our travels, we met many nice people and made many new friends.

Granddaughter Kathryn "Katie" graduated from Michigan Center High School in 2015. She attended dental school for a year before transferring into a nursing program. Katie received her Licensed Practical Nurse license in April 2021. She is currently applying at the Veterans Administration Hospital. Katie plans to continue her education to obtain the Registered Nurse degree.

Grandson Wyatt graduated from Michigan Center High School in 2018. He is attending a technical school at the University of Northwest Ohio and majoring in automobile mechanics. In the first six months of the program, Wyatt received his certificate for automotive heating, ventilating, and air conditioning. In February 2022 he received the associate degree in applied science with majors in Automotive Technology and High-Performance Motor Sports.

He became engaged to Megan Zimmermann in the fall of 2021. They plan to be married in 2024.

In 2020 Tim and I sold our RV. We are now happily settled in an apartment in Jackson close to both our families.

Tim and Noreen Litchard's Family 1985

Noreen and Tim Litchard 2016

THE WALTER AND ELEANOR GILLEN STORY

Chapter 10

$\sim$

Ginger and Jim Poole

By Virginia "Ginger" Gillen Poole and James "Jim" Poole

Fourth Daughter

I ATTENDED BROOKLYN High School in 1967 and Columbia Central High School in 1968 through 1970. 1970 was the first class to graduate from the new high school at Lake Columbia, on the outskirts of town. I was a B/C student. I loved school and had to work hard for my grades. I was a slow reader and didn't exactly have a quiet environment to be able to concentrate on homework at the Coffee Shop, or at home. My favorite classes were science, algebra, physical education, and art.

One year, my science class came to the farm to catch frogs in our swamp to dissect in class. It was a huge success. My muskrat skeleton project was not as successful. I cooked the carcass to get it clean before I could put the skeleton together. All I ended up with was a pile of bones I couldn't identify and complaints about the stench in the kitchen at home for a few days. My 4×6-inch toothpick bear art project turned out great. I have it today. I won first prize in the all-class art competition to design a record album cover. I remember the design on the cover today and how much thought and time it took.

I was a member of the Girl's Athletic Association and Ski Club throughout high school. I didn't know anything about football but played defense on the Powder Puff football team in 1969. I was good at track and hurdles, tumbling, trampolines, and the parallel bars. I didn't make the gymnastics team, largely because I didn't have the time to practice after school. I was thrilled when I was invited to attend the state championship with the team and watch them compete.

Linda Miller, Judy Choate, and I, were selected by the American Legion Auxiliary to attend Girls State in 1969. We spent a week at Markley Hall in Ann Arbor, Michigan, to learn the political process by running a mock government. We were in the mock Taylor City, where Linda and I ran for the County Board of Supervisors.

In 1965 and through high school, Noreen and I worked at Knutson's Bait Shop counting worms and night crawlers to get out of work at the Coffee Shop. We still helped at the Coffee Shop, but the Bait Shop paid piece rate and was the best paying job in town, if you could count fast. Noreen and I were the fastest counters at the time.

I mowed the lawn at home and babysat to make extra money. I babysat the Hardcastle family who had three sets of twins with a single child between each set of twins. The youngest of all the children was the only girl in the family. The family used to say they had a baseball team and a cheerleader. I also babysat for Jim and Jan Knutson; Don and Murphy Knutson; the Ksiazkiewicz children; and the Rose children. I went with the Rose family to the Shriner's clinic in Chicago, Illinois, on one occasion to help with Denise who couldn't walk. It was my first experience with big city traffic.

Many of my friends rode on our school bus. A few other close friends went to our church or lived in town. On one occasion, I went with the girls from town to a vacant house on the outskirts of town near M-50 and tasted liquor from the stash of booze the guys from high school had hidden.

I could go to Benny's Stock Car Races when we were invited, but Dad wouldn't let me date until I was 17 or 18. The older girls were dating at age 15. Mom said Dad thought I was too much like him and I might get into trouble. Noreen says she just explained her planned date to Dad, and he always let her go. When I could date, I usually met my girlfriends at the dance pavilion nearby at Wamplers Lake, and I went to my junior prom with Dale Stump. At the end of my senior year, I dated Mark Seifert before I left for airline school in Minneapolis, Minnesota.

One of the few pictures of me in the 1969 yearbook is taken in English class and my girdle is showing under my short skirt of the day. I had a solid but larger build than many of my classmates and struggled to fit in size-12 clothes, as they were sized in the 1960s. I have scars at my waist today from my tight girdles.

After high school, I attended the two-month Gale Institute Airline Training Center program. The airline schools at that time were separate from the airlines and near airline hubs. Our teachers were from Northwest Orient Airlines in Minneapolis and taught everyone stewardess, ticket agent, reservation agent, and airport operations classes. The school guaranteed 90 percent placement in airline positions. We graduated when Northwest Orient was on strike and the school helped us prepare resumes and get job interviews. At that time, the Federal Bureau of Investigation and the Department of Navy offered the Civil Service exam for positions in Washington, D.C. I was one of about 30 students who took the exam and accepted a job offer. We all arrived in Washington, D.C., on Halloween October 31, 1970.

I was one of four girls offered a job with the Naval Ordnance Systems Command (NAVORD) in the Crystal City area of Arlington, Virginia.

Crystal City was the U.S. Navy Headquarters and near National Airport, the Pentagon, and just across the Potomac river from Washington, D.C. We all reported for work on November 2, 1970. Four girls were sent to the U.S. Navy offices and began as GS-2 clerk typists, the lowest pay grade at the time. We aspired to making $10,000 a year. My job was in the Civilian Personnel Office with a desk just inside the office door where everyone congregated for morning coffee. I had to block out the conversation to do my job. This wasn't much different than trying to do homework at the dining room table during high school. The girls at the U.S. Navy loved their jobs. All our other classmates were offered jobs at the Federal Bureau of Investigation and hated their jobs. They had to get coffee for their bosses, open mail, run errands, and other minor jobs. They thought they would be doing something exciting.

Three of the four girls at the U.S. Navy rented a very low-cost apartment together for six months and dated the boys across the hall. When we became familiar with the area, all four of the girls moved to a town house and dated co-workers. I didn't find out for a couple of years that the co-worker I was with most often was homosexual. That's how steamy my relationships were. One of my roommates practically had sex on the doorstep with her boyfriends. One of her girlfriends in Michigan was pregnant and her parents sent her to live with us until she had the baby and could put it up for adoption. Another roommate's boyfriend dried marijuana in our kitchen stove at night. At that time our carpool driver was the head of security at NAVORD. If we were late for a ride, Mr. Buxton would knock on the door to see if we were ready. We never invited him in because the front door was next to the kitchen and there might be a lingering odor from the night before. If he could smell marijuana outside, he never said anything. I didn't smoke marijuana. I drank bourbon and Coke and switched to scotch and water when I was dieting. The guys from work came over after work at 3 p.m. and we often drank until early hours in the morning. At one point I could drink a fifth of scotch a night.

I bought my first car from my brother-in-law Dave's friend Dave when I was home in Michigan for a visit in 1972. The car was an 8-cylinder, blue 1970 Camaro with a soft black top. I am still sad today that it was totaled in a six-car collision on I-95 in 1979. I was on my weekly commute home to New Jersey when someone on their way home from "happy hour" crossed the six-lane highway. Luckily, I ended up with only bruises. The only car I have liked as well as the Camaro was the white 2006 ES300 Lexus I had from 2009 to 2018.

In 1975, I applied for the Department of Navy's new Upward Mobility Program along with 100 other applicants. The selection was to be based on potential and experience rather than education. After the interview I told my boss if I didn't get the job, it wouldn't be my fault because I wasn't asked any questions during the interview. An African American woman was selected for the position, and I was second. Because of my comment and the interview process, I was given the job. My new job was in the Naval Sea Systems Command (NAVSEA), AEGIS Weapon System Project Office, where I began a one-year training assignment as a budget analyst in the building next door.

My first major relationship was with Larry Blow who worked in one of the naval engineering departments. Every weekend, and sometimes during the week, we went somewhere - to a movie, bars, dinner, nightclub, party, holiday event, or sightseeing. Larry went to Michigan with me in 1975 and met my family. Our biggest trip was to the Summer Olympics in Ontario, Canada, for a week in 1976. One time Larry called me late at night and asked me to pick him up in Richmond, Virginia, a couple of hours away. I called his brother, and he picked up Larry. Another time Larry painted the NAVORD Commander's office with red paint. I found out Larry was bi-polar, and this type of behavior could happen when he didn't take his medication. We broke up shortly after these incidents. Larry was happily married when he came to my retirement party in December 2006. Larry was invited by Mike O'Driscoll, a previous boss of both of ours at different times. I was happy to see them both.

In my early 20s, I thought I was in love with everyone I had a steady relationship with. I would have accepted a marriage proposal from any of my boyfriends at the time. When they ended the relationship, I cried and continued with my life. Later, when I received two marriage proposals, I declined. The first proposal was from a divorcee who seemed to just want to be married. Also, I was Catholic and marrying a divorcee was not acceptable in the eyes of the church. The second proposal was from an older man who was infatuated with me and treated me very well. He drank a lot. His hands shook so much in the morning, he couldn't drink his coffee. I could only think of the life I would be living, and I didn't want it. Later, while I was still in my 20s, I met my future husband, although I didn't know it until much later.

I was on a business trip in 1976 conducting an audit at the Naval Ship Missile Systems Engineering Station in Port Hueneme, California, with my boss and co-workers. My boss, Billy Love, stopped to talk to a newly reported officer at the AEGIS Program office in Crystal City. Commander Poole was in California working on an AEGIS missile test at the nearby Pacific Missile Test Facility in Point Mugu. My boss invited Commander Poole to dine with him and his co-workers that evening and asked if anyone wanted to ride with Commander Poole to show him the way to the restaurant. I was happy to offer. As a result, I was seated next to the Commander at dinner and received a ride back to the hotel from him after dinner. After our acquaintance in California, we chatted occasionally back at the office in Crystal City and worked together on a couple office Christmas parties. We had more opportunities to get to know one another at other work functions and parties.

Commander Poole was older and married with two children in high school. I remember him saying it seemed like he couldn't do anything right with his wife. I was in my late 20s and had plenty of dating opportunities. Commander Poole (Jim) was in his 40s when we began seeing each other. He didn't want to leave the children while they were still in school, but they were rarely home and didn't seem to need him. I didn't want to be an old maid and told Jim I couldn't wait for him. He then told his wife he thought he had fallen in love with another women. His wife filed separation papers in 1978 and they were divorced in September 1980. Jim was promoted to Captain in 1978 and assigned as the NAVSEA Technical Representative for the AEGIS Shipbuilding Project at the RCA Engineering and Production Facility in Moorestown, New Jersey, for three years.

Father Fitzgerald at Saint Joseph's Shrine, in Brooklyn, Michigan, was able to get an annulment for Jim's marriage, and we planned a large Catholic wedding in September 1980. When the divorce wasn't finalized in time for the wedding, we went on our planned honeymoon for a week touring the New England coast. We were married in December at God's House of All Faiths & People in Thorofare, New Jersey, and hosted the reception at our apartment.

I am an excommunicated Catholic. Jim was raised as a Methodist. When we weren't married in the Catholic church, and we didn't have children of our own, we both remained committed to *God* and practiced our faith. I remember asking Grandma Wood why she didn't go to church. She said she didn't have to go to church to believe in *God*. I never forgot her response. When church services became available online due to the COVID-19 scare, we started attending church service every Sunday at the Washington Farm United Methodist Church. When we were home for a memorial service in April 2022, we watched the Brooklyn Presbyterian Church service online where Irene and Benny attend. We have been attending this service ever since.

I continued to work in Crystal City and commuted to our apartment on Hickory Street in Mount Laurel, New Jersey. Jim received a highly sought assignment at the U.S. Naval Academy in Annapolis, Maryland, in November 1981. As the Deputy for Operations, he served as third in command after the Superintendent and Commandant of Midshipman. This was a very fun and exciting duty station for three years. We had our choice between a mid-1800's quarters with eight bedrooms on Parade Circle, or a seven-bedroom duplex on Porter Road behind the chapel next to the academic dean. We chose the seven-bedroom quarters because it had fewer rooms. We later learned it had two kitchens with a dumb waiter between them that was very handy when Jim became the senior Surface Warfare Officer, and we hosted parties for 100 or more guests.

The bedrooms were well-used. In addition to many guests at our quarters, Jim's son Mark was a midshipman at the academy. He graduated in 1982 and married Jennifer Ternet in the chapel in 1983 when we were still in quarters. Jim's daughter Ruth was attending Radford College and spent the summers with us commuting with me to her summer job in Crystal City. One of our carpool members served on one of the original battleships and was called back into active duty to work on the USS Iowa (BB-61) reactivation in 1982.

In 1984, I was selected for a program analyst position in the AEGIS Shipbuilding Program Office and had to respond immediately to program and budget inquiries from the Pentagon and Congress. It was extremely important to file program and budget information for multiple programs and appropriations for one fiscal year so they could be tracked, along with numerous changes, for five-to-20 years. I maintained the program and budget records the way I learned in this position from my boss, and longtime employee in the AEGIS Program Office, Bob Gray, through the end of my career in 2007.

In 1987, I applied for a position in the NAVSEA Ordnance and Combat Systems Office and was selected as the Plans and Programs Office Director and Planning and Development Manager. I traveled frequently to more than 30 U.S. Navy field offices and contractor sites, mostly in California, Indiana, and New Jersey. During this assignment (1989) the battleship USS Iowa (BB-61) forward gun turret misfired and exploded while conducting a drill at sea, killing 47 sailors. Cousin Jim Gillen was assigned to the aft gun turret and was not hurt. Captain Miceli, a former shipmate of Jim's, worked in my office and was assigned to the investigation team. Jim and I visited Norm and Margaret frequently when they were stationed in the Norfolk, Virginia, area. Jim Gillen also visited when he was in port. We have exchanged Christmas cards with Jim and his wife Vicki ever since.

I worked for the AEGIS Program Office in Crystal City from 1993 to 2000 when it was the Program Executive Office for Theater Air Defense (PEO TAD) and later when it became the Program Executive Office for Theater Surface Combatants (PEO TSC).

Throughout my Navy career, civilians were required to take a minimum of 40 hours training each year to meet peers in our related field of work and to get a break from the office. I loved the training opportunities. Early in my career I also attended night classes at the University of Virginia and Indiana University and received credits equivalent to an associate degree. After later attending several senior level Department of Defense (DoD) sponsored leadership courses, I had more master's-degree credits than bachelor's-degree credits. I worked very hard in every class, just like I did in high school.

DoD leadership courses were highly competitive. At the time, classes were generally 70 percent military, 30 percent civilian, 8 percent women, and 4 percent African American. I was fortunate to be accepted without a degree. Jim loved attending functions as my spouse and my classmates and instructors loved having him. Jim was one of the few male spouses, and often the only one, to accept invitations when they were offered.

The 1986 six-month Program Management Course for acquisition professionals was held at the Defense Systems Management College at Fort Belvoir, Virginia. One of our keynote lectures was given by Admiral Grace Hopper who developed one of the first computer programming languages (COBOL) in 1959. She was a delight to talk with after her lecture.

In 1996 the eight-week National Security Studies executive program, normally held at the Harvard University Kennedy Center, was held at the Syracuse University Maxwell School of Citizenship and Public Affairs in conjunction with The John Hopkins University's Paul H. Nitze School for Advanced International Studies. The program was developed by the Honorable Sean O'Keefe, the Maxwell School's Director of National Securities Studies at Syracuse University and the Honorable Paul Wolfowitz, the dean of the School of Advanced International Studies at The Johns Hopkins University in Baltimore, Maryland. I knew of Sean when he was a presidential management intern at NAVSEA.

The National Security Studies program was designed two levels higher than the participants and required the class to act in positions or roles encountered by senior managers. My first position was as the Comptroller in the Office of the Secretary of Defense in a four-day peacekeeping simulation. My next two positions were even harder. I was chairman of the Subcommittee on Military Research and Development during the four-day information warfare simulation, and the Secretary of the Navy during the final four-day simulation where I had a lot of help but little time to react. Other participants were given equally hard roles as Congressional members, senior national security officials, Joint Chiefs of Staff, White House staff, and cabinet members.

To allow Syracuse University to accommodate other visitors the class had to vacate their hotel rooms every weekend. We put our belongings in a storage room at the hotel and packed a suitcase. Off-campus classes were held at the Canadian National Defense Headquarters in Ottawa, Ontario; Capitol Hill in Washington, D.C.; the Canadian Royal Military College in Kingston, Ontario; and Revolutionary War battlefields - Fort Henry, Fort Frederick, and Fort Ticonderoga and Fort Saratoga where we had to reenact key Revolutionary War battles. My role at Saratoga Springs was as Brigadier General Simon Fraser, commander of the British Advanced Guard under General Burgoyne early in the 1777 campaign. The class had one weekend off during the eight weeks, and it rained or snowed every day. Our spouses were invited to accompany us on the two trips to Canada.

The one-year Secretary of Defense Senior Executive Leadership Course (SELC) required my finding, interviewing for, and being selected for a position in a different branch of service from June 1997 to June 1998. I was selected to work in the Office of the Under Secretary of Defense, Acquisition and Technology, Acquisition Resources. My office was in the Pentagon in room 1E-474, next to the helicopter pad, and in the first section of the Pentagon being renovated. I was out of the office six months of the year traveling with my classmates to military installations for classes and tours of facilities and equipment. I was also required to complete a research project on a current DoD issue and have it accepted by a senior official. My research project was on Advanced Concept Technology Demonstration project transition into acquisition and was approved by the Under Secretary of Defense for Acquisition and Technology (USD (A&T)). Our final assignment was a Pacific Deployment to Honolulu, Hawaii, and Seoul, South Korea. One of our meetings in South Korea was held at the Demilitarized Zone with their military officers holding a rifle at every window during our meeting. After the meeting we were escorted through the tunnel crossing to the North Korea border and back.

I returned to my position in the PEO TSC in Crystal City until June 2000 when I was selected as the Business and Financial Manager in the newly established Chief Engineer's (CHENG) Office under the Assistant Secretary of the Navy (Research, Development and Acquisition). The first CHENG offices were in Crystal City until there was room for us at the newly renovated 197 building at the Washington Navy Yard. We had a second office in the Pentagon that was also being renovated. Our temporary office at the Pentagon was on the fifth floor. The fifth floor of the Pentagon was an addition to the original building plan and was often called the attic due to its limited aesthetics.

Thirty of my 36-year U.S. Navy civilian career required frequent trips to the Pentagon. On every visit I was in awe of the building beginning with its granite terraces, steps, and foyers at the Mall and River entrances. The Pentagon is a fabulous structure. Having offices in the Pentagon gave me many opportunities to explore the building and its history.

Inside the Pentagon are four smaller pentagons called rings. To walk the outer "E" ring, the location of my first and last offices in the Pentagon, is one mile. The most prestigious organizations were along the outer "E" ring that had windows. My last Pentagon office was in 1E-1165. I occasionally walked the outer ring for exercise and to see who I might know along the way.

There are five rings, 10 corridors, and extremely wide ramps between the five floors. Each floor is painted a different color and each corridor has exhibits of a different historical event. Offices are numbered by floor, ring, corridor, and room number. If we were lost, it was best to go to the center, "A" ring, facing the courtyard to get our bearings or find a ramp to the concourse where we could see all the ring and corridor numbers. Help was also available if we asked someone in the hall or in an office.

The concourse is a small mall with mini commercial shops, banks, and medical facilities. The large gift shop was my favorite. Food is available at the large cafeteria next to the concourse, in dining rooms (if you are invited), at one of many stand-up snack bars, vending machines, and at fast-food vendors.

The inner courtyard is a five-acre park where workers can get fresh air and exercise. Many ceremonies are also held here. I shook President Clinton's hand at one event. The courtyard was especially good for a short-cut to the other side of the Pentagon. There are 64 acres of parking. My assigned parking spot in 1996 was in the north parking lot. To walk to my office directly across the Pentagon on the south side was over a mile. I took the Metrorail instead with an entrance close to my office. Occasionally, I could use someone's parking space in the south parking lot.

The U.S. Capitol is also a favorite historical building of mine beginning with its granite steps and massive bronze doors leading to the rotunda. It can fit into anyone of the Pentagon's five wedges. On several occasions, I was able to attend hearings in the Capitol. I also loved having to make a delivery or attend a meeting at one of the House and Senate office buildings on Capitol Hill. After each new Congress, the office picked up a copy of the book with the current administration, representatives and senator's pictures, positions, and office locations.

I had many career highlights and attribute much of my success to my husband. Jim was my biggest supporter and promoter. Every day he would tell me how great I looked leaving the house in the morning and at the end of the day he supported my working and studying at home. With both Jim and I working on the AEGIS program we were able to attend many work and social events together and share many of the same acquaintances, travels, and friendships.

Rear Admiral Meyer was among my many other supporters. The AEGIS program was a very exciting office to work in under Rear Admiral Meyer. He is known as the "Father of AEGIS" for creating the finest air defense capability in the world and setting the standard for all future Navy weapon system and shipbuilding programs to be judged. The AEGIS program was second only to Admiral Rickover's nuclear program.

Admiral Hyman Rickover is known as the "Father of the Nuclear Navy" for his role in developing the first nuclear-powered submarine using a pressurized water reactor. He also developed the first full-scale commercial nuclear power plant for peacetime operation. Navy officers wanting to work in the nuclear field know Admiral Rickover for his legendary hiring antics. Admiral Rickover put interviewees in stressful circumstances to make sure the officers could adapt to any situation. One well-known antic was to hold the interview with the candidate seated on a chair with the front two legs shortened so the interviewee had to struggle to remain seated. If they provided unsatisfactory answers they were dismissed or sent to sit in a broom closet for hours to re-think their answers.

I knew Admiral Rickover from working in the same building and riding on the same elevators. His offices were on the second and third floors in the National Center 2 building. In 1975 my office was on the fifth floor and later the 10th floor. We were frequently in the lobby together, and on one of my first elevator rides with him he chastised my friend for his Afro-style hairdo. On another day he chastised someone for their short dress. Both were in style at the time.

Both Rear Admiral Meyer and Admiral Rickover were famous for their demanding management styles and doing whatever was necessary to see projects to completion. They often bypassed naval organizational hierarchies by finding sympathetic members of Congress and the media to promote their programs.

The AEGIS program began as a missile program and grew to become a weapon system, combat system, cruiser, and destroyer shipbuilding program. There were program reviews and tests for each program, ship trials, christenings, and commissioning ceremonies. They were all wonderful and historic events. Nancy Reagan christened the first AEGIS ship, USS Ticonderoga (CG 47) in 1981.

I had a great experience as one of the first women allowed to ride on a ship during pre-commissioning tests. The Leyte Gulf (CG 55) conducted a three-day Trial Bravo in 1987 and the ten women slept on cots in sick bay. One purpose of the trial was to check ship maneuverability by zig zagging under high speed while underway at night. All through the testing our cots rolled from one side of sick bay to the other side. When our cots bumped into the cabinets, the drawers opened above our heads before we rolled back to the other side of the room. We were asked to file a report.

Rear Admiral Meyer and Admiral Rickover are two of the few naval officers to have a ship named for them while they were living. The USS

Hyman G. Rickover submarine was commissioned in 1984, two years before his death. The USS Wayne E. Meyer (DDG 108) was commissioned one month after his death in 2009. I was extremely fortunate, and very proud, to have Rear Admiral Meyer as the keynote speaker at my retirement ceremony in 2006.

On September 11, 2001, the day of the al-Qaeda terrorist attack, the CHENG office was the only organization remaining in the three National Center buildings after NAVSEA completed their move to the Washington Navy Yard in August 2001. A couple of days before the 9/11 attack on the Twin Towers in New York and the Pentagon, the security guards in the National Center 2 building gave the keys to the front door of the 12-story building to the CHENG office before they relocated to the Navy Yard.

My office and staff were on the 5th floor. Admiral Paige and Mike O'Driscoll, my bosses' offices, were on the 10th floor. One of my staff members received a call of the attack on the Twin Towers and informed me of the attack. I ran up the stairs and informed Mr. O'Driscoll just as the Pentagon was struck. We looked out his office window and saw the smoke. Commander Lisa Avila, one of the midshipmen we sponsored when we were stationed at the Naval Academy and a good friend, was with Vice President Cheney in Texas on 9/11. She was the first of her flight crew to sense something wrong that morning and secured her plane and took off as soon as everyone was onboard. Having the Vice President onboard, she stayed in the air when all the aircraft across the United States were required to land. She flew as far as West Virginia and was then given an Air Force escort into Andrews Air Force Base.

September 11, 2001 was a frightening day. It took me four hours to drive 12 miles home after the Pentagon was struck by American Airlines flight 77. Almost everyone in Crystal City and Washington D.C. were sent home at the same time, around 10 a.m. At that time there was still a threat of another plane heading toward the Capitol. All the Metrorail stations and National Airport closed, and cell phone lines were overloaded. The only communication was the car radio and television. People from the airport carried their luggage and workers with briefcases filled both sides of Jefferson Davis Highway (U.S. Route 1) and walked faster than the cars could move. Jim was not allowed to enter Fort Myer, near the Pentagon, for a meeting and was working his way home. We happened to meet side-by-side at a stop light in Old Town Alexandria at 2 p.m., and he followed me the rest of the way home. I was so exhausted from the stress I slept the rest of the day, and it took me several days to calm down.

American Airline flight 77 hit the second and third floors of the Pentagon directly above my office next to the helicopter pad in 1997 and 1998. The newly renovated Navy Communications Center and Army offices received the most damage by the impact. Jim and I knew many of the Navy people who helped save others that day.

My office at the Washington Navy Yard from 2001 to 2007 was at the end of the corridor where the shooting on September 16, 2013, occurred. I walked this corridor several times a day and knew one of the 12 people killed that day.

I retired in January 2007 and began a volunteer career the same month serving on the Wessynton Homes Association Board (WHA). I worked just as hard as when I was paid a salary, but only 40 hours a week as a volunteer. I worked many fewer hours after one-acre of bamboo canes were removed in the wetlands area five years later. I was the WHA President in 2008 and continued as a Parks and Grounds Committee member or chair from 2010 to 2022. I joined the Fort Belvoir Ladies Golf Association when I retired and served on various committees before becoming the association's President in 2015 and 2016. I joined the Women's Golf Association Regional Team in 2010 and held key positions until 2017.

I explored Washington, D.C., sites, and the local historic districts by

Metro and by car when family and friends visited. I knew the roads in Washington, D.C., by carpooling to Crystal City from Annapolis. We each drove one day a week and listened to WMAL for news and accidents. When there was an accident WMAL provided alternate routes, which we took.

Mom visited most years. She loved to travel, sightsee, and being on vacation. When she was on vacation she expected to be waited on and taken someplace every day. She happily worked on any project she was given, mended anything she saw, looked at pictures, and knitted or crocheted. Jim catered to her. He would make her a drink, cook all the meals, and get anything she asked for. One of her favorite foods was rare steak. She would always tell Jim to just "wave it over the fire." One time he did this, and she had to admit she liked it more cooked. Jim loved that he finally caught her off guard. At this time Jim retired from his civilian career in 1996 and was the perfect "house husband" at our new home near George Washington's mansion in Mount Vernon. While I continued to work, he shopped, ran errands, and cooked. He was active with his 1957 United States Naval Academy classmates and community endeavors. He was the WHA President for two years, and in 1996 he established the USNA 1957 Golf Club that grew to more than 60 members with many playing monthly through 2022. I am thankful that Jim encouraged me to play golf. I made a hole-in-one playing in 2003 at the Class of '57 golf outing at Myrtle Beach, South Carolina. It was the golf group's first hole-in-one.

To summarize Jim's career before retirement he was a Naval Reserve Officer Training Corps (NROTC) student at The Ohio State University before his appointment to the U.S. Naval Academy. He served as a submarine officer until 1973, then became a surface line officer and commanded the USS Norton Sound, the AEGIS missile test ship home ported in Port Hueneme, California. He retired from the Navy in 1985 with the rank of captain after 28 years of service. He then worked as a consultant for Advanced Technology, Inc. / Black & Decker / EMHART. In 1988, he established Poole Enterprises, Inc., providing consultant services to the

Navy and others. From a previous marriage he has two children, three grandchildren, and four great grandchildren. During our careers we met many dignitaries including former President George H. W. Bush and entertainer Bob Hope.

Our travels through the years took us to 38 states in the U. S., Canada, the Bahama's, Bermuda, and Europe. Most of my experiences were wonderful. I will be forever grateful to my husband, my family and friends, and my mentors and co-workers, who have all shaped my life and made me a much better person.

Ginger and Jim Poole 1983

Jim and Ginger Poole 2009

Jim's Children 2019

Ginger and Jim Poole

Chapter 11

LINDA AND BILL THOMPSON

By Linda Gillen Thompson

Fifth Daughter

IN 1964, IN 5th grade, I was given the nickname Gilligan, by Mike Griffin. My nickname stayed with me until about the 10th grade.

I worked at Eleanor's Coffee Shop until it closed in May 1970. I babysat on weekends and took over babysitting for the Hardcastle kids when Noreen and Ginger left home. I also babysat for the Rogers in Onsted, and the owners of Camp O' the Hills girl scout camp on Pink Street across Stony Lake from our farm on Knapp Road.

Bill's IGA in Brooklyn held a teenage girl's contest. The contest started on April 8, 1968, and ended on June 1, 1968. The three girls with the highest points from all 50 States won a trip to New York City, New York, with their mothers. I was the first-place winner with over 73,000 points. The customers at the Coffee Shop signed my name on the back of Bill's IGA receipts and put them in a jar next to the donut case. The next two girls had 53,000 and 51,000 points. We left on June 10th for a week. We landed in Newark, New Jersey, and took a bus through the Lincoln Tunnel to New York City. We stayed in The Staten Hilton Hotel and toured New York City on a Double Decker bus. We took a ferry cruise trip around Manhattan Island and saw the Statue of Liberty, on Liberty Island. We saw the Empire State Building, the Rockettes at Radio City Music Hall, and the play *Happy Time* at The Broadway Theater. It was a great trip for a 14-year-old girl and her mother.

My favorite subject in school was geography and I worked on our class yearbook. My close friends in school were Veda Waldron, Karen Buskirk, and Gretchen Dermeyer. We had sleepovers and tee-peed the neighborhood with toilet paper, which we had to clean up. During my senior year, I had more friends - Debbie Munson, Gina Eshman, and Sharon Taggart. Sharon and I are still close friends today. I was also friends with Ramon, a foreign exchange student. I don't remember what country he was from.

After Eleanor's Coffee Shop closed, my first job was as a waitress at D&M Grill (formerly Christy's Grill) located on the corner of Onsted Highway and U.S. 12 in Brooklyn. I generally walked to the restaurant from our house, about one-half mile. I worked weekends and the summers during high school, and full-time after graduating until 1973.

Minnie and Dexter Layman were the owners of D&M Grill. After we moved to Onsted, they gave me a ride home to our house on Springville Highway. On our rides, Dexter taught me to drive a stick shift with their Volkswagen Beetle. Minnie and Dexter had two sons Phil and Eddie. Eddie and I are the same age. His birthday is in July and mine is in September.

I received my driver's permit during the summer before my senior year of high school. In November, I drove the family Ford Falcon car down Knapp Road and parked at the Twin Gables Tavern and Bar at the end of the road. I was planning to walk across U.S. 12 to D&M Grill to go to work. When I got out of the car, a policeman walked up to me and asked if I had just driven this vehicle. I said "Yes," and he asked me for my driver's license. I told him that I only had a learner's permit and didn't have it with me. He ticketed me, I had to give up my learner's permit and had to attend a two-week traffic class. After I completed the night class, I never asked for my permit back. I thought I had to repeat the entire Driver's Education program. Two years later Irene asked me about my learner's permit. She then drove me to the Driver's License Bureau. When I went to the desk, I was handed my driver's license, not my permit. As you can imagine Irene and I were very surprised. We didn't ask any questions at the time and thought the reason was probably my satisfactory completion of the traffic class or my age. By this time, I was almost 19 years old. I had just spent two years unable to drive due to a lack of communication.

In 1973 I was dating Ken Stites from Onsted, a customer at the D&M Grill. The Grill closed later in the year, and Minnie and I went to work at the Mark I Plastics plant in Jonesville, Michigan. Some things we made were plastic containers for hospitals and Dorell cigarette filters. We had to make sure there was no grease on the cigarette filters before we packaged them.

I bought my first car in 1974 while I was working at the Mark I plant. My new car was a maroon Pontiac Ventura. Minnie and I took turns driving to work. Minnie was driving one day in November when she hit a patch of ice and side-swiped a semi-truck in her Volkswagen Beetle. We were both bruised up a bit, but not seriously hurt. Minnie yelled my name, and I called out "Oh my God" when we hit the semi. Two days before the accident I gave her husband Dexter a set of keys for my car, and he was able to come and pick us up. How's that for timing?

The D&M Grill re-opened in 1975, and I went back to work as a waitress until 1977. One of the new customers I met was Bill Thompson. He worked on weekends in the local area building fiberglass boats and products with Jim and Clyde Gouldbury. Bill then, as now, always joked around when he came into the Grill and made me so nervous, I would always drop glasses in the sink. He always left me pennies for a tip in a glass of water, which the dishwasher (Eddie) often found in the bottom of the sink. One day Jim told Minnie that Bill liked me. Bill asked me out on a date, and we have been together ever since. Bill owned a small house on Brix Highway in Brooklyn that he purchased in 1969. He was always working on a remodeling project in the house and was building a kayak in the basement when we met.

Bill was born and raised in Toledo, Ohio, with his two sisters Suzanne (Sue) and Cindy. He drove to Toledo every day from Brooklyn to Haughton Elevator and Machine Company where he worked as a mechanical engineer on passenger elevators. After a while, he changed jobs within the company and became a field engineer. The company had many acquisitions and name changes over the 39 years that Bill worked for the company. Bill was a field engineer when the company became Schindler Elevator Corporation and did a lot of traveling, sometimes on a weekly basis, mostly in the United States. Schindler's main office was in Germany, and as Bill liked to say, "across the pond." When Bill was working in the Washington, D.C., area, usually on the Metro escalators, he called Jim and Ginger to meet for dinner.

I visited Ginger in Virginia for a week during the summer of 1974. While I was there, the apartment above Ginger's caught on fire during the night. Somebody was knocking on all the apartment doors and making the tenants leave the building. Ginger's apartment wasn't damaged but smelled smokey and all our clothes, linens and bedding had to be washed to get rid of the smokey odor. Ginger says she never heard the knocking on the door because of her hearing loss. She was grateful I was with her, and she is very afraid of fires to this day.

The following year was also very eventful. In April, I stayed at Cathy and Dave's home in Napoleon, Michigan, to watch Todd and Bryan for the weekend when they were 4 and 2 years old. I went to Chicago, Illinois, with the family for Norman's graduation from Navy boot camp. And Gary passed away on December 31st shortly after our family Christmas.

In May and June 1976, I was given three bridal showers. I married Bill on June 26, 1976, at Saint Joseph's Shrine in the Irish Hills in Brooklyn and moved into Bill's house on one-and-a-quarter-acre property at 11301 Brix Highway. We took a weekend honeymoon to the AuSable River in northern Michigan. Bill showed me where his grandpa Fred Thompson, lived and owned a cabin called *The Buckhorn*. Bill has the Buckhorn sign. In July, we took off for a one-month vacation out west to visit family. One of our stops was in Idaho Falls, Idaho, to spend time camping with Norm for the weekend when he was stationed there with the Navy.

Bill continued to remodel our house while we lived there. One of our favorite projects was assembling and installing a circular staircase made of cast iron that Bill was able to get from a razed building in Toledo. The iron was painted bright yellow. Bill refurbished it, scaled it to fit the space in the house, and hand-formed the handrail. Over the years he added a greenhouse, large decks, and a lot of landscaping. Bill and I never had children, but we have had German Shepherd dogs all our married life.

Our dogs were Panda, Heidi, Bridgett, Raven 1, Bailey, and Raven 2. We had Bailey the longest, 13 years. Bridgett was high-strung and our most difficult dog. We have also had 13 cats over the years. There were always a couple of house cats and many barn cats. We spoil all of them. The barn cats come to the front deck and let us know it is time for breakfast. We even have a heated water bowl in the barn in the winter to keep the water from freezing. We have named 11 cats over the years.

During 1976 -1977 I worked several odd jobs. I cleaned the St. Joseph's church rectory and was a census taker. In 1978, I began a 29-year career at the Brooklyn Products plant in Brooklyn. We made sponge bath mitts for Avon in the shape of animated cartoon characters, sponges for *Raindance* and *Turtle* car wax, and trim pieces and glove boxes for American Motors Corporation and other vehicles. One of our tasks involved hand-gluing the corners of sponge puppets and the glue we used made us feel a little "high." We called the work area the "happy corner." In the wintertime, we had a few snowball fights indoors and then had to clean up our workstations.

I was diagnosed with Becker's muscular dystrophy (MD) in 1995 when I began to have weakness in my right arm and left leg. I remained ambulatory and was able to go about my normal routine and work, but some functioning just became different. MD is a disease that progresses with more muscle weakness as time goes on. I continued to attend St. Joseph's Shrine and sing in the choir until 2018 when Bill became sick. In 2022 doctors said my disability is not MD, and they do not know what it is, although my symptoms are very similar to my brother Gary's.

On our annual vacations, we usually drove with the camper and had many families and friends join us. We went white water rafting on the New River in West Virginia for four summers in a row. On these whitewater rafting trips, the guides told us if we were tossed out of the raft and ended up underneath the raft, that there were arrows painted on the bottom of the raft to show us what direction to swim. I can tell you firsthand that there are NO arrows on the bottom of the raft. The last summer we rafted, another lady and I were thrown out of the raft and into the rapids. I went underneath the raft and used my hands to keep pushing my way to the edge. When I found my way out from under the raft, the river carried me away from the raft and the crew threw me a rope and hauled me back into the raft. Once inside the raft, I was still holding my breath until someone told me to breathe. After getting us both back aboard, the rafting trip continued, and I have never forgotten the name "Flee Flicker Rapids."

We took many short trips to the AuSable River in northern Michigan. At Buckeye Lake, near Columbus, Ohio, we often rented a cabin and played in the water and boated with Bill's sister Cindy and family. On other vacations, we traveled down the east coast to Florida and made several stops at Jim and Ginger's in Alexandria, Virginia.

We traveled to Alaska four times taking a month each time. We drove there through Canada or drove to Seattle, Washington, and drove our truck onto a ferry and enjoyed taking in the sights up the coast. Our neighbor's son lived in Alaska and ran a salmon guide business. We were able to salmon fish and have the canned fish sent home. Sherry, Jerry, and Kelly were able to join us on one of our Alaskan trips. Kelly was 13 months old and took her first steps in Alaska.

While I was fishing, Nigel Guest, our guide told me to yank hard on the line when I had a catch so the fish wouldn't get off the hook. I did this one time and there was no fish on my line. The heavy bobber and line went high up into the air and Bill covered his head jokingly. When he took his hands down, the bobber came down and landed hard on his head. We always laugh when we recall that incident.

We saw much of Canada on our drives back and forth to Alaska. Jasper National Park, British Columbia, was beautiful. Yellowknife in the Northwest Territory was desolate. When the spot we intended to camp had weeds taller than our truck we moved on to a better location. A stop at Long Lake in eastern Ontario had Bill hopping back in the truck quickly after a dip in the freezing cold water.

Most of our trips were to the West. We saw most of the national parks in Utah and the Grand Canyon. We rode mules down the trail from the North Rim of the Grand Canyon. I was saddle-sore for three days. While in the area around Olympic National Park in Washington, we rode a ferry to the San Juan Islands along the coast. We had many stops in Wyoming, Utah, and Idaho to see Sherry's and Norm's families and more recently, our nephew, Todd's family. We attended graduations and weddings for nieces and nephews and mom's surprise 80th birthday celebration in Idaho. While in Wyoming we joined my brother-in-law, Jerry, and his Uncle James in their elk and moose hunting expeditions. Our last western camping and road trip was in 2019 where we were also able to enjoy great-nieces and great-nephews.

We loved attending our immediate family gatherings across the country. The first family gathering was in 1993 in the middle of the United States at Lake of the Ozarks in Branson, Missouri. The family surprised both Dave and me for our birthdays. Dave celebrated his 50th and I celebrated my 40th. In 2005, 25 family members and friends went on a cruise to the Bahamas to celebrate Jim and Ginger's 25th wedding anniversary. The next family gathering was in 2014 at the Outer Banks in Kitty Hawk, North Carolina. It was an extra special treat to have the family gathering at Norm and Margaret's *Tintic Goldminers Inn Bed and Breakfast* in Eureka, Utah, in 2017. It was also great when the 2018 gathering was held at a lake house in Brooklyn only a mile from our house.

In 1998 we bought 20 acres north of our house from Don Novak, a race car driver from Florida, and I became a farmer's wife. We built a barn on the property right away. Bill had been cutting trees down for firewood from that property for many years. A short time later, we bought another 20 acres giving us 60 contiguous acres across U.S. 12 from the Michigan International Speedway.

Bill retired from Schindler Elevator Corporation on April 1, 2002. He continued to teach the Machine Repair Class for the company for another eight years as a contractor. When Bill finally retired in 2010, we became full-time farmers and beekeepers on Thompson Farm. In 2004, Bill started wood carving as a hobby.

In 2006, we began building our new house on our 20-acre property near the barn and moved in in 2007. I also retired from Brooklyn Products in 2007 and was able to receive disability as my muscular dystrophy began to make working difficult.

After completing our new 3,350 square-foot house, Bill grew alfalfa and clover for hay on 40 acres and sold round and square hay bales to local farmers. We had two large gardens and a pumpkin patch and began selling produce at the Walker's Tavern Farmer's Market in 2008. The next year, Bill started beekeeping. We sold honey, beeswax candles, and honey straws at the farmer's market, and to others locally. Later, Bill began selling his wood carvings at the farmer's market and continued to do this through 2020

Following this joyful life, Bill was diagnosed with cancer in 2011. For several years, the doctors were able to remove the cancer spots surgically. In 2018, cancer showed up in his liver and it was recommended that he begin chemotherapy. His final three years were a medical challenge. In the early summer of 2021, Bill finally decided he had had enough of the treatment and the negative effects on his body. He enjoyed the rest of the summer and ended up entering hospice care at the Hospice House in Adrian on September 23. He was there for six weeks and passed away on November 6, 2021.

Sherry visited us during this trying time in September and October 2021. After Bill was admitted to hospice, she frequently passed Bill's shoes at the house entry and realized that they would never see his feet again. She composed a tribute to him from this imagery.

Linda and Bill Thompson 2003

THESE SHOES

By Sherry Gillen Butcher Belmonte

THESE SHOES HAVE TRAVELLED MANY MILES

THEY SERVED MY COUNTRY, EARNED MY KEEP, AND KEPT ME GROUNDED

THEY CARRIED ME OVERSEAS AND ACROSS THIS COUNTRY MANY TIMES

THEY EXPLORED, HUNTED, FISHED, HIKED, BOATED, CANOED, AND RAFTED

THEY SPENT MANY HOURS ON THE GAS PEDAL PROVIDING PEACE OF MIND BETWEEN WORK AND HOME

HOME - A PLACE I NEVER RESTED FOR LONG - ALWAYS ONTO A NEW ADVENTURE, SO MUCH TO LEARN AND SEE AND ACHIEVE

EVERY TASK A NEW CHALLENGE TO CONQUER WITH THE LOVE OF CREATING, BUILDING, AND DESIGNING

NEVER OVERLOOKING THE BEAUTY ALL AROUND

– AN ANIMAL, A FALLEN FEATHER, A ROCK FORMATION, OR PECULIAR PIECE OF WOOD. A BIRDSONG OR BUZZING OF A BEE – ALL KNOWN AND SEEN

EVERY ELEMENT OF THE OUTDOORS, EACH SEASON A PLEASURE TO ENJOY AND CAPTURED ON FILM

THESE SHOES TOOK ME TO PLACES OF LAUGHTER, JOY, AND FULFILLMENT WITH THE PEOPLE WHOSE PATHS JOINED MINE - FAMILY, NEIGHBORS, COWORKERS, SKIERS, HOBBYIST – NEVER A STRANGER, NEVER AN AGE BARRIER

THE MAN IN THESE SHOES HAS BEEN A FRIEND, TEACHER, MENTOR, RESCUER, AND LEADER OF MULTITUDES

THE JOURNEY HAS BEEN FULL, AND IT HAS BEEN REWARDING.

THESE SHOES HAVE SERVED ME WELL

Chapter 12

NORM AND MARGARET GILLEN

By Norman" Norm" and Margaret Randolph Gillen

First Son

MY CLASS OF 1974 was the first to complete grades 9 through 12 at the new Columbia Central High School in Brooklyn, Michigan. During the transition, I attended classes in all the school buildings, including Cement City. Kindergarten through 4th grade were in the single-story elementary school, and 5th and 6th grades were in the old two-story brick building next to the elementary school. This was the old Brooklyn High School where Irene's husband Benny graduated in 1956. The 7th-grade students were bussed to Cement City, and the 8th-grade was in the "new" Brooklyn High School. I attended 9th and 10th grades at the new Columbia Central High School and finished 11th and 12th grades at Onsted High School after we moved to 7993 Springville Highway in Onsted, Michigan in 1972.

My cub scout leader was Phyllis McCloe. Her son Bill was my age, and we became best friends. I reconnected with Bill in 2020 and he reminded me of some of our activities. One was operating a library in our 5th-grade classroom. Another activity was creating an "Explorers Club." We explored the ruins of a cabin in the woods at the back of our farm and sorted for treasures in the ravine Dad used as the family trash dump site. We ended our daily activities when Mom called us from the house. One time we rode our bikes four miles from Bill's house to an old schoolhouse in Cement City where we climbed through a window to investigate the interior. Bill wrote a story of our adventure called *The Old School House*.

As a cub scout, I marched in Memorial Day and 4th of July parades with Dad and Noreen. I enjoyed band, marching during football games, and playing in the pep band during basketball games. At Columbia Central High School, I recall at least one trip to march in the Holland Tulip Festival parade. Not being a very good snare drummer, I mostly played other percussion instruments such as the triangle, bass drum, tympani drums, and cymbals.

I did not play sports. I tried running cross-country and competed in at least one meet but did not finish the season. My favorite subjects in high school were physics and band. Mr. Rice was the physics teacher, and I visited him at Onsted High School once while home on leave from the Navy.

My most memorable events from high school were the junior and senior plays at Onsted, directed by Mrs. Burt. *The Boarding House Reach* was the junior play. Girls in Mrs. Giroux's English class had been to the try-outs and said they needed more boys. I tried out and was chosen to play Wilbur, the lead. The cast was involved in the entire production, including building sets, painting, and locating and gathering stage props. It was great fun. The senior play *Finders Creepers* starred Wilbur. I won the part by default! Onsted housed 7th through 12th grades in the same building, and as a transfer student to Onsted High School between 10th and 11th grades more students knew me as "Wilbur" than as Norman.

With my new driver's license, I drove the county roads to and from Adrian, Michigan, in a 1968 Ford Galaxy fastback, passed down from Mom. On one trip I went too fast around a 90-degree curve and ran off the road into a bank three miles from home. There was just enough snow on the ground that the tires spun in reverse, preventing the car from getting back on the pavement. A nearby tractor rescued me, and I completed my trip. After returning home I parked the car in the driveway and went into the house. Linda came in later and said, "What happened to the car?" Busted.

As a "grounds keeper" at Saint Joseph's Shrine in the Irish Hills, Onsted, I worked with Wade Cash whose father Dick Cash was our boss. Wade's mother Gladys was Father Fitzgerald's housekeeper. Mom (Eleanor) was the church Secretary. Wade was a bit on the wild side – smoking and drinking. I smoked my one and only cigarette with him. It burned my throat, and there was no "buzz." There were rumors of hanky-panky between Father Fitzgerald and Gladys, and Gladys later committed suicide.

I became a beekeeper after moving to Onsted. Classmate Tim Hubbard's family-owned Hubbard Apiaries processed and sold honey. A subsidiary company owned and managed 30 "bee yards" throughout the local area. I worked weekends and summers putting empty "supers" (short for the superstructure on the beehive where bees store honey) on the hives in the spring, medicating the bees, and taking the honey-laden supers off in the fall. Hubbard Apiaries shipped the hives to Florida for the winter.

Tim's sister Betty Jo was Sherry's classmate and friend. Other friends included Marge Miller, brother and sister Terry and Cheryl Ferguson, Terry's girlfriend Gigi (Georgeanne) Crocker, and Sylvia Handy. I dated Jackie Koch, one year younger, and was introduced to tacos while eating dinner with her family. Her brother Rick was my classmate.

An ad on television stated, "Join the Army and receive $15,000 towards college," or something similar. I asked the Army recruiter in Adrian,

Michigan, about the promotion and he said, "Yeah, we got a program." He tossed me a brochure. I went down the hall to the U.S. Navy recruiter and mentioned I had applied to the University of Michigan engineering program. After hugging me and maybe even kissing me, the recruiter said, "Have I got a program for you." He proceeded to describe the Navy Nuclear Power Program. So, in February 1974, I enlisted in the Delayed Entry Program. Mom signed for me since I was only 17 years old. I was inducted into the U.S. Navy at Tiger Stadium on July 18 along with my entire boot camp company (Tiger Company #201) made up entirely of nuclear power and advanced electronics guys. After the baseball game, we boarded a bus for the Great Lakes Naval Training Center north of Chicago, Illinois.

I turned 18 while on leave from boot camp and returned to Great Lakes, Illinois, for Machinists Mate "A" School, and on to Mare Island Naval Shipyard in California for Nuclear Power School in January 1975. My next training platform was the A1W prototype reactor at the Nuclear Power Training Unit at the Naval Reactor Facility at the Idaho National Engineering Laboratory, Idaho Falls, Idaho, in June 1975. Upon graduation, I was selected to be a "Staff Pickup," a two-year instructor tour at the A1W prototype.

The Teton Dam near Rexburg, Idaho, failed while I was in Michigan for Sherry's high school graduation in June 1976. Flood waters from the Snake River came within four blocks of the house I was renting. One summer I visited Sherry at Cedar Point in Sandusky, Ohio, and had a great time with Sherry and her friends. I slept on the floor of Sherry's apartment (or dorm) and was shocked to hear one of her roommates use foul language, worse than sailors.

On completion of the A1W assignment in Idaho Falls, Idaho, in July 1978, I received orders to the USS South Carolina, a nuclear cruiser homeported in Norfolk, Virginia. USS South Carolina was deployed to the Mediterranean, so I flew to Naples, Italy, via New York City and

THE WALTER AND ELEANOR GILLEN STORY

Rota, Spain to meet the ship. The final leg required landing on board the USS Nimitz aboard a Carrier Onboard Delivery plane and taking a helicopter to the USS South Carolina. The seas were too rough for landing, so I was lowered to the deck in a "horse collar" while the helicopter hovered. My first port visit was to Venice, Italy.

My next duty station (March 1980) was the USS Carl Vinson, under construction at Newport News Shipbuilding and Drydock Company in Newport News, Virginia. In April 1981, I returned to Idaho Falls to visit neighbor June Erickson, and her daughter Cindy. Sherry picked me up at the Salt Lake City, Utah, airport, and we skied in Park City, Utah, on our return to Sherry's apartment in Evanston, Wyoming. Sherry had a volleyball game with her boyfriend Jerry Butcher that night, so she dropped me off at her apartment. Her roommate Margaret Randolph answered the door. I borrowed Sherry's car and drove to Idaho Falls to visit the Ericksons. After returning to Evanston, Sherry and Jerry and Margaret and I watched the Ice Capades at The Salt Palace in Salt Lake City where Randy Gardner and Tai Babilonia headlined the performance.

Margaret and I continued a long-distance relationship for five months with phone calls and letters. I used an airline voucher received on my return to Norfolk to visit Margaret and her family in Arizona in May for her brother Dean's marriage to Diana. After the wedding, I helped Margaret's family move to Belgrade, Montana. In August, I flew to Evanston and returned to Virginia with Margaret in her 1978 Ford Mustang. She moved into my old apartment in Newport News until we married on my 25th birthday, October 3, 1981. Mom, Ginger, and Jim attended our ceremony. We spent our wedding night at the historic Chamberlin Hotel at Fort Monroe, Virginia, and went to Ocracoke Island on the Outer Banks of North Carolina for our honeymoon.

We moved into the house I purchased as a foreclosure at 33 Westover Street, Hampton, Virginia, a month prior to meeting Margaret. I furnished the house with This End Up, crate-style furniture – couch, loveseat, chair, coffee table, and end tables. There was also a waterbed set, a teak drop-leaf kitchen table, and an oak roll-top desk. My roommate Troy Willauer moved to the ship's living quarters barge when Margaret moved in. We lived here while finishing my initial eight-year commitment to the U.S. Navy.

We left Virginia in July 1982, towing a 32-foot Holiday Rambler trailer behind a too-small half-ton Ford F-150. We visited *Mother Earth News,* a "back-to-earth" magazine, Eco-Village in Hendersonville, North Carolina, and attended the 1982 World's Fair in Knoxville, Tennessee, on our way to Michigan, where we parked our trailer behind Dave and Cathy's house in Napoleon, Michigan. The World's Fair featured a dome home and its signature structure, the "Sun sphere."

Who could have imagined that 40 years later we (and Lindsay) would be living less than 45 minutes from that location?

While on vacation with Mom and Father Bill McKeon over Labor Day weekend 1982 to Petoskey, Michigan, I met Bill's neighbor – the vice president of Nuclear Operations for Consumers Power Company and received a 10-minute job interview. I had a formal interview at the vice president's office in Jackson, Michigan, the following Tuesday, and an on-site interview at the Midland Nuclear Plant. I was hired as a technical writer in the Maintenance Department, with George Smith as my supervisor. I was "taught the ropes" by two contractors, Vic, and another guy, who both lived in Elmira, New York. Just a few weeks earlier I had applied for a job at Consumers Power Human Resources and received a polite rejection letter.

We bought our second house at 4405 Quincy Drive in Midland, Michigan, and moved there in October 1982. Daughter Andrhea was born on December 14, 1983. Mike and Helen Kostoff lived across the street and became good friends. Dennis and Sue Bishop lived in the neighborhood and had two small children. We learned how "not" to raise children from them. Dennis and I commuted to work together, and I helped Dennis replace the engine in his Volkswagen Beetle. We enjoyed cross-country skiing at a nearby park and volunteering at the Chippewa Nature Center. Midland Nuclear Plant was one of five "troubled" nuclear plants in the early 1980s and finally succumbed to economic and political pressure, halting construction in the summer of 1984. I was in the Naval Reserve, attached to the USS Shenandoah and in New Orleans, Louisiana, for my two-week active duty for training that summer and joked that I might not have a job to go back to afterward. The plant did close, putting 4,500 employees out of work.

I re-enlisted in the U.S. Navy, returning to Great Lakes Naval Training Center on November 2, 1984. I was in Great Lakes just long enough to receive orders to the USS Carl Vinson, homeported at the Naval Air Station in Alameda, California. We lived in an apartment in San Leandro, California, where Margaret worked at the Waldenbooks store. Mike and Helen had returned home to the San Francisco Bay area, so we saw them occasionally. I flew overseas to meet the USS Carl Vinson in Yokosuka, Japan, via Subic Bay, Philippines, in December 1984.

After my April 1986 re-enlistment, I was assigned to Engineering Laboratory Technician School at Ballston Spa, New York, in December 1986. Margaret and I became good friends with my seatmate Todd Petro and his wife Susie, who was also from Michigan. In March 1987 I was assigned to the USS Emory S Land homeported in Norfolk, Virginia. The submarine tender deployed to the Strait of Hormuz in the Persian Gulf via the Suez Canal and returned via the Panama Canal. I was promoted to Chief Petty Officer during this deployment.

In March 1987 we moved to 19 Edgemont Drive in Hampton, Virginia, on the Peninsula, across the Hampton Roads Bay Bridge-Tunnel from Norfolk Naval Station. Our first major home renovation project was here. The roof over the Florida room leaked, destroying the wood parquet floor tiles. A contractor properly attached the shed roof over the 10-foot-wide addition, and we did the interior work. The cement floor was uneven, so we trimmed 2×2 stringers and installed a subfloor to level it. We also hung and (poorly) finished the sheetrock and installed a wood-burning stove in the addition, where 5-year-old Andrhea burned her hand on the stovepipe while mimicking Dad holding his hand close to check the temperature. She didn't know about the "close" part. Daughters Lindsay and Kari were born while we lived in Hampton, Virginia.

Andrhea attended 1st grade at a Christian School, but it was too expensive to continue. Margaret felt it would be "dumbing down" to put her in public school, so she began homeschooling. There was a strong local support group, and we joined the Home School Legal Defense Association advocacy group. The homeschool movement was relatively new, and we did not feel like outcasts.

The two-story, two-car detached garage had to be dismantled because there was no way to correct construction errors. We had a very effective compost pile and a productive organic garden. We used Rodale books for guidance. One technique was "double digging" to loosen soil 20 inches below the surface. I chopped at a tree root with the shovel before realizing it was the underground electrical cable. A month later the house experienced a brownout. I was able to show the repair technicians exactly where the problem was. The cable was supposed to be 32 inches deep.

I transferred to the USS Dwight D Eisenhower in September 1989. This tour included deployments to the Persian Gulf for Desert Shield and Desert Storm. I detached from the ship during deployment and saw smoke from burning Kuwaiti oil rigs during my helicopter flight from the ship to Bahrain, United Arab Emirates.

In November 1991, I received orders to the Supervisor of Shipbuilding in Newport News, Virginia, for my shore tour. I assisted with contract changes for the 4th refueling overhaul of the four nuclear reactors on the USS Enterprise.

In February 1994, I found myself stationed aboard the USS George Washington at Norfolk Naval Station as the Reactor Laboratories Division Officer, a position normally filled by a junior officer. A giant retinal tear was discovered in my left eye in December 1994, and urgent surgery was performed to re-attach the retina. I returned to limited duty aboard the George Washington in January 1995 for a Mediterranean deployment. A recurrent detachment caused me to be medevacked to the Azores and to National Naval Medical Center in Bethesda, Maryland. I don't think there are many people who have flown off a carrier while prone in a stretcher and blindfolded. I spent the next four months in and out of surgery at Bethesda. Brother-in-law Jim Poole, living in Alexandria, Virginia, and working from home while running Poole Enterprises, Incorporated, was very gracious during this period, serving as my chauffeur, nurse, and companion.

In June 1993, we moved to 17807 Beale Place Drive, Windsor, Virginia. This was close to friends Todd and Susie Petro (and their daughters Mandy and Katie) and across the James River Bridge in a rural area west of Smithfield, Virginia. Our three-acre parcel included an older mobile home with an attached one-bedroom apartment and a shelled-in two-story addition. Margaret's brother Wade, and his friend Paul, visited and helped me replace the steel beam supporting the second story. Contractors completed the interior work - no more drywall hanging and finishing for us. Half of the downstairs was a living room with a wood stove, and the other half was a garage and workshop. There were three bedrooms upstairs. We raised chickens, milked goats, sheared sheep and bred Himalayan cats and Dalmatian dogs, and had the best garden ever! I was required to be in a "face-down" position for two weeks following surgery to repair a detached retina. I was "face-down" while pulling weeds and tending to the garden.

We purchased the mobile home across the road after the owner died. We sold it after performing minor repairs and giving it some "tender loving care." This was our first of 24 investment properties. A book I read in 1976, *How to Wake Up the Financial Genius Inside You* by Mark O. Haroldson, planted the seed in my mind for investing in real estate. This author was also a mentor to Wright Thurston, another real estate guru whose seminars I attended in Salt Lake City, Utah, in the 2000s.

We invited Mom to live in our mobile home after we moved into our "new" house. She moved there in August 1994. My letter to Mom about my deployment on the George Washington is at the end of my story – a great insight into the life of a sailor. Son Jayme was born on December 14, 1996, on Andrhea's 13th birthday. She didn't appreciate that birthday "gift." Thirteen-year-old Andrhea showed goats at the Virginia State Fair in Richmond in August 1996. We stayed at the fairgrounds for three days during the fair, a positive and interesting experience.

After the ophthalmologists stabilized my eye in April 1995, I was transferred back to the Supervisor of Shipbuilding in Newport News in a medical hold/limited duty capacity, and I medically retired from the Navy on May 17, 1997.

I was hired as an instructor for a Newport News Shipbuilding and Drydock Company subsidiary – Newport News Reactor Services (NNRS) in Idaho Falls. NNRS was located 60 miles west of Idaho Falls at the Naval Reactors Facility at the Idaho National Engineering Laboratory. I taught Radiation Safety to workers de-fueling the A1W-A and -B reactors [the USS Enterprise] prototype where I had qualified to be a nuclear operator 22 years earlier. NNRS also de-fueled S5G, a submarine prototype.

During a house-hunting trip to Idaho in 1997 we looked at six or seven houses with a Century 21 real estate agent. None of the houses worked out for us. After returning to Virginia the agent sent pictures of 574 Hanson Drive in Shelley, Idaho, and we signed a Real Estate Purchase Agreement sight unseen. The agent must have been on "pins and needles" during my first walk-through of the house. I moved in immediately upon closing while Margaret oversaw the packing of the Windsor house. I flew back to Virginia to drive with the family to Shelley in our Ford Aerostar van. Mom stayed in Michigan until we were settled. The moving configuration included a utility trailer with a "goat house" for a pygmy mama and baby goat and pets. Hopefully, no laws were broken by transporting livestock across state lines without a permit. Uncle Benny teased Andrhea that she was going to be a "potato spud" in Idaho. Andrhea quit homeschooling and attended Shelley High School in 10th grade – Shelley's mascot was The Russets! She transferred to Idaho Falls, Idaho high school for 11th and 12th grade, and graduated in 2000.

Lauris, our next-door neighbor in Shelley, had a team of horses that 5-year-old Jayme loved riding. We were very active in Berean Baptist Church in Idaho Falls. Church members were meeting in the Idaho Falls Public Library while building their own house of worship in Ammon. I was one of the deacons overseeing the construction, and all members helped with the new building, led by a missionary who specialized in construction. After Lauris died, a Native American lady moved into his mobile home and proceeded to give us "nasty neighbor" grief until we sold the house.

I became a postal clerk in Idaho Falls after Newport News Reactor Services completed the de-fueling in September 1999. This was my only non-nuclear job since joining the Navy in 1974. The mail volume dropped due to increased electronic and digital communication and so did the part-time flexible worker hours. I found a job as a Radiological Controls Technician with EG&G Technical Services Incorporated in Utah. EG&G had a contract with Envirocare in Clive, Utah, 50 miles from the Nevada border and 280 miles from home. I stayed in our Trail Manor camper in Lakepoint, Utah, during my 60-hour work weeks, and traveled home to Shelley on weekends.

After a few months, I accepted a position as a night operations supervisor and became a permanent Envirocare employee. In March 2001, we moved to 449 South Main Street in Tooele, Utah, where we converted the house to a duplex while living in it. This included removing a portion of the roof to expand the second floor. A frequent question during construction was "Where are we sleeping tonight, Mom?" Margaret's father, Carol, and Andrhea's fiancé, Lucas Ray, helped me jack up sagging floors in the 70-year-old house to scab on 2×8-foot boards to reinforce floor joists and install concrete pads and steel posts to support the new second-floor addition and roof. I also built a 20×30-foot garage from the ground up, including footers. We converted this garage to an apartment for Jayme after he graduated from Tintic High School, Eureka, Utah, in 2014. We purchased the house next door at 437 South Main Street in Tooele, Utah, another foreclosure, and converted it to a duplex (two one-bedroom units) where newlyweds Andrhea and Luke lived for a few months.

In January 2003 we moved to 761 Upland Drive in Tooele, another foreclosure. This house required extensive concrete work – the driveway, sidewalks, and digging and cutting three window wells to add egress windows into basement bedrooms. Removing drywall exposed a beautiful stone chimney and fireplace (where we installed a pellet stove), and an apartment was created in half of the basement. The covered patio along the entire length of the house had an awesome view of the Great Salt Lake 15 miles distant and was a great setting for our Bullfrog Spa hot tub. Lindsay graduated from homeschooling in 2006 and lived in the basement apartment for a short time. Kari attended Grantsville High School and graduated in 2008. Jayme continued homeschooling.

I left Envirocare in August 2003 and returned to the Idaho National Laboratory as a Radiological Controls Technician working four days on/four days off 12-hour shifts. The four-day weekends allowed sufficient time for the 200-mile commute and quality home time. Andrhea's Gate Agent job at Skywest Airlines made this easier, enabling me to frequently fly round trips from the Salt Lake City airport to the Idaho Falls airport, using "parent of employee" non-revenue privileges.

"Bungalow mansion for sale, Eureka, Utah." An ad in the *Tooele Transcript Bulletin,* was the introduction to the next phase of our journey. Owner Lamar Penovitch showed the house at 331 S. Beck Street in Eureka in 2005, but no offer was made. Lamar contacted us in spring of 2006 when we agreed to purchase terms. We spent the summer removing old furniture and carpets from the house, while the property was being remediated as part of an Environmental Protection Agency Superfund cleanup site, and finally closed in October 2006. Margaret was the general contractor for renovating the house interior – insulating exterior walls, installing new wiring, potable water lines, and sewer drains, re-plumbing cast-iron radiators and running one-inch polyethylene piping to them, installing a wood-pellet boiler, replacing windows, adding two bathrooms to create six guest rooms, and adding a two-bedroom apartment in the basement. Jon Goodman was our "jack-of-all-trades" contractor, performing a lot of the work himself while overseeing a local crew, when they weren't in jail.

We licensed the Tintic Goldminers Inn Bed & Breakfast (B&B) in Eureka, Utah, and opened in August 2008, during the Great Recession in the United States. Despite the economic downturn, we had steady customers, the majority coming for weekend scrapbooking retreats. This idea was inspired by Irene's scrapbooking activities. We partnered with Cathie Rigby who conducted workshops in Salt Lake City, Utah, on using a Cricut, an elaborate decal maker for scrapbooks. The business was always good for a tax write-off, and even generated a positive cash flow when operations were suspended in 2019 in preparation for my pending civilian retirement. Jayme enrolled in Tintic High School for 7th grade and graduated in June 2014.

Many guests stayed at the B&B while visiting relatives in Eureka, or Mammoth, Utah. We hosted a Mormon movie production crew annually while filming at their Jerusalem movie set 10 miles away. Other guests were in town for funerals, including Bill Stewart's funeral. We bought Bill's Mammoth cabin, built in 1898, on Sioux Street in Mammoth when his estate was settled in August 2017. We demolished everything but the original 12×24-foot cabin, built a proper addition for the kitchen, dining room, and bathroom, and added another addition for a second bedroom. Some floor joists had completely disintegrated, requiring the cabin to be jacked up to replace them. Jayme and his friend Leneisha Seeley did much of the work over a two-year period.

Lindsay followed my footsteps and became a Radiological Controls Technician in 2010, eventually working at the Oak Ridge National Laboratory near Knoxville, Tennessee, where she and her husband Ryan put down "roots" and purchased their home in Knoxville in 2016. Margaret and I bought a five-acre parcel at 344 Keck Road in Maynardville, Tennessee, in January 2019, to be near Lindsay, Ryan, and their girls, Gemma and Priya. Our property included a mobile home, and a two-story, weathered-in 3,600-square-foot house, with no interior walls. We designed the floor plan, and Jayme and contractor Ben rebuilt the stairs, installed walls, built a 10×20-foot deck, ran electrical wiring, installed electrical fixtures, and completed other work on the house. I wired the circuit breaker panels, and Jayme, Margaret, and I installed polyethylene piping and ABS drain lines. Contractors sprayed foam insulation and installed and finished drywall in the spring of 2021. It was a joyful day when the occupancy permit was issued in January 2022, the culmination of nearly three years of hard work.

I quit my permanent job at the Idaho National Laboratory in May 2019 to become a contract Radiological Controls Technician, beginning my transition to retirement. Margaret also "retired" from hosting guests at our Tintic Goldminers Inn Bed & Breakfast in Eureka to free up time for travel to visit her children and grandchildren, and her mother Francis in Montana. The B&B and the adjacent Chief Consolidated Mining Company Office and Guest House were leased to the High-Power Exploration (HPX) mining exploration company, which was prospecting for copper in the historic Tintic Mining District. This arrangement continued through the COVID-19 fright of 2020 and into 2023, even though HPX had suspended work for most of 2021.

I was hired by my son-in-law Luke's company (EnviraChem) to work with Luke at the Santa Susanna Facility Laboratory (SSFL) site in Ventura County, California, in October 2019. Jayme was hired in June 2020 as a laborer, and then as a Radiological Controls Technician six months later. I transferred to Hunters Point Naval Shipyard, San Francisco, California, in October 2020 for my final professional job – an Environmental Protection Agency oversight contractor for soil remediation. I retired from this position in July 2022. Lindsay was hired as a temporary employee at (SSFL) by Luke, working intermittently beginning in January 2021. It was a proud day for me when all four Radiological Controls Technicians in the family were on the same job site at the same time in April 2021.

We have lived in eight states, owned 10 residences in six states, and have owned an additional 23 investment properties. In 40 years of marriage the only companies I worked for while commuting daily from home were - Midland Nuclear Plant (1982-84), Newport News Reactor Services (1997-98), United States Postal Service (1998-2001), and Envirocare (2001-03), a total of 10 years. I worked a 4-day 10-hour shift or 5-day 8-hour day shift schedule only 15 of 48 working years. The rest of the time was spent "on watch" (U.S. Navy), rotating days and nights on 4-day 12-hour shifts at the Idaho National Laboratory or working straight mid-shift at the United States Postal Service and Envirocare.

Our oldest daughter Andrhea met her future husband Lucas Ray at church in Idaho Falls. They were married in Salt Lake City on April 6, 2002. Andrhea and Luke's two sons Malachi and Titus were born in Salt Lake City. Daughters Eden and Evie were born in Fairfax, Virginia, and Eliana was born in Thousand Oaks, California. Second oldest daughter Lindsay met her future husband Ryan Foran through the Young Adult ministry at their Oak Ridge, Tennessee, church. They were married in Oak Ridge on August 23, 2014. Their three daughters, Gemma Ruth, Priya Rose, and Zora Leigh were born in Knoxville. Youngest daughter Kari met her future husband Jason Weimer at a house party in Sugar

House in Salt Lake City in 2016, and they were married at Solitude Mountain Resort in Solitude, Utah, on June 19, 2021. Son Jayme is unmarried and working as Radiological Controls Technician in Simi Valley, California.

I did not continue in the Catholic faith after joining the Navy. All students at the Nuclear Power Training Unit in Idaho Falls were assigned a "sea-dad" (mentor). Mine was Steve Sternburg, who attended the Christian Center, an independent Evangelical/Charismatic church in Idaho Falls. I started attending and was "born-again" and baptized there. I was a faithful member there for two-and-a-half years until receiving orders to the USS South Carolina in February 1978. I continued to worship throughout my time in the Navy. All my ships had a chaplain and conducted Sunday Services, as well as Bible studies throughout the week. A publication, *The Navy Christian Link-up,* provided contact information for various ministries in Navy ports around the world. It was a valuable resource that gave liberty calls significance for me. A summary of my visit to some of these ministries is at the end of my story. (God's Vessel(s)).

Margaret and I were active with The Navigators, a ministry to sailors while living in San Leandro, California. When we moved to 19 Edgemont Street in Hampton, Virginia, in 1987 we joined Harbor Baptist Church, an Independent Baptist church. We were very active in the church and continued worshipping in Baptist churches: Calvary Baptist in Smithfield, Virginia; Berean Baptist in Idaho Falls, Idaho; Cornerstone Baptist in Tooele, Utah; Santaquin Baptist in Santaquin, Utah, and New Testament Baptist in Maynardville, Tennessee.

*Norm and Margaret
Gillen 2006*

*Norm and Margaret's Children
2009*

The Old School House

One night after school Norman ___ came over to my house to play. After a while we couldn't find anything to do so we decided to explore the old school house on Cement City Rd. When we first started out it was ___ day, ___ we ___ on our ___ bikes that all it ___ work. When we finally got there we hid our bikes in the cornfield and then had to climb in a window to get in.

When we got in we found a real old piano out of tune, some old magazines, a ___ and a boot. In another room we found a pile of ___ some canning cans, and a juice ___ when we went back in the other room we found something that we didn't see before. It was a small cardboard box with a couple clamps on it. I tried to get one off but it ripped then I tried the other clamp and it came right off and then I ___ in my pocket.

Then when we went back through the window we decided to look around a while. First we went in a shed a found some old desks. Next we went around on the other side of the school house and found some cement blocks. Then We went over to look at the teeter-totter and came down on Norman's head.

After that we looked around and didn't
find anything interesting so we started home
Norman was the first to get home It took me a
while to get home because the chain broke
on the bike. When we got home we looked
to see if the stamp we found could go in
my stamp book.

The

End

by

Bill

Aug 21, 1994

Hi Mom,

How are all of you doing? I just wanted to drop a line to let you know what's happening in my world. I reported aboard the USS George Washington (CVN-73) on Feb 18. My job here is similar to the one I had on the USS Eisenhower from Sept. '89 to Nov. '91. I recently completed the 5 month qualification phase for Propulsion Plant Watch Supervisor. The propulsion plants are manned 24 hours a day, as we generate steam which is used for propulsion, electrical generation, and production of fresh water. We stand 5 hour watches, usually one watch per day. In addition to that every one is assigned to a work center which is responsible for cleanliness, preventive and corrective maintenance. I am the Reactor Laboratories division officer, in charge of 25 men, overseeing the administration and coordination of my division. There is plenty of work to do - enough to keep one going 24 hours a day if you're not careful!

That's the business end of the ship. The "cruise ship" aspect is quite a bit different. Three weeks after leaving Norfolk on May 20 we anchored in Portsmouth, England for three days. The city was bristling with activity as there were tens of thousands of tourists in town for the 50th anniversary of the D-Day invasion at Normandy Beach. I was duly impressed by the USS Constitution, a restored sailing ship from the 18th century, commanded by Lord Nelson, and the Naval museum in Portsmouth. Before we left Portsmouth we were honored to "hail the queen" as she, President Clinton and 13 other heads-of-state passed in review aboard the queen's yacht HMS Britannia. President Clinton and Hillary came aboard that afternoon for our transit across the English Channel to Normandy Beach. While here, he re enlisted 60 crew members and shook hands with hundreds of the crew, including me! He also had a news conference with Wolf Blitzer, Tom Brokaw, and Sam Donaldson and presided over a memorial service to those who died on June 6, 1944. The best part of that whole experience for me was spending two hours listening to first-hand accounts from 2 veterans who were part of the invasion. We had 12 veterans on board for our transit from the states to England.

We left from there and went to Brest, France where we were warmly received by the French. I went on a tour there to centuries-old villages and churches. On to Antalya, Turkey where I saw Roman ruins, some in excellent condition, and a carpet factory. I bought a beautiful Turkish rug - you will have to come visit after Nov. 20 if you want to see it! Our next port visit was to the island of Corfu, Greece. It is a European tourist destination, primarily for its beaches. I just walked around and window shopped, and drank cappuccino while I ate baklava, a pastry. My favorite port this deployment has been Haifa, Israel The ship sold over 2,000 tours to holy land destinations such as the Sea of Galilee, Nazareth, the Jordan river, Jerusalem, the Dead sea and Masada. I have seen most of those places during previous visits, so this time I spent my three days off with missionaries I met at Bethel Tourist Hostel, and some Americans working at the B'ahai World Center. The missionaries invited me and a buddy to picnic and swim with them at Gan Hashelosha (the place of the 3 springs), in sight of Mt. Gilboa, where King Saul was killed (as described in 1 Samuel). The next day we gave our 8 new friends tours of the ship, including lunch. They all enjoyed their time aboard very much. We are currently in Rhodes, Greece and scheduled to visit Cannes, France and Cartagena, Spain before we return to Norfolk on Nov. 20.

The best aspect of shipboard life is the spiritual one. I am aware of more than 200 practicing Christians on board The chapel is booked 24 hours a day with services or bible studies for members of all denominations, and many groups meet in any out-of-the-way space they can find. I hear reports of men accepting Jesus Christ as their personal Savior at an average of 1 or 2 each week. Praise the Lord! I am attending a MasterLife bible study on Saturday evenings. The study is loaded with memory verses to help us walk closer to the Lord. Do you know Jesus as your Savior? Someone you can turn to in times of joy and sorrow? I pray this is the case, that you have followed the steps of Romans 3:23 (all have sinned), Rom 6:23 (wages of sin is death), Rom 5:8 (God has provided a way to salvation), Rom 10:13 (those who call upon the Lord will be saved) and Rom 10:9 (confess that Jesus is Lord). With that done, there is hope in living, and no despair in death. The Apostle Paul says to die is gain! But until then, we can live our lives as a witness to Jesus Christ, and tell others about the good news of the Gospel!

As you knew, the worst thing about deployment is being separated from Margaret, Andrhea, Lindsay and Kari. They have been keeping plenty busy, settling into our "new" house, preparing for Mom's arrival, and keeping up with the goats and chickens. Time to go now, BYE!

I hope this reaches you before you leave Michigan. Margaret tells me everything is ready for you. Are you excited? Many second thoughts? You're kind of moving backwards, aren't you - from the city to the country. more people should make that move, I think. See You in November, Norm

God's Vessel(s)

T291401
Norman Paul Gillen

God's Vessel(s)

The Places

The Navy Christian Link-Up magazine led me to many wonderful experiences at ports-of-call the world over: Subic Servicemen's Center in the Philippines; Trans-World Radio station in Monte Carlo (where the station manager and his family invited us to a Mediterranean beach picnic on Bastille Day beneath choreographed fireworks!); A church in St. Thomas; Toulon, France; Perth, Australia (where I spent 3 days as a house guest of an older couple who I met in church. Anyone for Vegemite?); Palma de Majorca; London; Youth With a Mission, Singapore; Bahrain and a dozen others.

The Hostel

Haifa, Israel's Bethel Hostel stands out from the others because that is where God would use me as His vessel. I discovered this refuge 1 mile from fleet landing in 1990 when the USS Dwight D. Eisenhower anchored in Haifa's bay, 2 hours after liberty call (queuing for liberty boats, the ride ashore, walking, etc.). A group of us enjoyed interacting with the permanent and temporary staff, and they enjoyed touring our aircraft carrier.

The Cargo

I returned 2 years later aboard the USS George Washington with 20 - 25 boxes of bibles from the American Bible Society - in Arabic! They belonged to Christian Egyptians ministering in the West Bank of Jerusalem.. I learned of the missionaries request to have their bibles brought overseas through Harbor Baptist Church in Hampton, Virginia.

The Question

How were these bibles going to get ashore, past an armed Israeli guard at fleet landing and down to Jerusalem 3 hours from Haifa?? Store them at the hostel…ride bus to Jerusalem…return with missionaries to Haifa…but what about bringing them ashore??

The Delivery

2 hours one way, 2 boxes per sailor, 2 round trips. Okay, I and 5 fellow Christians could transport all the bibles in one day. Nope- duty or scheduled tours/plans reduced the available helpers to zero, I was on my own. The only help available from the ship's chaplain and the Sixth Fleet chaplain was moral support (a political "hot potato", you see). I committed to God to do whatever it took. Saturday came. I borrowed a cart and a guy to help load it. A work party appeared from an adjacent store room with two full mail carts and loaded my cart. Next they took all 3 carts to the fantail to be lowered to the boating dock. A work party there loaded the "books for charity" on the work boat and my cargo and I were bound for fleet landing!!! A third work party there unloaded my cargo – Phase I complete!

I borrowed a luggage cart from a nearby passenger terminal, loaded the books and pushed it through a gate manned by an armed Israeli soldier – No questions asked! I phoned the hostel, which sent a van to collect me and the books. Two trips later we completed stowing the boxes at the hostel. Fait Accompli before liberty call even commenced!!

Phase II complete.

I arrived in Jerusalem via bus at 1800, where the missionaries waited, and waited, and waited. We finally connected at 2100 when I asked a man sitting on a retaining wall if he was looking for Norman Gillen. The color of my clothes under the street lights was completely different than my description of them. I received a wonderful one-on-one tour of Jerusalem (including the West Bank, an area off-limits to sailors due to political unrest) and Caesarea-Phillipi during my 2-day visit, and return to Haifa. The missionaries loaded their bibles and returned to Jerusalem, while I returned to the USS George Washington.
Phase III complete.

Chapter 13

✦

GARY GILLEN

By Catherine "Cathy" Osborn, Noreen Gillen Litchard,
Virginia "Ginger" Gillen Poole, Linda Gillen Thompson,
Norman "Norm" Gillen, and Sherry Gillen Butcher Belmonte

Second Son

WE WERE ALWAYS amazed at Gary for his infinite patience. We were also so proud of him because he never complained about his muscular dystrophy (MD) disease. He simply accepted his plight in life and did his best. We never saw Gary get mad. He may have gotten upset a few times, like the rest of us, and he was a great brother.

Throughout Gary's and Sherry's elementary school years, the family went to the Mother of Twins Club picnics in the summer, and in December there was always a local Muscular Dystrophy Chapter Christmas party for the MD kids and their siblings in Jackson, Michigan.

Gary was in the Boy Scouts of America during his elementary school years. When he was 10 years old, he was in the Brooklyn Fourth of July parade with his scout pack, and they pulled him in a wagon. He was not in a wheelchair yet, but he couldn't walk that long distance.

Gary attended the Crippled Children's Camp for two weeks every summer for at least five years. All the camps were in Jackson, except one year when it was in Benton Harbor, Michigan. The camps were amazing. The staff was so compassionate, and the activities list went on and on. Gary had the accessibility to get into the swimming pool at camp, and always came home with many craft projects. When Gary was at home, he spent many hours at a desk in his room painting, assembling model cars, and sketching homes.

Gary was just finishing 7th grade in May 1972, in Brooklyn when the family moved to Springville Highway in Onsted, Michigan. He repeated 5th grade because he missed many school days one winter due to colds and ear infections. Gary had fun meeting Norm's and Sherry's new friends. We had several parties at the house so that Gary could participate. There were May Basket parties, a '50s Sock Hop, and a Halloween party that we hosted.

Gary was enrolled in the Tecumseh School District starting in the 8th grade, 15 miles away. The Onsted schools did not have handicap access, or the special assistance Gary needed. A bus with a lift picked him up and dropped him off at the house on school days.

Gary began using a wheelchair full-time by the time he was 12. He didn't get a power wheelchair until he was 17 in 1975. A bed was set up along a wall in the dining room for him to use when he could no longer get up the staircase to his bedroom. When Gary no longer attended church services with us, he watched Billy Graham on the television. This program was always on when we arrived home during the years we lived in Onsted.

Gary was able to go out into the yard and function with the use of his wheelchair. He was independent enough when he had his electric wheelchair to get outside and wait for his bus on his own. After we moved to N. Main Street in Onsted, Linda was outside when one of our new neighbors asked her if Gary could talk. She said, "Of course, he can. He just can't walk." The neighbor had seen Gary sitting out on the sidewalk waiting for his bus.

Gary was very smart and was inducted into the National Honor Society at Tecumseh High School when he was in the 10th grade. He loved school, and the kids and teachers loved him because he was smart and funny. His favorite subjects in school were shop and drafting. He made a set of bookends in shop class that he gave Ginger for Christmas one year. They are very functional. She treasures the bookends and his last Christmas gift to her, a pair of star-shaped pierced earrings with crystal in the center.

We were all together at the family Christmas party in 1975, in Onsted when Gary didn't seem to be feeling well. Mom even commented that we should try to convince Gary to eat a bit more and he might feel better. Little did we know that Gary would pass away 10 days later on New Year's Eve. Gary was saved from his crippled body and taken home to eternity and to Dad in Heaven. Mom always said that Dad blamed himself for Gary's affliction, for whatever reason. We don't know if that is true and if that revelation is about the time that Dad seemed to give up on himself and went into a downhill spiral from which he never recovered.

Gary's 18th birthday was on December 21st, and he died on December 31, 1975, from the effects of his muscular dystrophy disease. He was a junior in high school, a member of St. Joseph Shrine in the Irish Hills, and a member of the Lenawee Chapter of the Muscular Dystrophy Association.

Gary Gillen 1974

Gary, Sherry, and Irene 1971

Chapter 14

‌

SHERRY AND BRIAN BELMONTE

By Sherry Gillen Butcher Belmonte

Sixth Daughter

I AM THE youngest sibling of the family albeit by two minutes. My twin Gary was just a touch ahead of me. Our childhood through 8th grade was spent at the farm on Knapp Road in Brooklyn, Michigan, and was quite different than the four older sisters (Irene, Cathy, Noreen, and Ginger).

Mom and Dad bought the Coffee Shop when we were going into first grade. The older sisters were in their teenage years, and all had a part in helping at the Coffee Shop. The four younger kids (Linda, Norman, Gary, and Sherry) were all about playing. Gary and I were ages 10, 11, and 12 when Irene, Noreen, and Cathy married. The advantages of having older sisters were many. The younger sisters and brothers were able to participate in many of their activities. Benny raced stock cars every Friday and Saturday night. Irene frequently picked up the kids at home to take them to the races. Tim had some siblings the same age as us younger kids.

Noreen picked Norm and me up many times and took us to play with his brother and sister our age or go to the Jackson High School football games. Noreen and Tim took us younger kids to the Cedar Point amusement park in Sandusky, Ohio, for the first time when I was just barely tall enough to get on the rides. It rained a little and they closed the rides. When the rides reopened, Noreen and Norm went on the double Ferris wheel. It took the operators four or five tries to get the top wheel down to the bottom to let the riders off due to the wet gears. They were on that top wheel and ended up with a much longer ride than anticipated. I'm guessing they were getting a little nervous by the time it worked correctly.

I was 12 and in the 6th grade when Noreen had Dawn, the first grandbaby in our family. The next year Mark and Todd came along to Irene and Cathy. I babysat for Mark every Friday night and stayed overnight at Benny and Irene's. On Saturday mornings Cathy picked me up to babysit for Todd for half a day. Dave came home at noon and drove me the 10 miles home.

When Mom and Dad moved to Onsted, Michigan, in May 1972, I was just finishing the 8th grade. I began Onsted High School in 9th grade. During our first summer in Onsted, we met Gene and Judy Martin and their family who were our new next-door neighbors. Judy was the housekeeper at Saint Joseph's Shrine and had two young girls (Sherri and Lori). I babysat for the girls often during high school.

My Onsted High School years were very happy. I met a great group of friends early on and have stayed in touch with several of them throughout my life. I knew several students from catechism classes at church where both Brooklyn and Onsted kids attended. Lisa Coberley was one of the Onsted "church" girls and became a very good friend. She and I were also roommates at Eastern Michigan University together. Norm and I hung out with several of the same friends because some of them were in the band with Norm and in my class, and some of my friends dated Norm's friends. One of our most fun activities was having May Basket parties.

The party started with filling a cardboard box with popcorn and candy and leaving it on a friend's doorstep. The group rang the doorbell and then hid close by. The recipient had to find everyone, and then host the party at their house for the evening. Many of the dating couples stayed hidden for quite a while longer than the rest of the group. Gary was able to participate in the parties at our house.

I attended most of the Friday night sporting events, riding the school pep rally buses to the away games. After the games, my friends and I drove into Adrian to MacDonald's or a pizza parlor. At red lights, we played Chinese Fire Drills. Everyone in the car jumped out, ran around the car, and jumped back into the car before the light turned green. One evening on our return drive to Onsted, a car full of Mexican kids started following us. We were using back roads and got scared. We pulled into the driveway of a house with lights on and rang the doorbell. The home-owners allowed us to stay there for several minutes until we were all sure the car left the area.

My friends and I frequently toilet-papered trees in yards after football games. One homeowner shot a gun in the air to chase us away. It worked. We all ran. Another time a homeowner blocked my car in with his trac-tor. With some tricky maneuvering, I was able to get my car out, and we all headed for home. After those 'messages,' we quit playing pranks.

I played sports all through high school - basketball and softball for four years and volleyball for three years. Softball and volleyball both became sanctioned sports for the first time in our district during the years I played. I also loved helping build the class float every year and partici-pated in the junior-year play. It was called *Hillbilly Wedding* and I was one of the daughters.

I dated Tom Etter from my junior year through my freshman year in col-lege. During those years Tom and I visited Ginger in Washington, D.C., Tom's brother at the Kincheloe Air Force Base in the Upper Peninsula of

Michigan, and his brother in Detroit, Michigan. That was the only time I was in the Upper Peninsula.

During my high school summers, I worked at the Saint Joseph's Shrine gift shop, kept the family tradition going of working at Knutson's Bait Shop counting worms, and waitressing at the D & M Grill with Linda. I admired how well Linda did this job, but I did not enjoy it at all. Maybe it reminded me of all the times Mom fussed at me at Eleanor's Coffee shop to smile before I went to wait on the customers. The next summer, I worked for the Hubbard Apiary. I worked in the family's garage with Jo Hubbard, daughter of one of the owners, and Lisa Coberley. We built the frames to fit inside beehives and inserted the beeswax sheets that bees make the honey on. It was a good, fun job. When we finished for the day, we often hopped in the family swimming pool to relax. On one of these days, we helped ourselves to a cold beer out of Jo's parents' refrigerator. Of course, Jo's mother came home and was not happy with us. Jo talked fast stating that there was no pop to drink, and she avoided getting in trouble.

I enjoyed bicycling and took a couple of big rides during the summer. Jo and I rode our bikes seven miles from home in Onsted to the Walter J. Hayes State Park on Wamplers lake. The next time, Sylvia Handy and I pedaled 12 miles from home to my sister Cathy's home in Napoleon. One of Cathy's friends passed us while she was driving and thought it was Cathy on the bike. I was exhausted after returning home from that ride. All the locals know about the long, steep, incline hill heading into Onsted which is about half-a-mile long. Ugh!

When I was a junior in high school, Norm was graduating from boot camp near Chicago, Illinois. During the second week in September, I was driving to school when I turned east, and the sun blinded me. I turned the car away from an oncoming bus that had just turned the corner onto the street I was on. I ended up hitting a car parked parallel along the street and pushing the parked car into another parked car. Wouldn't you know? Both car owners were teachers of mine. Then I was absent for the next two days because of the family trip to Chicago to see Norm. The teachers and other students must have thought I was too embarrassed to show my face around school. At least the trip to Chicago with Mom, Linda, and Gary, and getting to see Norm was rewarding.

I bought a Mustang with a manual transmission from Tim and Noreen. Tim gave me a short lesson on how to drive a stick-shift car. During the week while Mom was at work, I took the car for a short drive to Adrian, Michigan, using back roads. I had to stop on a slight slope to turn onto US-223. I was so afraid of stalling the car that I sat at the intersection waiting and waiting for oncoming cars to clear. Meanwhile, the line of cars behind me kept growing. I finally had to move forward and figured out how to drive it.

On another day I took Gary in the car and went to the Adrian Mall. Coming out into the parking lot, I got Gary's wheelchair off balance going off the curb. It was a slow-motion tumble to the ground for Gary. Someone ran over and helped me pick Gary up.

When I was a senior and began planning for college, I intended to go to Jackson Community College in Jackson, Michigan, the local junior college, to stay living at home and help Mom with Gary. He passed away on December 31 of that year. As plans progressed, I ended up attending Eastern Michigan University in Ypsilanti, Michigan. With Mom's low income, I was able to attend college free on a government grant. I worked throughout all four years of college. I lived in the dorms my first two years and in an apartment my last two years. Lisa Coberley was one of my roommates for three of the four years. In the early spring of my freshman year, a recruiter from Cedar Point amusement park in Sandusky, Ohio, came to the college. I signed up to work at the amusement park during the summer and took off on this adventure in mid-May as soon as classes ended.

I worked in food services at Cedar Point for three summers. We worked hard and long hours but played and had great fun during our off hours. There were sports teams we could join, the Lake Erie beach, competitions between the various food booths, parties, ferry trips into town, and free access to the park at any time. I took the ferry to Put-In-Bay Island several times. During my growing up years at home I had heard of Put-In-Bay from Mom and her childhood stories. It was interesting for me to see where Mom spent parts of her childhood summers. It was many years later while looking through family photo albums that I saw how frequently Mom went to Cedar Point during the summer. Even though I worked there for three summers, she never mentioned this pastime of hers.

During my second summer at Cedar Point, I was an assistant food booth supervisor, and during my third summer, I was the head supervisor. During my third summer, I also worked for the recreation department, which provided staff activities. The recreation work was outside of my daily food service job and allowed me to receive credit for a required on-the-job practicum unit for my recreation degree.

I made friends with many Ohio college students, which turned into huge football rivalries during the fall. Especially huge were the Ohio State and the University of Michigan games. A large group of Cedar Point friends went to Columbus, Ohio, when the game was there, and everyone went up to Ypsilanti, Michigan, when the game was in Ann Arbor.

During the fall of my sophomore year, Lisa Coberley and I went to Columbus, Ohio, for the big Michigan and Ohio rivalry game. We stayed at the sorority house with a Cedar Point friend, Kathy Rothacker. On Saturday morning she woke Lisa and me up at 7 a.m. to go bar hopping. We then went to the game which I remember very little. We went back to the house to take naps and at 7 p.m. Kathy woke us up to go bar hopping again. There also were several other friends in town. A favorite hangout was Papa Joe's. They served beer in two-gallon red plastic buckets. It was a crazy town on game day.

The following year the gang went to Michigan for the game. Sororities have "brother" fraternities. Kathy had several of the gang go to the fraternity, go in the front door, and steal one of their three-foot by four-foot composite pictures. Her sorority kept it in Columbus at Ohio State, for one full year, and the next fall the fraternity boys had to sing the sorority song to redeem their picture.

In May 1980, I received a Bachelor of Science degree from Eastern Michigan University in Therapeutic Recreation with a minor in Psychology.

After graduation, I took on another huge adventure. My roommate, Linda Wilder, and I decided to "Go West, young girls" for a few years and find our first jobs. Linda was a Hearing-Impaired Specialist and wrote to the State Board of Education in the inter-mountain states. I said I would go to any state with Linda. We did not want to go to California. Linda was hired in Wyoming. We found an apartment in Kemmerer, Wyoming, and after moving in we went to the neighboring town of Evanston, Wyoming, to buy a television. We were driving past the Wyoming State Hospital and decided to stop to see if there were any job openings in my field. I went to the personnel office, and they had two vacant Recreation Therapy jobs. I was hired and started work immediately after Labor Day.

Soon after moving to Wyoming, I laid out in the sun reading a book and was sunburned so badly that I couldn't let any clothing touch my legs. I didn't know anything about living at a high elevation. Evanston, Wyoming, has an elevation of around 6,000 feet. There were several other things to learn about living in the West. Most of the vehicles on the street were four-wheel-drive, pickup trucks with gun racks in the rear windows. There are large grates across the roads. We learned the grates are called "cattle guards" and used to keep cattle from crossing the roads, as opposed to fencing used in Michigan and Ohio. Many men out there also wore large belt buckles and cowboy boots. We had moved to cowboy country. We attended our first rodeo and experienced the great, wide-open spaces outdoors.

Before either of us began our first jobs, we visited Yellowstone National Park which was only a four-hour drive from Kemmerer. This is one of the things that helped me to really appreciate the beauty in the western United States. The landscape in Wyoming is arid, dry, and rocky with very little natural vegetation outside of sagebrush. There are a few rivers in the area, but they are small and often have little water in them. There are mountain ranges all around Evanston. These were a minimum 30-minute drive, and it was always worth the drive. It is very different than southern Michigan's trees-and-lakes landscape.

After a couple of months, Linda and I chose to live in Evanston instead of Kemmerer and found a three-bedroom apartment. One of my co-workers, Rosa Jackson, had a sister, Margaret Randolph, who was interested in sharing the apartment. Margaret became our roommate and a lifelong friend and a future sister-in-law. She and Norm met at our apartment in April 1981 and married later that year.

I was invited to play on a women's volleyball team by another co-worker, Angela Lowe. After a couple of weeks of playing, teammate Jolene Janway said the referee was her cousin and wanted to meet me. Jerry Butcher asked me out for a cup of coffee, and then we continued to date. A year-and-a-half later he became my husband. I wore Ginger's wedding dress and married Jerry on April 17, 1982, at Hillcrest Southern Baptist Church in Evanston, Wyoming. When our wedding party members flew into Salt Lake City, Utah, we picked them up at the airport and headed straight to the mountains to ski. I took my bridesmaid, Kathy Rothacker to ski in Jackson, Wyoming, and we got stuck in the snow. A moose, taller than the car walked over to check out the car. We stayed in the car until help came. Many of the people at our wedding had 'raccoon' faces from skiing for several days with ski masks. After the wedding, we went on a honeymoon to Oahu, Hawaii.

When I began dating Jerry, I went to the Catholic church on one Sunday and then to his Southern Baptist church with him the next Sunday. I alternated for a while and then I began to really like the Baptist church because they took the time to open the Bible and read scriptures as part of the service. I began to grow and understand so much more than I ever had before about the Bible. I learned that salvation is the role Jesus plays in our lives, not simply that God created our world and exists.

Jerry was a construction worker, contractor, and bricklayer. He ran his own business for many years and later worked on construction projects for the Amoco Oil Production company in Evanston. Jerry's aunt and uncle lived in town, and Jerry and I spent several holidays with them. The kids have always claimed Uncle James as their grandpa, since both Jerry's and my father had passed away before they were born. Jerry's mother Mildred lived in Sidney, Nebraska. We traveled to see her three times a year and she came to our house twice a year.

Mom flew out to visit from Michigan almost every year. The year after we were married, Mom came out in May for Mother's Day. I took her on a road trip to the north rim of the Grand Canyon just south of the Utah border, about a six-hour drive. After we passed into Arizona, a sign read "road closed due to snow." I thought this was surely a mistake, and the road crew must have missed taking down the sign. I continued driving and met a six-foot wall of snow just around the curve. We had to turn around and ended up spending the night together at a tiny resort that was right there. It was the first time we ever paid $8 for one hamburger. We spent the next day heading back home. Someone told me about a short-cut without going all the way back to the interstate. It meandered all through the countryside, not a house in sight. We drove up on a plateau and down along a riverbed. This drive went on for a couple of hours. I was so glad when I finally saw Provo, Utah, ahead. Another lesson about high elevation living for me.

Several years later Mom planned to visit us following a trip to Ginger's in Virginia. The kids and I went to Salt Lake City airport to pick her up. Every passenger got off the airplane, but Mom was not among them.

I asked the gate attendant if she could give me any information. She looked the information up on her computer and told me that she could not give out confidential information, but that if I came back the following week, I might have more success. I then phoned Ginger and nonchalantly asked what they were up to. Ginger replied that she, Mom, and Jim were playing a game of Scrabble. The kids and I went back to the airport the following week and picked Mom up.

In 1983, Jerry and I planned to travel to Alaska with Bill and Linda. They postponed the trip for a year when I became pregnant with Kelly. We all made the trip the following summer, where Kelly took her first steps and began walking. The trip started with driving our trucks onto a ferry in Seattle, Washington. The ferry stopped at ports along the waterway until the ferry ride ended at Haines, Alaska. We drove through the Anchorage area and made our way to the home of a friend of Bill's and Linda's on the Kenai River. Nigel Guest was an outfitter for salmon fishing and took our group out on the water for a day. Kelly and I stayed on shore and listened to all their stories when they returned. The trip continued with a drive and camping through Fairbanks and the Canadian Rockies. We parted ways at Calgary in Alberta, Canada. Bill and Linda headed east toward Michigan and Jerry, Kelly, and I headed south to Wyoming.

Our family continued to grow with Dustin and Stacey and our life was busier in Evanston. A favorite family activity was camping in the Uinta Mountains about 30 miles away. Everyone also had an opportunity to learn to ski in Park City, Utah, although we didn't get to do it frequently. The kids all played sports, attended church functions, and played with neighborhood friends. The kids loved going to see family in Michigan and we all loved the visits from our out-of-state family members to our house.

Another element of Wyoming living is experiencing antelope, elk, and moose hunting expeditions. I shot an antelope one time and got absolutely no joy from it, so I didn't shoot another one. Elk camps and hunting were a big function. There were campers, cook tents, horses, varying sizes of hunting parties, and all kinds of weather conditions. The men stayed up at the camp for seven-to-10 days.

I am not a morning person but the stillness of the mornings at 4:30 a.m. is unbeatable. The cook tent smells come alive. The horses are whinnying as the men start to get them fed and saddled up. The snow is crunching underfoot, and you can see every breath you take. Beautiful is the start of the ride with everyone in their winter gear and orange vests, moving in single file on the trail with no conversation and enjoying the cold, crisp mountain air and sights.

One year Jerry and I both had a moose license. This was significant because we could not reapply for five years. It was a big deal. We set up a hunting date with Uncle James and Aunt Ruth, and a couple of their older grandkids, and Bill and Linda came out from Michigan to join in the adventure. Stacey was only 7 months old, and we took all three kids. I told the men that I only had this one weekend to spare for the hunt. The hunting party found a moose on the first morning. I had the perfect shot and all I could do was say, "Oh my gosh. Oh my gosh!" I could not pull the trigger, so Uncle James standing next to me shot that big boy.

I worked at the Wyoming State Hospital from September 1980 to November 1991. Stacey was almost 2 years old when I quit to stay home. I then ran a daycare for six years from 1991 to 1997. During this time, I learned tole painting and sold my work at a consignment shop in Ogden, Utah, and at many area craft shows on the weekends. In 1997, I went to work for the United States Post Office as a mail carrier. I worked as a mail carrier for 20 years and retired from the Postal Service in 2017. Stacey was 7 years old when I went to work outside of the home. She called me every day to ask when I was coming home.

It was so nice when Norm and Margaret's family moved to Idaho. They were only four-and-one-half hours away, so our family had a lot of visits back and forth to see them and Mom, who lived with Norm and Margaret. Margaret and I rendezvoused at the McDonald's about two hours between Evanston and Shelley, Idaho, to transfer Mom between our homes. Margaret and I were also able to meet and play with the kids at Bear Lake on the Idaho border. Kelly, Dustin, and Stacey were able to have a few week-long visits in Idaho during these years.

In June 2000, our family moved to Cheyenne, Wyoming. Kelly was going into her junior year of high school, Dustin was going into the 8th grade, and Stacey, the 5th grade. Kelly had been selected to attend the High School Institute Camp, which was held at the University of Wyoming in Laramie where students learned how the government is organized. The family moved from Evanston to their new home in Cheyenne while Kelly was attending this camp.

The house was not ready to move into, so we stayed in our camper for the first month while Jerry and I began our new jobs. Dustin and Stacey stayed with their Grandma Butcher for one week. Then all three kids had to hang out in the camper during the day by themselves. Everyone was thankful when the house was ready to move into and there was space to spread out.

Jerry took a job with a construction company in Cheyenne, and I transferred to the Post Office and continued to carry mail. This was a huge transition. Evanston had seven mail routes and Cheyenne had 50. I never worked less than 45 or 50 hours a week. In 2001, we bought 10 acres of land and began to build a new house. It was a lot to juggle.

Kelly graduated from Central High School in 2002 and attended the University of Northern Colorado in Greeley, Colorado. She majored in Kinesiology and became an Exercise Physiologist. Her first job at Cheyenne Regional Hospital was in the Cardiac Unit. Kelly married Mike Liddle in June 2004 after her sophomore year in college. Kelly went back to school and received her master's degree in Education in 2014.

She was then able to put her two areas of expertise together and became an educator for the hospital.

Kelly and Mike's son Caleb was born in 2011, and they divorced in 2014. Kelly married Tom Harmsen in 2019. Kelly, Tom, and Caleb continue to live in Cheyenne.

Dustin graduated from Central High School in 2005 and attended Casper College for Fire Science. After three semesters, and struggling with his grades, he left college. Dustin became a volunteer fireman and stayed steady with that work for nine years, working in Casper and Cheyenne. He then began working as a welder's hand in Rock Springs, Wyoming, for a year. He returned to Cheyenne and began work as a laborer with several construction companies. While working as a fireman, Dustin met Chelsea Newton. They married in December 2014, and moved to Mesa, Arizona. They were divorced in February 2016, and Dustin moved back to Cheyenne. Dustin received his commercial driver's license in 2020 and works for the City of Cheyenne driving trucks.

Stacey was 10 years old when we moved to Cheyenne. She barely remembers Evanston and calls Cheyenne home. When Stacey graduated from Central High School in 2008, she already had her Certified Nursing Assistant (CNA) certificate and was working at a local nursing home. She remained in Cheyenne and attended Laramie County Community College. She became a Licensed Practical Nurse (LPN) and then a Registered Nursing (RN) and continues to work in the nursing field. Stacey married her high school sweetheart Jake Reiber in November 2011. They have a daughter Emmalynn, and fraternal twins Rylee, and Everett.

In early 2003 Jerry and I separated, and I moved into an apartment. We divorced in April 2004. I met Brian Belmonte at the Post Office. He retired from a 21-year career in the United States Air Force and after his retirement, he went to work at the Post Office as a mail carrier. He was raised outside of Philadelphia, Pennsylvania.

Brian and I were married on May 1, 2005, at the home of our good friends Marv and Millie Goldhammer's in Cheyenne. After our wedding, we had a house built in Cheyenne. I retired in 2017 after carrying mail for 20 years and Brian retired in 2019 after carrying mail for 20 years. We spend a lot of time traveling to friends and family who live scattered throughout the U.S. We spend time with our church family, playing and watching sports, and being Pop and Nana to seven grandchildren, all living in Cheyenne. We continue to live in Cheyenne along with Kelly, Dustin, Stacey, and Brian's son, Brandon, and their families. We feel so blessed to be part of this family and love how frequently we get to see everyone.

Jerry and Sherry Butcher's Family 2002

Sherry and Jerry's Children 2020

Sherry and Brian Belmonte 2021

Sherry and Brian Belmonte

Chapter 15

THE IN-LAWS

By Sherry Gillen Butcher Belmonte

SEVERAL OF OUR spouses come from small families and several come from large families. These are their memories of first meeting the Gillen family based on Sherry's interviews with each of the in-laws in October 2021.

Benny, married to Irene, is the oldest of three children, one boy and two girls. He ate breakfast every morning at Eleanor's Coffee Shop and lunch daily at Carmen's Restaurant. He met all of Irene's siblings at the Coffee Shop at various times. Gary and Sherry were not yet 10-years old, and he remembers Gary having a funny gait when he walked.

Benny said Mom was a hard worker and always had a lot of energy. He only knew Dad as an alcoholic. He was upset with him when he had a car accident. Dad ran into the feed mill with the car, and he had Gary in the car with him. Benny invited our entire family over to his lake house for strawberries and ice cream.

Dave, married to Cathy, is the oldest of 10 children, six boys and four girls. He met all of us on Christmas Eve. Cathy had invited him to go to midnight mass with her. When he arrived at the house around 10 p.m., everyone was sitting on the floor playing with new games and toys that they had recently opened. He said the scene looked just the same as his house, which he had just left after opening gifts. So, it was quite familiar for him to go from mixing with one big family to another.

Tim, married to Noreen, is the fifth of 10 children, six boys and four girls. He has very little recollection of meeting each of us individually. He just remembers meeting us at the house on Knapp Road. He said he was so smitten with Noreen that he paid very little attention to anyone else.

Jim, married to Ginger, is the oldest of two children, one boy and one girl who is 24 years younger. Jim met Eleanor, Cathy, Norm, and Sherry when they visited Ginger at her apartment in Alexandria, Virginia, for a week in April 1978. On one of the days, Jim took all six of us to Annapolis, Maryland, in Ginger's Camaro, with Ginger sitting on the console. Jim met the rest of the family - Irene, Noreen, Linda, and Gary - at Christmas time in 1978 when Eleanor (Mom) lived on 4th Street in Onsted, Michigan.

Jim most remembers Mom looking exactly like the Quaker lady in one of P. Buckley Moss's prints, Cathy being very welcoming, Sherry being very guarded because of Ginger's and Jim's age difference and talking to Norm about the U.S. Navy. When he met the rest of the family at Christmas, he saw the Gillen family was a group of independent thinkers, but the family came first.

Bill, married to Linda, is the oldest of three children, one boy and two girls. He met everyone at a family Thanksgiving at our home on Main Street in Onsted and thought, "Who are all these people? They just kept coming." On another occasion, Sister Lorenzo looked at Bill's black and white cat and called her a Dominican cat. Sister was a Dominican nun.

Bill met Linda after Dad died. Bill had met Dad many years earlier while working at the Irish Hills Ski Resort. Bill worked on the Ski Patrol and Dad's job was running the tow rope. Bill said that Dad always helped the kids and paid a lot of attention to them; and he was easy to get along with. Dad worked out of a little warming shack. Bill said that Dad had a "hooch" bottle hidden in the shack with him and often offered a swig to him on cold nights.

Margaret married to Norm, is the fifth of seven children, two girls and five boys. Margaret was a roommate with Sherry and met Norm when he visited Sherry in Evanston, Wyoming. Later that year, in August, Norm flew into Salt Lake City, Utah, to help Margaret move to Virginia where he was stationed in the U.S. Navy. On their way to Virginia, they stopped in Michigan first so she could meet the family.

They stayed at Mom's apartment. Mom gave Norm her bedroom, and she and Margaret shared a pull-out couch bed in the living room. Margaret tried hard not to wiggle too much while sleeping. The next day, Bill and Linda hosted the family at their house for a Hobo dinner. That is when Margaret met most of the rest of the family. Everyone was nice to her, but she was shy and didn't know what to talk about. Grandkids Todd and Bryan were there. They were about eight and 10-years old, so Margaret began playing with them. She played with them for about an hour in the yard. The next day Norm and Margaret visited Tim and Noreen at their double-wide trailer and met grandkids, Dawn, and Andy. Their family had just gotten a new computer and they all talked easily about that. She met Jim and Ginger after they got to Virginia.

Jerry, divorced from Sherry, is the youngest of two children, one boy and one girl. Jerry's first impression of the family was that everyone was really short. He said that he was always a foot taller than everyone in photos.

Jerry met the family at a backyard barbecue at Benny and Irene's house in the summer. He was sitting in a chair on the patio amused at the constant chatter going on around the table between the sisters. At one point, Cathy made a statement that Jerry didn't talk much. He told her that when he had something to say, he would say it. Bill began laughing at his statement and that was probably the beginning of their lifelong friendship. Jerry always said that he would never move east of the Mississippi because there were too many people on that side of the country.

Brian, married to Sherry, is the 10th of 14 children, 11 boys and three girls. They were married in early May and Sherry's son Dustin graduated over Memorial Day weekend. Most of Sherry's family came to Wyoming for his graduation. Brian worked that day. He came home, opened his front door and the whole room was full of new brothers and sisters-in-law. He said he almost stepped back outdoors to check and see if he was in the right house. He enjoyed everyone but he was a little intimidated at the time.

Chapter 16

Eleanor's Retirement Years

By Sherry Gillen Butcher Belmonte, Norman "Norm" Gillen,
Margaret Randolph Gillen, Noreen Gillen Litchard,
Virginia "Ginger" Gillen Poole, Cathy Gillen Osborn

1976 – 2002

AFTER SHERRY LEFT for college in 1976, Eleanor (Mom) continued to live in Onsted until 1982. Sherry worked at Cedar Point Amusement Park in Sandusky, Ohio, during her college summers. Mom made it a point to visit Sherry there each summer. It was a two-hour drive, so Mom went with various family members and friends. On one of these visits, the family convinced her to go on the Corkscrew roller coaster. It does a full 360-degree loop and a few corkscrews. Mom had never been on a roller coaster and didn't want to go on one now. The family talked her into it. When the ride stopped, her face was as white as a ghost, and she almost had to be assisted out of her seat by the staff. She acted like she was in shock. We all sat down on a park bench nearby to get Sno-cones to help us take a break. Everyone felt awful afterward and learned a huge lesson - do not bully people into something they don't want to do.

Sherry never returned home to live, only visiting during the college breaks. She graduated from college in 1980 and moved to Wyoming. Mom rented a bedroom in the house to a male friend of hers, Andrew. He had two daughters who lived in Indiana. He seemed to drink quite a bit and as time went on, Mom couldn't watch the TV shows she enjoyed or enjoy her home much. In 1982 with these observations and encouragement from Linda, Mom chose to move.

Mom moved to an apartment in Brooklyn. Her first apartment was on an upper floor and then she moved to the first floor. She was annoyed in the first apartment because the lady across the hall always kept her door cracked open and watched all the comings and goings-on their floor. The sons-in-law were annoyed with Mom because they had to move her piano again. She lived at this apartment until 1986 when she retired from her job as the secretary at St. Joseph's Shrine after 16 years.

Mom then moved to an apartment in Jackson, Michigan, that offered subsidized billing. While in Jackson, Mom worked part-time at St. Joseph's Day Care Center as a caregiver and a secretary. She did this for the next five years. In 1991 Sherry's family from Wyoming visited and stayed at Bill and Linda's home in Brooklyn. Mom was living at her apartment and invited seven-year-old Kelly to spend the night with her. While there, Kelly asked Grandma what would happen if there was a fire as she had been learning "Kid Safety Tips" at school that year. Grandma just chuckled and told her she would be fine and to get ready for bed. Nope. Since Kelly didn't get a real answer to her question, she made Grandma drive her back to Brooklyn at 10 o'clock that night.

She lived in Jackson until 1993. Norm and Margaret bought a home in Virginia and invited Mom to move there with them and she accepted their offer.

Throughout her life, Mom had always loved social gatherings and being in group activities. She resumed many of these activities again. She was part of a Secret 12 Club, which met once a month. She remained on the church Altar Society until 1993; on the Bishop's Council on Alcoholism/Chemical Dependency from 1983 to 1993, and the National Council of Catholic Women from 1989-1992. Every year she worked at the Muscular Dystrophy Labor Day Telethon answering phones. Mom began taking art classes and Spanish classes for adults at Jackson Community College. She made each of her children a painting of their choice.

Mom also started traveling again. She put her Spanish to practice by taking two trips to Mexico. Mom continued traveling to other locations as well. She went on short trips to northern Michigan with her friend Ruth Cote or friend Bess, and Indiana with Andrew to visit his daughters.

When Ginger, Norm, and Sherry relocated around the country, Mom was able to enjoy traveling to more new places. Ginger lived in the Washington, D.C., area. Norm moved with his Navy assignments and lived in Virginia, California, Idaho, and Utah. Sherry lived in Wyoming. Mom often made a travel loop for three to four weeks to visit us all.

In June 1993 Sherry coordinated a mini family reunion for the family at a central location to make it easier for everyone to come. We met at a campground at Lake of the Ozarks in Missouri. Everyone had a wonderful time. There were recreational vehicles (RVs) and tents, family members cooking and telling stories, filling water balloons, and playing games with the youngest ones. There was talking or playing cards with the adults and grandkids created great memories. One event created the laughter of a lifetime. Sherry and Jerry filled rafts with air to use at the lake. Mom tried to get on one of the floats and fell into the shallow water. She was laughing, the ones trying to help her stand up were laughing, everyone watching was laughing, and then the entire process happened with two more attempts - a very hilarious memory.

In August 1994, Benny and Irene drove Mom to Norm and Margaret's home in Windsor, Virginia, in their RV towing her car. Toward the end of their first day, they were going to the campground and then decided to get food first. It was getting dark when Benny went down a dirt road that was a dead end. He had to unhitch Mom's car, back up until he found a place to turn around, and then re-hitch mom's car. It was pitch black by the time they were able to get off the dead-end road.

Once they arrived at Norm and Margaret's home, Benny helped Margaret finish installing trim in their mobile home. He cut his thumb with a utility knife, which required a trip to the emergency room for stitches. What a rough trip for Benny. The best part about the trip was that it was the last time the sons-in-law had to move Mom's piano.

Norm and Margaret's property in Windsor had a mobile home attached to their two-story house with a connecting breezeway. Mom moved into the trailer and had a place of her own to call home. Mom's major activity was watching television and checking in with Margaret and the kids each day. She attended Calvary Baptist Church with the family in Smithfield, Virginia, where she made a profession of faith in Jesus Christ. She drove to Smithfield weekly to shop, get her hair done, and go to the senior center for various activities. Mom taught seven-year-old Lindsay to sew, and she helped Margaret when she came home from the hospital with her new baby Jayme. She cooked dinner on Wednesday nights and everyone ate together at Mom's residence, at least until the girls said they were very tired of the "Hamburger Helper" cuisine.

Norm's family moved to Shelley, Idaho, when Norm retired from the Navy in May 1997. They again invited Mom to move with them or to go back to Michigan. She chose to go with them. The new house had a second kitchen which Norm and Margaret converted, along with the garage, into a studio apartment for Mom. She ate evening meals with the family, assuring at least one healthy meal each day (versus ice cream, bologna, potato chips, and cookies). Mom's major activities included watching television, doting on toddler Jayme, attending Berean Baptist Church with the family in Idaho Falls, Idaho, and going to the senior center. She had a male friend, Fred, who she socialized with occasionally. Norm's new home was only four hours from Sherry in Evanston, Wyoming.

In November of that year, Sherry and her kids visited Mom to surprise her for her birthday. Sherry put on her mailman jacket and pulled her cap down low, trying to disguise herself. She rang the doorbell and handed Mom her package and turned away quickly. After taking a few steps Sherry didn't hear the house door close and looked back. Mom was still standing in the doorway holding the screen door open. She said, "You look like my daughter in Wyoming." We all had fun the rest of the weekend.

Norm and Margaret successfully organized a surprise 80th birthday for Mom in 1998. Even two-year-old Jayme didn't give the surprise away. The Ameritel Inn in Idaho Falls, Idaho, graciously allowed the family to use their lobby on a Sunday afternoon for "family pictures." Irene, Cathy, Ginger, and Linda's families flew into Salt Lake City, Utah, rented a van, and went to Sherry's in Evanston for the first day. Then they all traveled the four hours to Idaho. It was easy to pull off the surprise because we held the party in October instead of closer to her birthday in November trying to avoid any possible bad weather for the travelers. Mom was so shocked when she walked into the lobby and saw all the family, that when she saw Benny she said, "That man looks like my son-in-law." We knew then that the surprise was a success.

The party was a grand tribute to a "Grand Mother" while she had her full faculties. However, the surprise backfired on us. Mom had always been a part of the planning throughout her life. This time she felt left out. We all arrived at once, and we all left together after the long weekend. There were so many of us at one time that she was overwhelmed and sad that she didn't have enough time to spend with each of us. It had such an impact on her and the family we will never leave an elder out of the planning in the future. The buildup and anticipation of the event are half the fun for everyone.

Mom was diagnosed with breast cancer in the late spring of 1999. The doctor did a lumpectomy as treatment and then radiation. No chemotherapy was necessary. Sherry was able to visit and help with some of her appointments, and Cathy flew out from Michigan to help.

Early in 2000 Mom's behaviors showed that her health was deteriorating. First, her hairdresser Janeel phoned Margaret concerned that Mom had signed her check, Eleanor GillenGillenGillen. One day she inadvertently overdosed on cough syrup with codeine, thinking each time she woke from a cat nap it was a new day. Another event was cooking bacon on the stove while going into another room to watch TV and not hearing the smoke detector alarm. Thirteen-year-old Lindsay heard the alarm at her Grandma's and turned off the burner. Later in the year, Ginger was visiting when she stopped Mom from walking into the shower fully dressed, including her shoes.

Mom's care soon became too much for Margaret and Norm to handle. She was unable to stay home alone. These events inspired discussions amongst siblings and Mom for her future care. She chose to go home to Michigan knowing she would need to be in an assisted living center. So, in August 2000, Mom moved back to Michigan. Margaret relayed her from Idaho to Sherry's new home in Cheyenne, Wyoming, now a nine-hour drive. Then Sherry rendezvoused with Irene and Benny in Des Moines, Iowa, and finished the relocation trip to Michigan.

The first in-home care facility for mom was Sprucegate in Brooklyn. Even though she was aware that she would not be living with one of the daughters when she returned to Michigan, she put up quite a bit of resistance to settling in there. Although it was a small family-style residence, Mom wouldn't participate in many of the daily activities she always liked. They had a large sunroom, gardens, and other amenities. She wouldn't play the piano they had available. She didn't want to follow the schedule set for showers. She wouldn't work crossword puzzles, and family members couldn't get her into her normal happy state of mind. One of the reasons for her state of mind was her initial impression when she entered the licensed facility. Her first vision upon entering the facility in mid-morning was everyone sitting in the living room sleeping with their heads down. This seemed to cast a gloom over her. We wouldn't allow the nurse to give Mom a drug after her morning meal. After a short time and due to the cost of the facility and her resistance, the girls still in the area found another location for her.

Mom moved to another in-home care facility on Wolf Lake Road in Grasslake a few miles away. While at this house, she began to get close to one of the male residents there and then too close, getting into his bed one night. Mom fell trying to get back to her room. When this behavior started to take place in the living room the staff called Cathy to say Mom had to leave.

In 2001, we moved Mom to the Jackson County Medical Care Facility in nearby Jackson. She was placed on a locked ward for dementia patients. While several indications of dementia had started in Idaho, these continued during her last two years in Michigan. She couldn't list the names of her eight children, and she couldn't stay engaged in a conversation. She was seen with her underclothes over her clothes, laying on her bed naked, and again, not amenable to the staff. She fell and hit her head quite hard and almost seemed to have stroke-like behavior afterward. She didn't want to take her medications and finally had little desire to eat or get up out of bed.

During these two years, the sisters living in the area visited Mom frequently. She was able to go on outings in the community with the care facility staff. Noreen and Tim took her to the weekly music program at the facility, Cathy visited weekly, and the others took her to church at times and brought her to their homes for big holidays. Ginger, Norm, and Sherry's families were all able to get visits to Michigan during this time.

Irene, Cathy, Noreen, and Linda celebrated Mom's 83rd birthday with her in November 2001 when they all attended a picnic at the Jackson Care Facility in the spring.

When Mom passed in June 2002, most of the siblings were in Wyoming at Sherry and Jerry's to celebrate Kelly's high school graduation and Andrhea and Luke's recent wedding. Ginger and Jim were at home in Virginia and received the call of Mom's death. Tim and Noreen were in Michigan and were able to take care of her final details.

With the life of servitude that Mom lived, she finished this way as well. She opted to have her body donated to science and it was sent to the University of Michigan. When they were finished, she was cremated, and her ashes were returned to Cathy. A memorial was held for her in July, and she was interred at the St. Joseph's Shrine Cemetery in the Irish Hills next to Walter and Gary.

Eleanor had the great privilege of watching her children grow up to be well-adjusted, responsible, and happy adults. Her greatest joy, which she mentioned frequently, was that her children remained friends and stayed in touch with one another.

She had a full, eventful life. She lived it well and with a steady, consistent display of quality character. She dealt with multiple traumas, hardships, and circumstances and yet continually met the family's needs. The many qualities that she passed on to her children are respected and remembered to this very day by all of us.

Eleanor Gillen 1989

THE WALTER AND ELEANOR GILLEN STORY

Tribute To Mom

By Sherry Gillen Butcher Belmonte

Never regret what you wished
you'd done differently.

The day you had children,
you began a legacy.

The errs you think you made weren't errs.
They were living as it comes daily.

The "lack of"
finances – created humility in us
individual time – made us resourceful
emotional sharing – created sensitive adults

You gave us so much more than you ever neglected!
All our past becomes who we are now.

Think of all the talents and abilities and
qualities we have between us.
You created quality adults without a doubt!

The only thing to say is THANK YOU!
For being a mother and helping us to become
who we've all become.

May we all be a blessing to you every year out,
as you have been to us every year in!

WE LOVE YOU

Walter Gillen 1968

Remembering Dad

By Virginia Gillen Poole

Dad was one of our biggest teachers
and helped shape us into who we are today.

He set goals, dreams, and aspirations for himself,
And for his family.

His home meant the world to him.
He provided for the family,
And he gave us the needed guidance.

Our dad was:
A very private and loving man.
He was deeply religious and a family man.
He was smart and intuitive.
He was courageous and resourceful.
And he was a jokester.

Yes, he could get angry or disappointed,
and picked up some bad habits.
And we are still grateful for our dad.

He had long-term health issues
that redirected his life.
And he died at the early age of 56.

His memory remains in our hearts and mind.
And we continue to miss him today.

PART FOUR
MEMORIES

Our parents
and
brothers and sisters

Chapter 17

Favorite Family Memories

Irene's Memories of Mom and Dad

I LOVED WHEN Mom played the piano and we all had songbooks so we could sing along. This tradition began in Ohio and continued in Michigan.

I remember that when we moved from the Metamora farm to the Assumption farm, the men had put a piano in the back of a truck. They didn't fasten it. It fell out going down the driveway and smashed to pieces.

When I was four years old Dad had Mom, me, Cathy, Noreen, and Poodle on the back porch during a storm. He had a microphone and was recording our reactions. Cathy thought it was funny, but I didn't.

Saturday was bath night for me, Cathy, Noreen, and Ginger in Ohio. All of us were in the bathtub at the same time.

Dad loved being involved in the Catholic War Veterans (CWV) group in Assumption, Ohio, and going to Michigan in the summer to one of the lakes for their annual picnic.

Grandma and Grandpa Wood visited us quite often and were included in a lot of our pictures.

I remember Mom and Dad's ability to raise such a large family that had good times together. Their 25th Wedding Anniversary party was also a favorite occasion of mine.

I inherited Grandma Wood's mandolin and tried to learn to play it. I play the accordion, piano, and bells, but I couldn't master the mandolin. I passed it down to Sherry.

... and Siblings

Cathy and I played together at our Ohio farm near Metamora in 1949-1951. We had a big empty corn crib that Mom and Dad put us in to play when they were busy in the field. Mom had us dressed alike sometimes.

Cathy and I got dolls for Christmas that were as big as us. Dad came into the living room one day when the dolls were laying on the floor. He was scared that the dolls were one of us, so we couldn't play with them anymore.

Cathy was always where she wasn't supposed to be. She climbed the pear tree and fell out. She was sitting on top of double doors in the barn while they were loading cattle, and she fell out of Poodle's car because she was messing with the door handle with her feet.

Noreen usually ended up sitting in the pantry in Ohio because she didn't eat all her meal. When we were older, she always disappeared when it was time to do the dishes.

Ginger climbed halfway up the windmill when she was little and was afraid to come back down. Dad had to go up and help her down. One winter in Ohio she got her tongue stuck on the metal handrail. Mom or

Dad poured water on the handrail so she could remove her tongue without getting hurt.

I was in grade school when Linda was born. Linda was almost three when Mom and Dad took her with her four older sisters and Grandpa and Grandma Wood to Oak Openings Park in Swanton, Ohio, for a picnic. Later that August the five girls had fun at the CWV picnic at Posey Lake near Hudson, Michigan.

Norman was born on October 3, 1956, and Linda was three on September 12, 1956. This was the largest age gap between all of us.

I was at a birthday party when the twins were born. Cathy and I helped take care of them - folding diapers, feeding them, and playing with them. When the twins were in cribs in my bedroom, they got a hold of my flip-flops and chewed the back off.

Cathy's Memories of Mom and Dad

Mom loved to go dancing with Dad. She loved to watch television after everyone else had gone to bed. She loved old movies and was the biggest movie star buff I have ever known.

Mom had a love for traveling anywhere and at every chance she got. She taught us to take every opportunity to travel, too. Mom made a point to tell us that opportunity knocks but once. So "take it" every chance you get. I can still hear her saying it. I did go on a few trips as the babysitter so the family could enjoy the occasion a little more.

Some of us in the family are directionally challenged as to where east, west, north, and south are. Mom was at the head of the class on this point. So, some of us may have come by it honestly. Mom always pointed her right arm straight out to the right and said, "That's north," no matter which direction she was facing.

Mom loved to share innate details whenever telling a story. I was amazed by all the details she knew when I did a story of her life in an album. I called Mom almost daily once I started the album. I loved that she could answer almost every question and was even able to date almost everything correctly. The album became two albums by the time it was finished. The first album ended as Mom left her mother's home to go off on her own. The second album started out as Mom began her life with Dad, Walter Gillen. This album was about Walter and Eleanor's children and their growing-up years. The two albums were divided at this point, without any planning on my part. I was as surprised as anyone by this fact. I had a lot of help from Irene, Noreen, Ginger, Linda, Norm, and Sherry during the process of the albums coming together so nicely. I totally appreciated every ounce of help.

Dad loved to dance, and I loved to watch Dad dance with Mom. Most often at family weddings and Twin Gables bar on Saturday nights. He taught me how to slow dance by following his arm and foot lead.

He also loved to entertain us, and our relatives. On the farm in Michigan one Sunday, Bernard and Betty and their kids came for a visit. Dad decided to take all of us for a ride down the lane. He hooked up the small stock trailer to the tractor, loaded up all the kids and guests, and away we went down the lane. When we got to the next pasture Dad turned around. He decided to give us a little thrill and veered off the lane along a slight hill. The thrill turned out to be way more than he bargained for. The trailer tipped over on its side and spilled some of us out and onto the ground. Noreen was the only one to get hurt, luckily not seriously. Noreen was at the bottom of the pile of kids. It was a scary scene, I am sure. Dad lucked out that no one was seriously injured. Apparently, Dad lived up to his childhood nickname "Lucky."

Dad always said a 10-minute nap is the best pick-me-up.

Mom taught us if we have a problem with someone, go straight to the source of the issue (usually, the someone) and have a discussion. This lesson has served me very well throughout my life.

Mom and Dad taught us many skills we would need in life as we grew up. Together they taught us respect, kindness, taking turns, and helping each other. They taught us physical labor and we learned a great work ethic. If it needs to be done, just do it.

Not so sure the items I have are inherited, but I have a couple of items of Moms from my childhood. I have the crystal creamer that might have been set on the buffet. I also have the mother-of-pearl teapot and sugar bowl from Grandma Wood.

. . . and Siblings

Irene always did her homework. At every family party or event, Irene always played her accordion. We would sing along with some of the songs. I, however, didn't sing much. I can't carry a tune. Dad called it tone-deaf (deef). It was obvious, others were also tone-deaf.

Irene liked making Hermit cookies. I don't think I have ever made Hermit cookies. Hmmm. Maybe I should sometime.

Irene is very kindhearted. There is nothing she wouldn't do for you. She always means well. We have a great appreciation for each other.

My own favorite memory is when I began the hugging greeting and saying, "I love you." It's something we didn't hear much when we were kids. It started on a day Norm came to visit while on leave from the Navy. It occurred to me that he should have a proper greeting. So, I gave him a hug and said, "I love you." After that day I made it a point to greet each of you the same way. I love it. Now it doesn't feel weird or unnatural.

Noreen always did her homework too. She was the prettiest of the bunch,

I think. We always got along well. But if we were fighting, it was intense.

Noreen had a strange spot on her leg - like a black hole. One day Mom decided to check it out. When she squeezed it, Noreen fainted. The rest of us weren't in the room with them. Mom yelled for us to come quickly, but we didn't know what was going on. We thought we were in trouble for something, so we didn't hurry. By the time we got to them, it was over, and Noreen had recovered from the faint. We had never seen anyone faint, so I am not sure what kind of help we would have been. To my knowledge, the cause of the spot was never discovered.

In high school, Noreen and I were about the same sizes, and we both had long brown hair. Kids were always calling us by each other's names, maybe because we wore each other's clothes on some days.

I finally began to appreciate Noreen's love for *God*. She taught me forgiveness. After that, we got along very well after a few years of not being sure what was going on or why we didn't seem to get along. She came through a bad horse-kick accident. I am sure her faith brought her through it. And I'm so thankful that Noreen is still with us.

Ginger is the one child who didn't have hair until she was two years old. Ginger is probably the hardest worker of the bunch. She has a drive that never quits. She is a bit directionally challenged though. I learned that one day when I drove her to Ann Arbor to visit Dad in the Veterans Administration hospital. If Ginger said turn left, we should have turned right and if she said turn right, she should have turned left. It just seemed to work out a lot better that way. It took us over two hours instead of 50 minutes to get there.

Linda was a bit quieter than most of us and a bit unsure of herself at times. She was always the kind one, she would do anything you would ask of her. I loved that sweet quality about her. She didn't like the lake much. I'm guessing because she couldn't swim. So, we older girls decided it was time she learned she could be safe in the water. We forcefully got her to Randall's raft by boat, onto the raft, and into an inner tube, and eventually into the water without the inner tube. She learned how to swim, at least enough to save herself. We were successful, and she did learn to swim and was even proud of herself in the end.

Linda is way smarter than she gets credit for. She chose to not argue with Bill, for example, on most occasions. That plan served her very well for many years. Now is her time to shine. She is now making decisions on her own, for her wants and needs. It is quite amazing to see her in her own element.

Norm was always creating things to make the jobs he had to do easier. I remember seeing him riding his bike with a rope attached to the little red wagon to haul something. He's always had that entrepreneurial spirit. And still has the entrepreneurial spirit. He invented a mobile weed-sprayer unit that he could wear on his back. He should have gotten it patented because someone else had the same idea and did get a patent. They are in every home and garden store these days. Norm had an amazing career in the U.S. Navy.

Gary always seemed content with his lot in life. He never complained, although he surely had plenty to complain about. I believe we all learned compassion through Gary. We learned to be compassionate for all people who are among the less fortunate. Gary taught me to be more patient. He was easy to hang out with, he always had something good to talk about.

Unfortunately, Gary didn't get a chance at adulthood. However, he did live his best life possible. He helped a lot of kids with health issues along the way. He helped them understand how to work with the disease that they had and how to be able to roll with it. He was a giver and would have made a difference in the world if he had the chance.

Sherry was always very energetic as a child. She always had something going on. She was always full of ideas for what to do next. She was fun to be around. I do remember being shocked that the twins were no longer the "babies" once they turned four years old. She was Todd's babysitter while Dave and I both worked on Saturday mornings. She was shy around Dave especially on the drive home after babysitting. He wasn't much of a talker either. It was a quiet ride home.

Sherry is still full of energy. She is always ready with solutions to any problems that arise. There is always another way to get around it. No more problem. She and I love that we look so much alike and are surprised to find that we share some mannerisms as well. She is a wonderful "Nana" to seven amazing grandkids. It's a good thing she is energetic.

Noreen's Memories of Mom and Dad

Mom enjoyed watching old movies and soap operas on TV. On Sunday afternoons, she enjoyed playing the piano and having the family sing along.

Mom taught me how to knit and crochet. She was a very strict teacher. When I was about 10, I wanted to learn how to knit. When she told me to rip out what I had done, I wasn't very happy about it. She told me to come back and when I was ready to learn and follow her directions. When I was 15, I made myself a sweater. I have been knitting ever since. To learn to crochet, Mom taught me to crochet edging on handkerchiefs. I have made many doilies, stuffed animals, and angels since she taught me to crochet.

After I found out that Andy had muscular dystrophy, I could talk to Mom about it. She understood what I was going through having helped Gary.

Mom was always baking. I especially remember her baking cookies for the nuns at Sienna Heights in Adrian for Christmas. She would start baking in November. I liked helping decorate the cookies. I picked up my love of baking from her.

Dad liked going to the bar every day. He enjoyed watching TV. His favorite shows were *Bat Masterson, Red Skelton, and Gunsmoke.* He enjoyed playing cards with the older siblings. We would play "I Doubt It," "Hearts," and "Spades." He liked to go fishing with friends on the lake. When he came home with a bucket of fish, he would give them to the older girls to scale and prepare for dinner. We usually ate them pan-fried.

When I was five or six in Ohio, I liked to go with Dad in the big farm truck. The truck didn't have very good shocks. When we would go over railroad tracks or a bumpy road, I would bounce on the seat and hit my head on the ceiling. The only thing you had to remember was to be ready when he was, or he would leave you behind.

On Sundays, Dad played Croquet with us. He liked to see how far he could "send" everyone's ball. We could end up anywhere in the yard. One time he tried to tighten up the heads on the mallets by slamming the head down on the ground, which ultimately split the heads. I enjoyed spending time with Dad on Sundays because he worked 2nd shift and wasn't home during the week.

Mom liked Cloisonné jewelry. I have a couple of pieces. I have a butterfly pin that she wore quite a bit.

. . . and Siblings

Irene always got better grades in school than I did. She helped me with my homework. Irene and I were in the band together and went to the Holland Tulip Festival every year.

Cathy seemed to always be in charge, telling us what to do. I could ask her about anything that maybe I didn't want to ask Mom or Dad. Cathy liked to do my hair for the prom and my wedding. She was my Maid of Honor at my wedding.

Ginger always ran around with the "rich" kids at school and seemed to be in a different league than me. She always seemed to be in trouble with Dad because she liked to do her own thing, even if we weren't supposed to.

When Linda was younger, she was always afraid of animals. When we moved to Michigan, she was afraid of the water at the lake. She eventually overcame her fears.

Norm had very curly hair (ringlets) when he was little. He was very cute. Mom insisted that all of us call him Norman. I don't think he liked it once he started school. When he was in high school, everyone started calling him Norm.

I remember feeding Gary and Sherry when they were babies. We took turns.

Tim and I played a lot of board games with Norm and the twins when we were dating. After we were married, we took them to Cedar Point in Sandusky, Ohio.

Ginger's Memories of Mom and Dad

Mom loved baking, playing the piano, pinochle, dancing, traveling, and working in the garden and flower beds. As a small child in Ohio, I mostly remember her at the stove cooking for the day when I was up early in the mornings. I also remember her spring cleaning the house and doing the laundry outdoors in the summer while we played in a small kiddie pool. She was very good at buying thoughtful gifts.

I learned a dieting technique from Mom. When she learned portion control at Weight Watchers, she didn't have to give up a favorite food - potato chips. When Pringles came out, she bought them so she could count how many she could have for her snack.

Dad loved raising his family, working on the farm, drinking, smoking, playing cards, dancing with Mom, and visiting relatives, and sightseeing. He bought us a big swing set in Ohio and made us stilts in Michigan. He took us to church events, fairs, swimming, and played games with us in the yard. When Dad was in the Veterans Administration Hospital in Ann Arbor, Michigan, he always gave us money to buy candy from the vending machine.

After I left home and returned on holidays, I enjoyed sitting and talking with Dad at the kitchen table. On my first visit home, I told Dad I wanted to drink coffee at breakfast. When I reached for the cream and sugar, he said "as long as you are learning to drink coffee, learn to drink it black." I did, and I drink it black today.

I bought my first car in Michigan in 1972. I was petrified to drive the 10 hours back to Virginia by myself. I had only been on a few several-hour trips by car, and never as the driver. I thought I might take the wrong exit. Dad color-coded a map for me and wrote out each direction that we reviewed in detail. I woke up with hives in the morning, but I made it back to Virginia without a problem.

I have the 3×5 inch "Bless us O Lord" plaque that hung on the kitchen wall at home. Mom had the plaque in her purse when she was in Idaho, shortly before she moved back to Michigan. I thought it must have a significant place in her heart. I asked her if I could have it because her memory was failing, and I wanted to keep it safe for her.

I have three of Mom and Dad's wedding presents that remind me of our home. I have the crucifix that Mom received from her in-laws when she made her First Communion in the Catholic church. It always hung in Mom and Dad's bedroom. I have the metal tray the family used daily to serve bread at the dinner table, and I have a 4-inch deep, 12-inch round, etched, clear glass bowl. I don't remember how or when we used this dish.

. . . and Siblings:

I remember Irene being in the mix with everyone else doing chores, playing, enjoying family life, and attending family events. When Irene and Benny were raising Mark and Kristi, I worried that Irene was not cooking healthy meals for the family because she "cooked from a box." I later learned she is a very good cook and used prepared foods to save time during their very busy parent, racing, and working lives. Irene and Benny were wonderful hosts to Jim and me on our annual visits to Michigan after Mom died. Irene is a very conscientious and successful sister. She is a perfectionist, and loves socializing, shopping, and organizing.

As a preteen growing up on the farm when we had sheep, pigs, and horses, Cathy could answer my questions about animal behavior when I asked. She was also quick to let me know when I had bad behavior. I loved for her to comb and style my hair and polish my nails. Cathy is very outgoing, loves to travel, and loves to tell jokes. Cathy was a wonderful mother. She made sure the boys knew what to expect and how to behave when they were growing up. When the boys were adults, she never questioned their actions. She was just there for them when they called. Cathy likes to keep up to date with current events, family, and friends. I think she was one of the first networkers. She is very artistic. Her creativity shows in her home decorating and in the gifts she buys.

Noreen is only 12 and a half months older than me. We had the same chores, shared the same bed, wore each other's clothes, and both played the clarinet. She was 19 when she married Tim. I worried that her marriage wouldn't last because she was so young. She and Tim are going strong after 53 years together. Noreen stayed very close to her family and missed a lot of the Gillen family events because of her job with Toyota and Tim's job at the State prison. It was like being reacquainted after they retired. She didn't change. She has a lot of hobbies and interests, offers to help, and can talk over the top of everyone else, just like the rest of us.

I was considered an older sister and often participated in "older girl" activities, both fun and work. Linda was often at home and in charge of the three younger kids. They were all very playful and happy to interact with their older sisters when we were home, and when especially when they could go with us to a movie or bowling.

Linda had many friends through work and her husband. She was a farmer's wife and always had popsicles, cold drinks, and cookies for Bill when he was working in the field. We stayed with Linda and Bill after they built their new house in 2012 and liked to stay on their farm and help Linda in the garden or wherever we could. During our work years, I called at least once a year to say hello and we saw each other at family events. She was always proud of herself when she remembered to call me first. We called much more frequently after we both retired.

Norm, being the first boy in the family after five girls, received a lot of attention from everyone in the family, and everyone else who knew the family. He was cute, extremely playful, smart, and independent. He did boy things. He enjoyed comic books, played cowboy and Indians, and received toy tractors and animal gifts. He was happy to follow Dad around and to help in the house. One of his favorite chores was taking over baking the bread for home and the Coffee Shop after Noreen.

Living in Virginia, we enjoyed the many holiday weekends with Norm and his growing family during the 13 years they were stationed in Norfolk and Newport News, Virginia. We loved being so close when the children were little. Norm and Margaret are engineers to the core and can do anything mechanical, electrical, construction (except drywall), electronic, driving long distances in big or little vehicles, buying, selling, entertaining, and having fun. He is always doing or learning something new.

Gary and Sherry being the first twins in the family, also received a lot of attention. They were both very cute, playful, and smart, and had older sisters to help with the baby chores and parenting. When Gary was diagnosed with muscular dystrophy in kindergarten, he began to receive more attention than Sherry. Sherry, being the true baby of the family by two minutes, could do almost anything she wanted, and at a much younger age than anyone else. She was always charming, independent, and very helpful. I learned during our book writing that she was always looking for attention and affection. Something I never noticed because I was so busy doing my own thing when I had a little time.

Sherry was extremely proud to be the first child in the family to graduate from a four-year college – Eastern Michigan University. As a trained recreational therapist, she gives praise and encouragement to everyone quietly in the background when offering advice and seeing that things run smoothly. Sherry is a very good listener, and very good at keeping thoughts to herself until she thinks you are ready to hear them. She is a people person, very loyal to her family and friends, and always busy but never too busy to read or work on crafts.

Linda's Memories of Mom and Dad

Mom liked to work on crossword puzzles, play the piano, and bake.

Dad liked to fish and taught us how to clean fish and clams.

. . . and Siblings

We all went to Irene's high school graduation in the blue station wagon. Benny's dog Butch always sat on the porch with both feet in front of him.

Cathy woke up from a nap and threw a hairbrush at the kids downstairs. She was mad at everyone for letting her oversleep. She thought she was late for work, but it was 9 p.m.

Noreen's marble hit the window and made a small hole. She blamed it on Linda.

Ginger was cleaning the house and the younger kids were in the way. She made us all sit in a chair.

Linda was coached into throwing Buffy, the cat, into the lake. Buffy was able to swim.

Norm and I were by the garage putting gas in the lawn mower when it shot flames into the air.

Sherry went through a stage where she hit Linda in the back with her fist for no reason.

Norm's Memories of Mom and Dad

Mom loved to garden, play the piano, and work crossword puzzles. I love them too.

Mom's frequent comments: when we carried an over-sized load it was a "lazy man's load." If someone stood in front of the television, they "made a better door than a window." If we left an outside door open or ajar "We live in a house, not a barn."

My fondest memory of Mom is being comforted after an injury. She bandaged and splinted my left index finger after I ripped my fingernail 80 percent off when I was 11 or 12 years old.

I got an excellent work ethic from Mom. She kept the family together through good and bad times. There were many ups and downs.

I don't have memories of many chores, just empty farm buildings that were a grand playground for Linda, Sherry, Gary, and me.

I don't have many positive memories of Dad. I wonder if his greatest lesson to me is what not to do? Don't drink to the point of becoming an alcoholic. Don't smoke. Don't take a new job frequently. Don't live beyond your means.

As a farmer, I am sure Dad was a "jack-of-all-trades." I don't recall him farming, only driving the Farmall tractor occasionally. I did help him repair the water pump a couple of times. The pump house was down the hill past the Quonset. I was fascinated by the sparks thrown off by the grinding wheel when he sharpened a blade. He had a jury-rigged gas tank on a lawnmower that caught fire and shot flames 10-feet high.

Dad liked to sit at the kitchen table with beer and a whiskey chaser, rolling long cigarettes and using a cutter to cut five individual cigarettes. He liked playing shuffleboard at Twin Gables bar, one-half mile down the road, and drinking beer at the American Legion in Brooklyn.

My favorite memories of Dad are - playing "horsey" with us in the living room, hollering from downstairs "shut up and go to sleep or get a spanking," and the kids laughing even harder. I also liked playing pinochle with him, Mom and Sherry, and their friends Frank and Julia Szabo.

Items with the most meaning for me are - Dad's ring he created from a silver 50-cent piece. He and his buddies made the rings while they were in the service; Mom's paintings made from our photographs; the buffet from the dining room on Knapp Road; and the slates from Grandma Wood with tiny chalk drawings and words apparently written by spirits during Grandma's seances in the 1930s.

. . . and Siblings

Irene playing her accordion during family piano and sing along sessions, mostly on Sundays. Attending stock car races in Lansing with Irene.

I remember horsing around with Cathy and her boyfriend Larry Wibbler; Margaret and I flying home from Idaho to surprise Cathy for a birthday

THE WALTER AND ELEANOR GILLEN STORY

party - Kristi sent us an invitation. I didn't recognize Cathy when she and Brian Belmonte, whom I had not met, picked me up at a car dealer in Cheyenne, Wyoming; Margaret and I had our van towed there for an engine replacement.

Noreen and Tim played a lot of strategy-style board games and were early "innovators" buying the newest gadgets and electronics. Margaret and I enjoyed their visits during their cross-country RV trip.

I visited Ginger in Virginia prior to getting married. Margaret and I, and the kids, visited Ginger and Jim often after getting married. They lived three hours away, so it was an easy drive. They were fantastic hosts. We all enjoyed the great meals they served. They also hosted multiple Thanksgiving dinners for our family after our children were married.

I remember tickle-torture from the older girls.

I played a lot of indoor and outdoor games with Linda growing up. After she was married, it was always fun to see Bill's latest activities – their new house, haying, beekeeping, wood carving, when we visited in the 2000s

I had fun pushing Gary around on a hand truck before he got his wheelchair.

Sherry and I had fun with our mutual friends "the Gang" during high school in Onsted. During the summer of 2019, Sherry and Brian opened their home to me every other weekend while I worked as a subcontractor in Denver, Colorado.

I remember playing Elvis Presley and Beach Boy records. I guess they were left behind after the older girls left home.

Sherry's Memories of Mom and Dad

I think I saw Mom get the absolute most joy out of her creative endeavors. She spent many, many hours baking and decorating cakes and creating her sugar Easter eggs. She created school scrapbook memories for each one of us children, and was very precise in her cutting, gluing, and spacing. She was organized in her photographs, making sure each of us had copies of special occasions, and documenting names and dates with each photo. I think all of us write the dates and names of people and places on the backs of our photos to this day. For her quiet time, she loved to read and watch old movies.

Dad enjoyed playing cards. He played cards with the older girls on Sunday afternoons. In later years, friends came to the house on Saturday nights and played pinochle. Norm and I learned from them when we were in junior high school. Dad also loved playing cards at family reunions. The men had card tables set up in the barn where they played.

When Dad took the family for Sunday drives, he would find steep hills to drive up. He would pretend that the car couldn't make it up unless we all pushed on the back of the seats. We pushed with all our strength, laughing the whole time. He would also pick up speed going up hills and then pull his foot off the accelerator. This made our stomachs roll and feel like we were on a rollercoaster.

Once in a great while, something would just get Mom giggling so hard that she would have tears running down her face. She didn't laugh much when we were young, so this was a joy when it occurred.

Mom was steadfast. She stayed strong through every financial circumstance, Gary's handicap, moves to new homes, being a working mom and raising eight children, through Dad's alcoholism and his and Gary's deaths. She was a strong woman and I seldom throw in the towel on any project or commitment I make. I'm sure much of this is from observing her strength.

I saw Dad care for Gary, and I saw how sensitive he was with his siblings passing away. So, I know there was a good character in him. What I lived through, was observing a person who didn't follow through on many things, wasn't steady for his family, and communicated very little with the kids. I never had conversations with him as a child. He did provide transportation, but that was not on a personal level. I was a young teenager when he passed away. As an adult, it took me a lot of years to learn how to communicate on a true level with men. I had a view of them being the head of the house, but not an awareness that I had a valued opinion in the home.

I knew that Dad drank too much and that he had medical issues. I just accepted this as the way life was. We appreciated what we had and asked for very few things. I am still very accepting of most individuals and their shortcomings with very little criticism or judgment. I do not need things, even now, to make me happy.

... and Siblings

Irene is the perfect eldest child in my mind. She has always seemed so organized and put together. As a child, when we went to the racetrack with her, she always had a cooler with snacks, blankets to sit on, and extra jackets for cool evenings. When eating at her house, she got the plates ready in the kitchen and then served them. She has always had up-to-date and current styles in her home and clothing. Serving people and making them feel comfortable all the time is just second nature to her.

The word that comes to mind when I think of Cathy is motion! She is always on the go, off to do her errands, off to her next project, or to her next social gathering. She loves being around people. She tries to visit with everyone and make them comfortable at any gathering. She is organized, follows through on her commitments, and keeps track of everything going on in family members' and friends' lives. While sometimes hasty in her thoughts of a situation, she is always willing to listen to a different perspective and adjust her thinking. Throughout her life, she has continued to grow and learn and take on new projects joyfully. She is very dedicated to all her family members.

I think of Noreen as being a doer. She willingly does any task that is being asked of her without attitude. She is very talented in her sewing and yarn work and very generous in sharing them. She is adaptable to her living situation. She and her family have lived in many different homes, from living with in-laws, a mobile home park, building a home, and traveling full time in an RV and apartments. She has never been frustrated in any of these environments. She and Tim have had many hobbies and interests over the years, and they commit to them wholeheartedly at the time. She gets on board with each new endeavor and does so willingly. She is a giver of her time and talents, especially with church and mission projects.

Ginger always seemed 'bigger than life' to me when I was growing up. I loved her clothes, the friends she had, and how busy and active she was. She was always out doing something. When she went to airline school in Minnesota and then on to Washington, D.C., this just continued the image. As I got older, however, it was a joy to get to know her as a person, have conversations with her, and continue to respect her professionalism. She is very dedicated to any project she chooses to do, and she does it with every 't' crossed and 'i' dotted. She has always loved company and treated them like royalty in her home. She has had the most life experiences of any of the siblings with her travels and high-level job, but she has stayed humble, gracious, and dedicated to her family.

Linda has always been right by my side. The closest sister to me in age, she allowed me to be the playful younger sister, probably 'getting away' with a lot more than she ever did. Linda was the oldest of the 'younger' kids and we were glad to have her on 'our side' of the lineup. The four of us younger kids played easily with each other and had very few squabbles. She was and is, a steady, constant, quiet supporter for me. She has moved through life quietly and patiently doing her own things; jobs, marriage, gardening, traveling, and never making a big show of any of it. She let everyone zip around her and then was right there to listen and laugh at all the stories and circumstances as they played out around her. Linda is very aware of what is going on with her friends and family and is always just a phone call away.

While Norm was the other busy, more active playmate for me, he kept himself busy doing his own thing much of the time. Maybe this was his youthful way of functioning in a house full of girls. He was on the quiet side conversationally, although he enjoyed cards and games along with the rest of us. He always seemed studious to me and got good grades without trying overly hard. Joining the US Navy right after high school gave him the independence that seemed to be a part of his nature anyway. Throughout his life, he has continued to read, study, and learn new techniques for every facet of being a homeowner and creating efficiency. He is smart, still easygoing, mellow, and easy to hang out with.

I have a 16x24 photo of Gary and me as newborns. It was featured in the local photographer's store window as a display for a time.

PART FIVE
OUR HERITAGE

1719 – 1946

A view into the
lives of our ancestors

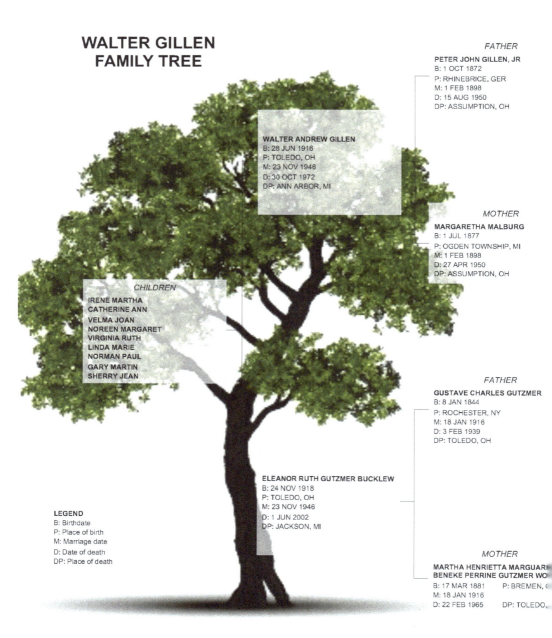

WALTER GILLEN FAMILY TREE

FATHER
PETER JOHN GILLEN, JR
B: 1 OCT 1872
P: RHINEBRICE, GER
M: 1 FEB 1898
D: 15 AUG 1950
DP: ASSUMPTION, OH

WALTER ANDREW GILLEN
B: 28 JUN 1916
P: TOLEDO, OH
M: 23 NOV 1946
D: 30 OCT 1972
DP: ANN ARBOR, MI

MOTHER
MARGARETHA MALBURG
B: 1 JUL 1877
P: OGDEN TOWNSHIP, MI
M: 1 FEB 1898
D: 27 APR 1950
DP: ASSUMPTION, OH

CHILDREN
**IRENE MARTHA
CATHERINE ANN
VELMA JOAN
NOREEN MARGARET
VIRGINIA RUTH
LINDA MARIE
NORMAN PAUL
GARY MARTIN
SHERRY JEAN**

FATHER
GUSTAVE CHARLES GUTZMER
B: 8 JAN 1844
P: ROCHESTER, NY
M: 18 JAN 1916
D: 3 FEB 1939
DP: TOLEDO, OH

ELEANOR RUTH GUTZMER BUCKLEW
B: 24 NOV 1918
P: TOLEDO, OH
M: 23 NOV 1946
D: 1 JUN 2002
DP: JACKSON, MI

LEGEND
B: Birthdate
P: Place of birth
M: Marriage date
D: Date of death
DP: Place of death

MOTHER
**MARTHA HENRIETTA MARGUARI
BENEKE PERRINE GUTZMER WO**
B: 17 MAR 1881   P: BREMEN, (
M: 18 JAN 1916
D: 22 FEB 1965   DP: TOLEDO,

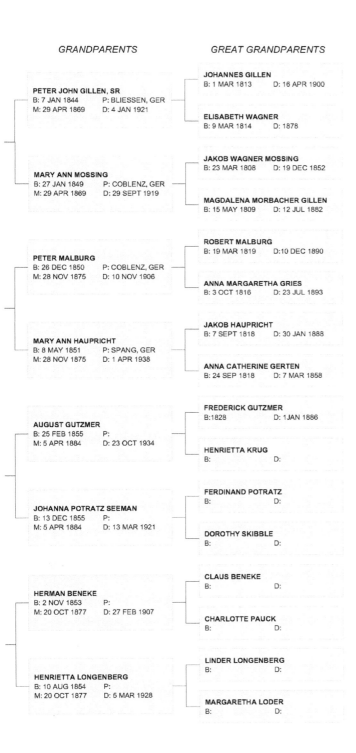

GRANDPARENTS

GREAT GRANDPARENTS

PETER JOHN GILLEN, SR
B: 7 JAN 1844   P: BLIESSEN, GER
M: 29 APR 1869   D: 4 JAN 1921

JOHANNES GILLEN
B: 1 MAR 1813   D: 16 APR 1900

ELISABETH WAGNER
B: 9 MAR 1814   D: 1878

MARY ANN MOSSING
B: 27 JAN 1849   P: COBLENZ, GER
M: 29 APR 1869   D: 29 SEPT 1919

JAKOB WAGNER MOSSING
B: 23 MAR 1808   D: 19 DEC 1852

MAGDALENA MORBACHER GILLEN
B: 15 MAY 1809   D: 12 JUL 1882

PETER MALBURG
B: 26 DEC 1850   P: COBLENZ, GER
M: 28 NOV 1875   D: 10 NOV 1906

ROBERT MALBURG
B: 19 MAR 1819   D:10 DEC 1890

ANNA MARGARETHA GRIES
B: 3 OCT 1816   D: 23 JUL 1893

MARY ANN HAUPRICHT
B: 8 MAY 1851   P: SPANG, GER
M: 28 NOV 1875   D: 1 APR 1938

JAKOB HAUPRICHT
B: 7 SEPT 1818   D: 30 JAN 1888

ANNA CATHERINE GERTEN
B: 24 SEP 1818   D: 7 MAR 1858

AUGUST GUTZMER
B: 25 FEB 1855   P:
M: 5 APR 1884   D: 23 OCT 1934

FREDERICK GUTZMER
B:1828   D: 1JAN 1886

HENRIETTA KRUG
B: D:

JOHANNA POTRATZ SEEMAN
B: 13 DEC 1855   P:
M: 5 APR 1884   D: 13 MAR 1921

FERDINAND POTRATZ
B: D:

DOROTHY SKIBBLE
B: D:

HERMAN BENEKE
B: 2 NOV 1853   P:
M: 20 OCT 1877   D: 27 FEB 1907

CLAUS BENEKE
B: D:

CHARLOTTE PAUCK
B: D:

HENRIETTA LONGENBERG
B: 10 AUG 1854   P:
M: 20 OCT 1877   D: 5 MAR 1928

LINDER LONGENBERG
B: D:

MARGARETHA LODER
B: D:

✺

Chapter 18

WALTER AND ELEANOR'S LINEAGE

By Sherry Gillen Butcher Belmonte, Noreen Gillen Litchard,
and Virginia "Ginger" Gillen Poole

OUR FAMILY IS descended from courageous German immigrants who left for America searching for a better life for their families. Our ancestors were hard-working and determined. They had faith in God and were devoted to their families. They experienced success, failures, joys, and sorrows and left the family with values and traditions rich in faith and love.

Walter's family has been traced back to the early 1700s to Johannes Jacob Gillen and Catharina Klein, Walter's fourth great-grandparents. Eleanor's family has been traced back to 1830 to Frederick Gutzmer and Henrietta Klug, Eleanor's great-grandparents. Members from both families immigrated to America between 1852-1885 at varying ages. Some were young children with their parents, some were single men and women, and some were married couples with, and without, young children.

There was tremendous change occurring in Central Europe when many of our ancestors were born. Those born before 1806 lived when Germany was known as the Holy Roman Empire. Those born through 1871 lived when the area was known as Prussia. Family members are also listed as being from Allemagne, the French pronunciation for Germany. Much of the immigration to America occurred because the area was experiencing civil unrest, crop failure, land, and job shortages, rising taxes, and famine.

Most of the Gillen family was born in what is currently the German states of Saarland and Rhineland-Palatine in southwest Germany. Most of the Gutzmer family was born in Hamburg and Bremen in northern Germany. While both families were from what is now Germany, Walter often said the family spoke two different languages, meaning dialects. Families from the north spoke Low German and the families from the southwest spoke High German.

Walter's maternal great grandparents Robert Malburg and Margaretha Gries were our first family members to immigrate to America. They traveled as a young married couple in 1852 with two small sons. Walter's Grandfather Peter Malburg was one of these children. Walter's maternal Grandmother Mary Ann Haupright was 21 when she came to America in 1872. Robert's and Margaretha's three additional children were the first Malburg's born in America. Walter's mother Margaretha was one of these children.

Walter's paternal grandparents Peter John Gillen, Sr. and Mary Ann Mossing immigrated to America in 1875 as a young married couple sailing with three small children. Walter's father Peter John, Jr. was one of these children and was 3 years old at the time. Six more children were born to this family once they were settled and were the first Gillen's born in America. The family arrived at Ellis Island on the S.S. Oder on April 8, 1876, and settled in Assumption, Ohio, in Fulton County where they raised their family.

Eleanor's paternal grandparents, August Gutzmer and Johanna Potratz, did not come to America as a couple. August was 26 years old when he immigrated in 1881. Johanna was 16 years old in 1871 when she immigrated. Eleanor's father, Gustave and his siblings were the first Gutzmer's born in America.

Eleanor's maternal grandparents Herman Beneke and Henrietta Longenberg immigrated as a young married couple. He arrived first in 1884 at age 31. Henrietta followed one year later at age 31 in 1885 with their four children. Eleanor's mother, Martha was one of these children and 3 years old at the time. Two more daughters were born after they settled in America.

We are fortunate that Eleanor was such a history buff and the family historian. She collected much of our family history at reunions and other gatherings and would then organize the photographs and record the stories. We have many stories of strength and stability along with traumatic and heartbreaking events. This compiled history reveals that our human nature is to survive, grow and prosper. As children, we were taught that hard times come along with the good times. This strength comes from strong family ties bound by deep love and acceptance. What a perfect gift!

Walter's Paternal Lineage

Generation No. 1 (Walter's fourth GREAT-GRANDPARENTS)

JOHANN JACOB GILLEN was born February 3, 1725, in Heisterberg, Trierland, Holy Roman Empire and died in Bliessen, Trierland, Holy Roman Empire in 1778 at age 53. Johann married **MARIA KATHARINA** "Catharina" **KLEIN** on January 17, 1750. Catharina was born in Bliessen, Saarland, Germany in 1719 and died in 1799 in Oberthal, Saarland, Germany. They had seven children: Margaretha (1750), Margaretha (1752), Maria (1753), Elisabetha (1755), Catharina (1758), **Johannes** (1760), and Petrus (1763).

Generation No 2. (Walter's third GREAT-GRANDPARENTS)

JOHANNES GILLEN was born in Bliessen, Trierland, Holy Roman Empire in 1760 and died in Bliessen, Prueben, Germany in 1820 at age 70. Johannes married **ANNA PLATTNER or** "Plettener" on February 21, 1786. Anna was born in Bliessen, Saarland, Germany in 1761 and died in Bliessen, Saarland, Germany in 1843 at age 82. They had six children: **Peter** (1786), Maria (1789), Margaretha (1791), Anna Maria (1794), Elisabeth (1797), and Maria (1801).

Generation No. 3 (Walter's second GREAT-GRANDPARENTS)

PETER GILLEN was born in Bliessen, Saarland, Allemagne in 1786 and died in Bliessen, Preussen, Allemagne in 1822 at age 36. Peter married **JOHANNA JUNG** on February 8, 1809. Johanna was born in Bliessen, Trierland, Holy Roman Empire in 1788 and died in Wallesweilerhof, Preuben, Germany in 1857 at age 69. They had four children: Matthias (1810), **Johannes** (1813), Johan Nikolaus (1815) and Peter (1818).

Generation No. 4 (Walter's GREAT-GRANDPARENTS)

JOHANN (JOHANNES) GILLEN was born in Wallesweilerhof, French Republic in 1813 and died in Wallesweilerhof, Saarland, Germany in 1900 at age 87. Johannes married **ELISABETH WAGNER** on February 18, 1841. Elisabeth was born in Bliessen, Saare, Allemagne in 1814 and died in Bliessen, Sarre, Allemagne in 1878 at age 64. They had eight children: Anna Maria (1842), **Peter John** (1844), Barbara, (1846), Johanne (1848), Johann Nikolaus (1851), Jakob (1854), Nikolaus (1856) and Catharine (1857).

Generation No. 5 (Walter's GRANDPARENTS)

PETER JOHN GILLEN, SR. was born in Bliessen, Saarland, Germany on January 7, 1844, and died January 4, 1921, in Amboy Township (Assumption) Fulton, Ohio, three days shy of his 77th birthday. Peter married **MARY ANN MOSSING** on April 29, 1869, in Oberkirchen, Preuben, Germany. Mary Ann was born to Jakob Wagner Mossing and Magdalena Morbacher Gillen on January 27, 1849, in Oberkirchen, Preuben, Germany, and died September 29, 1919, in Amboy Township, Fulton, Ohio, at age 69.

Peter and Mary Ann immigrated in 1875 and had nine children: Magdalina (Lena) (1870), **Peter John Jr.** (1872), Mary Ann (1875), Catherine (Kate) (1877), John (1880), Anthony (Tone) (1882), Mariam Elizabeth (1885), Francis (Frank) Joseph (1888), and Rose Anna (1892).

On April 24, 1876, Peter purchased approximately 40 acres of land on a building site one mile south of Assumption on Highway 20 (Central Avenue) for $1,350 from John Bettinger. This became the family farm with a farmhouse and outbuildings. The land was one half mile deep with woods and a stream at the back. In October 1888, Peter bought another 80 acres of wooded land from D.E. and Elizabeth Swank for $2,400 across Central Avenue to add to his building site. This 120-acre farm remained in the family until 1959.

In May 1879 Peter purchased 40 acres for $1,400 from Peter and Mary McGrory. This property was later the home of his daughter, Lena, and Charles Eisel's family. In September 1888 Peter purchased 40 acres across the highway from the farmhouse for one dollar from Thomas and Elizabeth McKinney (nee Caragher). This property was passed on to his son, Tone.

Peter, Jr. remained on the 120-acre farm and raised his family there. A gate was built between the farm and Tone's property on Sylvania Avenue as the two brothers worked hand in hand on both farms. Tone and his sister Kate never married and eventually bought a house in Assumption and lived there together.

PETER JOHN GILLEN, JR. was born October 1, 1872, in Rhinebrice, Germany, and died August 15, 1950, in Assumption, Ohio at age 78. Peter married **MARGARETHA MALBURG** on February 1, 1898, in Assumption, Ohio. Their wedding day was minus 17 degrees, the coldest day ever recorded at that time. Margaretha was born July 1, 1877, and died April 27, 1950, in Assumption, Ohio, at age 72.

Peter was three years old when he immigrated to America with his family in 1875. He didn't speak English when he started school and continued to speak German at home throughout his life. Peter and Margararetha "Maggie" had nine children: Cecilia (Cely) (1899), Edward Peter (Eddie) (1900), Louis John (McGrory) (1902), Martin Joseph (1903), Arnold John (Spike) (1905), Leslie Robert (Poodle) (1907), Marcella Rose (Sally) (1910), Cletus Frederick (Charlie) (1914) and **Walter Andrew** "Walt" (1916).

Peter was a very innovative man. To improve the farm productivity, Peter and Tone created irrigation ditches. They hitched scoops to the horses to dig up and dump a load of dirt, then backed the horses down for another load. After they dug these ditches, they tiled them. It was really hard work.

The farmhouse was two stories and lit with kerosene lamps and lanterns until sometime in the 1920s when Peter generated his own electricity before lighting was available in the rural areas. He had Duco Electric lights, the forerunner to General Electric. He used a generator in the basement with batteries he had to keep charged and ran wires into the house. This provided electric lighting in the house. Peter built a cistern in the cellar. Pipes connected to the cistern provided running water into the kitchen and bathroom for washing and cleaning. A hand pump outside provided drinking water.

Peter also built a windmill over the milk house where he placed cans of milk so a stirrer could agitate the cooled milk. He then took the milk cans in the cart out to Central Avenue to sell. Central Avenue was the main highway built on an Indian trail that went from Monroe, Michigan, to Toledo, Ohio, to Chicago, Illinois.

Approximately 70 of the 120-acres was farmed. There was no machinery in the early years. Plowing and discing were done by the farmer walking behind the plow or disk drawn by two horses, and then the fields were ready to plant. This was Peter's favorite way to plant the fields. The farm was quite productive, in part, because of the stream running through the property. Crops were mostly corn, wheat, and oats.

Farming was a year-round occupation that varied with the seasons. The family raised hogs, cattle, and chickens to provide meat, dairy products, and eggs. They grew field crops to bed and feed the livestock and sold what was not needed. The harvested crops were stored on the farm in the barn, corn crib, granary, silo or sold. Over the years tractors and other farm machinery were added.

Once or twice a year, Peter went to Toledo with a team of horses and a wagon to sell and trade. He went as far as Talmadge Road (Franklin Park today) and stopped at the home of his friend George Shetter to rest and water the horses. He spent the night and had breakfast with George and his wife before continuing to Toledo. He often sold pigs and bought salt and staples needed on the farm. Peter was said to be a good money manager. He returned to George's home to rest again before heading home and arriving around midnight. The wagon could travel over the snow and sometimes the wheel tracks remained all winter.

After the farm work was done for the day, Peter often went one mile into Metamora to have a beer. One of his favorite drinks was a Blind Robin – a small fish that was drunk with the beer. He also enjoyed smoking a pipe.

When the grandchildren were older, Peter paid them five cents to kill the sparrows in the barn. He did not like the sparrows fouling the hay with their droppings. He had a trap with a door and food. When the sparrows went through the door for the food they were trapped. Once the sparrows were in the trap, the adults and children grabbed the birds and twisted their heads. Peter also paid the children to clean out the chicken coop.

Peter walked with a cane due to an amputated toe. He retired from farming when he was almost 50 because of heart problems and let his sons run the farm. He often sat outside the local bar in Metamora and tried to hook the school kids with his cane as they passed by.

Peter loved automobiles. He and his brothers always had the most up-to-date car. Peter bought each of his sons a car on their 18th birthdays. He, however, was not a good driver and drove through the back of the garage more than once. He was killed driving through a barricade and into a deep roadbed on Central Avenue.

Generation No. 7

WALTER ANDREW GILLEN was born June 28, 1916, in Assumption, Ohio, and died October 30, 1972, in Ann Arbor, Michigan, at age 56. Walter married **ELEANOR RUTH GUTZMER BUCKLEW** on November 23, 1946, in Toledo. Eleanor was born November 24, 1918, in Toledo, Ohio, and died June 1, 2002, in Jackson, Michigan at age 82.

They had nine children: Irene Martha (1947), Catherine Ann (Cathy) (1949), Velma Joan (1949), Noreen Margaret (1950), Virginia Ruth (Ginger) (1951), Linda Marie (1953), Norman Paul (1956) and twins, Gary Martin, and Sherry Jean (1957).

Walter's Maternal Lineage

Generation No. 1 (Walter's GREAT-GRANDPARENTS)

ROBERT MALBURG was born March 19, 1819, in Klotten, Rheinland-Palatinate, Germany, and died December 10, 1890, in Toledo, Ohio, at age 71. Robert married **MARGARETHA GRIES** on September 5, 1843, in Coblenz. Margaretha was born October 3, 1816, in Coblenz, Rheinland-Palatinate, Germany, and died July 23, 1893, in Toledo at age 77. They had five children: **Peter** (1850), Nicholas (1852), Mary (1855), Anna (1860) and John (1861). Peter and Nicholas were born in Germany and the youngest three children were born in Toledo. Mary died at age 16.

Generation No. 2 (Walter's GRANDPARENTS)

PETER MALBURG was born December 26, 1850, in Coblenz, Rheinland-Palatinate Germany, and died November 10, 1906, in Ogden Township, Michigan, at age 55. He married **MARY ANN HAUPRICHT** on November 28, 1875, in Toledo, Ohio. She was born May 8, 1851, in Spang, Rheinland-Palatinate, Germany, to Jakob Haupricht and Kathryn Gerten and died November 4, 1938, in Ogden Township, at age 75. Peter came to America with his family in 1852 when he was two years old. They had six children: **Margaretha** (1877), Robert (Rob) (1879), Joseph J. (Joe) (1881), Ann (1883), Rose Magdaline (Rose) (1886), and Frederick Leo (Fred) (1897).

Mary Ann's mother died when she was six years old. She arrived in America as a young woman of 21 in 1872. After they married, Peter and Mary Ann settled their family in Ogden Township, (now Blissfield), Michigan. Their son, Fred served in World War I.

MARGARETHA MALBURG was born July 1, 1877, in Ogden Township, Michigan, and died April 27, 1950, in Assumption, Ohio at age 72. Margaretha married **PETER JOHN JR. GILLEN** on February 1, 1898, in Assumption. Peter was born October 1, 1872, in Rhinebrice, Germany, and died August 15, 1950, in Assumption at age 77.

Margaretha was known as Maggie or Mag most of her life. She and Peter were blessed to celebrate their 50-year Golden Anniversary together. They both died the same year.

Margaretha and Peter raised their nine children on their farm in Assumption, Ohio. The farm was a typical, busy place with fields, animals, gardens, and children to care for. Margaretha raised chickens in a brooder house to sell. She cooked on a wood-burning stove with a tank on the side to heat water. She baked eight loaves of bread two-to-three times per week to feed the large family. They had doughnuts for breakfast, and cookies, cake and pie were always available. Before school, the older children packed school lunches while the younger children cleared and washed the dishes.

During the threshing and harvest season, neighboring farmers moved from farm to farm to help everyone harvest their crops. The women went to each other's homes to help prepare food for the men working in the fields during the harvest.

The farmhouse ceilings were high, and the kitchen cupboards were floor to ceiling. In later years, Maggie's arthritis made it difficult for her to reach the higher shelves, so she kept the everyday dishes on the lower shelves.

She was diagnosed with bladder cancer just a few months before her death.

WALTER ANDREW married **ELEANOR RUTH GUTZMER BUCKLEW.** They were married for 25 years.

Eleanor's Paternal Lineage

Generation No. 1 (Eleanor's GREAT- GRANDPARENTS)

Frederick Gutzmer was born in 1828 and died in 1886 in Berlin, Germany, and married Henrietta Krug.

Generation No. 2 (Eleanor's GRANDPARENTS)

AUGUST GUTZMER was born February 25, 1855, in Germany and died October 23,1934, in Toledo, Ohio, at age 79. August immigrated in 1881 at age 26 and married **JOHANNA POTRATZ SEEMAN** on April 5, 1884. Johanna was born December 13, 1855, in Germany to Ferdinand Potratz and Dorothy Skibble and died March 13, 1921, in Toledo, Ohio, at age 65. August married Mimmie Radtke on March 22, 1922, at age 67.

In Germany, as a young girl, Johanna fell in love with August Gutzmer. Her parents forced her to marry JOHN SEEMAN, an older gentleman who was established and could provide security. He was born in 1831 in Prussia and was 25 years older than Johanna. Shortly after her arrival in America in 1871 she married John (known as Henry in the family) on January 6, 1872, in Toledo. John had an 11-year-old son, William, at the time of their marriage.

August and Johanna had four children together: Mary (1875), Henry (1877), Charles (1879), and Emma (1880). Emma died at age 36. John (Henry) and Johanna were married 12 years when he died. Johanna was said to have had 16 pregnancies and 10 children raised to adulthood. Four children were from her marriage to John Seeman and six children were from her second marriage to August Gutzmer.

John died in 1881 as listed on his daughter Mary's Ohio Marriage Record. After his death Johanna married August. They had seven children together: **Gustave** (1884), Alma (1889), Bertha (1892), William (1894), Eleanor (stillborn), Lillian (1897) and Della (1899).

In 1887, August and Johanna moved the family to the German section of Toledo and raised their blended family there. August was a cabinet maker. Eleanor was 16 years old when August died. She remembered annual family reunions being held at her grandfather's home and many Christmases being shared with the Seeman and Gutzmer relatives.

Generation No. 3 (Eleanor's PARENTS)

GUSTAVE CHARLES GUTZMER was born January 8, 1884, in Rochester, New York, three months before his parents married in Toledo, Ohio. He died on February 3,1939, in Toledo at age 55. Gustave married **MARTHA MARGUERITE HENRIETTA BENEKE PERRINE** on January 18, 1916, in Pasadena, California, at age 32. Martha was born February 17, 1881, in Bremen, Germany, and died February 22, 1965, in Toledo at age 84. They had two children, **Eleanor Ruth,** and Harold Leroy.

Gustave was the eldest of his siblings and had five half-brothers and sisters from Johanna's first marriage. When Gustave was 3-years old, the family moved to the German section of Toledo known as Der Hugel (The Hill). He later moved to Pasadena, California. Gustave worked in a glass factory at this time. While in California, he met Martha while visiting an alligator farm. She was taller than he and moved behind him so he could see. This started their courtship, and they were married six weeks later.

Gustave and Martha returned to Toledo to live. Gustave was 34 when Eleanor was born. She was named after his baby sister who was stillborn. Harold was born a year-and-a-half later. Gustave was an acetylene welder at the Willy's Overland Automobile Factory. When he was 46, he fell 25 feet from a scaffold and landed on his feet. He shattered his left ankle and split the femur in his right leg. He spent 18 weeks in the Toledo Hospital with a 50-pound weight on his ankle. He made a brace for his leg to be able to walk with one cane instead of two.

When he was unable to go back to his job after the accident, he and Martha opened a sidewalk business in front of their house. The backyard was used as parking for Willy's Overland Automobile Factory. Within three years they built a small storefront onto the house with the name "The American G. Gutzmer and Son" and was successful enough to hire a young girl named Olga to work for him. Olga was said to be able to cause objects to fly around the room with a Ouija Board.

Gustave loved fishing, traveling and woodworking. When he went fishing it was an all-day outing. He got up at 4 a.m., took a streetcar, then the Interurban to Point Place, rented a rowboat, and fished in the Maumee Bay on Lake Erie. The family went to Greenwood Lake in Long Island, New York, annually for many years. While there one summer, Gustave built a porch on Catherine and Otto Sakat's (Martha's sister) lake house. The family went on many local outings together. The Gutzmer family had an annual family reunion at his parent's house on the south side of Toledo. These were large gatherings as there were 25 cousins on the Seeman side of the family and eight cousins on the Gutzmer side of the family.

After Eleanor's marriage to Arnold Bucklew the new couple went together with her parents to Cedar Point, Ohio, and Clear Lake, Indiana, throughout the summer. Gustave passed away unexpectedly from a heart attack one year after Eleanor's marriage. After he died, lawyers proved the heart attack was caused from his work accident, and Martha received workers compensation for many years.

Generation No. 4

ELEANOR RUTH GUTZMER was born November 24, 1918, in Toledo, Ohio and died on June 1, 2002, in Jackson, Michigan, at age 83. Eleanor was married to Arnold Bucklew from February 2, 1938, to February 18, 1940. Arnold was born January 20, 1909, in Toledo, and died February18, 1940, at age 31. They did not have any children. Eleanor married **WALTER ANDREW GILLEN** on November 23, 1946, in Toledo, Ohio, and they had nine children together.

Eleanor's Maternal Lineage

Generation No. 1 (Eleanor's GREAT-GRANDPARENTS)

Clause Heinrick Beneke and Charlotte Friedrike Pauck were Herman's parents as listed on his German Death Certificate in 1907.

Generation No. 2 (Eleanor's GRANDPARENTS)

HERMANN (HERMAN) BENEKE was born November 2, 1853, in Bremen, Germany, and died February 27, 1907, in Hamburg, Germany, at age 53. Herman married **HENRIETTA LONGENBERG** on October 20, 1877, in Bremen. Henrietta was born August 10, 1854, in Germany to Linder Longenberg and Margaretha Loder and died March 5, 1928, in Coney Island, Brooklyn, New York, at age 73. Herman and Henrietta had four children while living in Bremen: Herman (Tom) (1879), Reinhardt (1880), **Martha** (1881) and Alexander (1884). Two more children were born after Herman came to America in 1884 and Henrietta joined him in 1885: Catherine (Bep) (1888), and Marguerite (1890) who died when she was 3-months old.

Henrietta is listed as Margarethe Auguste Henrietta on her son's birth certificate from Hamburg, Germany. Henrietta's father, Linder, belonged to an aristocratic German family. He fell in love with an upstairs maid and was disinherited. He left the family, married Margaretha Loder, and became a farmer. They had two daughters: Henrietta and Marie. When he was 31, he drank ice-cold milk on a hot summer day and died.

Herman was a mathematician and got into legal trouble in Germany. He moved his wife and four children to Hamburg, Germany, where they stayed for one year before joining him in America. Herman's sister Catherine "Tante Teenie" arrived from Germany with the family. They settled in the Tenement District of New York City.

Herman was an alcoholic. At times when he came home in a drunken rage, he made Henrietta sit at the table across from him. He threatened to kill her with a butcher knife if she moved. The children would hide behind the couch or Tante Teenie would hide them.

In 1893, Herman went to prison for embezzlement. He was arrested in Canada and initially incarcerated in Sing Sing Prison in Ossining, New York. He was moved to a local county jail three days later. His jail sentence was five years, but he was released 18 months early for good behavior. He never returned to live with his family. The last time he was seen was in 1897 along the Bowery in New York City. His 16-year-old daughter Martha saw him on the streets in New York and gave him a dollar. At some point after his release from jail he returned to Germany where he then died.

In 1896, with Herman in jail, Henrietta petitioned the courts for a divorce. The divorce was denied because the youngest child was only seven-years old. The family lived in many areas of New York, including Oakwood Heights, Queens, Long Island, Woodside, and Staten Island.

Henrietta worked hard to raise her children. She bought and renovated houses and raised rabbits for their pelts. Her son Reinie died at age 12 from a ruptured ear drum after his schoolteacher boxed his ears and caused them to become infected. Reinie was a young artist. Ginger has his drawings today.

Her son Herman Jr. "Tom" changed his name to Tom Bennett because their father was in prison. Tom also made his two sisters Martha and Catherine "Bep" change their names. People called them the Bennett sisters. They later changed their name back to Beneke, although Martha's name also shows up as Bennett in some later documents.

Henrietta's son Alex was a New York policeman. He married and was later divorced. During WWI he was a conscientious objector and on Christmas Day, 1917, he was sent to Mineola Prison. He was mentally unstable after his release and died in the Brooklyn State Hospital in Brooklyn, New York, at age 48.

Henrietta was very close to her family. In later years, one of her grand-daughters was molested and Henrietta took her to Florida to have some time away. Henrietta visited her adult children for holidays and went on vacations with them. She visited Martha and her family in Toledo and vacationed at Put-In-Bay, Ohio, with them in 1927. She ended her life in 1928 by committing suicide from gas poisoning using the stove in her home.

Generation No. 3 (Eleanor's PARENTS)

MARTHA MARGUERITE HENRIETTA BENEKE PERRINE was born March 17, 1881, in Bremen, Germany, and died February 22, 1965, in Toledo, Ohio, one month shy of her 84th birthday. Martha was married to John Perrine from 1913-1915 when he died. She was married to **GUSTAVE GUTZMER** from January18, 1916, until February 3, 1939, when he died. Martha was married to George Wood from July 25, 1947, until her death.

Martha was 3 years old when her family emigrated from Germany in 1884. Her family initially lived in the tenement section of New York City Martha was raised in Staten Island and Long Island, New York. She only completed the fourth grade. Later she attended night classes at the Pratt Institute of Art and the Toledo Museum of Arts. When Martha was 14, she went to work as a nursemaid for a wealthy family who owned a hotel on Long Island.

Martha helped sew tents for the Spanish American War (1898) when she was 19. Later she was a designer of ladies' neck wear at the Triangle Shirtwaist Factory. The shops were located on the 8th, 9th, and 10th floors of the Asch/Brown building in New York City. On March 25, 1911, a fire broke out and 146 workers died. It was common at the time to lock the stairwell and exit doors to prevent workers from taking unauthorized breaks, and to reduce theft. Tom was worried that Martha was in the fire, but she was not. Martha continued a life-long career of designing women's clothing.

During these years, Martha met a young woman, Julia, who had been beaten and mistreated, and the family took her into their home as a boarder.

Martha married John Perrine when she was 32 and became a widow two years later. John was accused of molesting Martha's niece Catherine. He was not guilty of this act and was exonerated. However, he was tormented by the accusation and drown himself near Newfoundland in 1915. Following his death, Martha moved to California.

Martha was in Los Angeles near Angels Flight (a landmark incline railway). While visiting an alligator farm, she moved toward the back of the crowd so a shorter man could see better. The man was Gustave Gutzmer.

Martha was 37 when **Eleanor** was born and 39 when Harold was born. Martha was strict and very involved with the children's lives. She sewed all of their clothing, including winter coats and hats made from rabbit skins. Eleanor had her first store-bought dress when she was 12. Her mother also made many Halloween costumes for the children and herself. They enjoyed this holiday. One year Martha sewed a nun costume for herself and had a difficult time getting her photos developed when she was criticized for mocking nuns.

Martha taught both of her children to embroider. She had a belief that 'Satan finds mischief for idle hands to do." Eleanor embroidered a dress at age 6-and-a-half.

The family was very active. They visited Martha's sister Bep on Long Island, New York; New York City; Cedar Point, Ohio; the Port Clinton Lighthouse in Ohio; and many neighboring parks. Some of Martha's good friends: Mother Ruth, Mrs. Sara Poole, Lillian Trautwein or Ernie and Beulah were often with them on these outings. In 1928, Martha took a summer-long job on Put-In-Bay Island, Lake Erie, Ohio. Each of the kids came and stayed with her for two weeks at a time. Martha was a strong swimmer. When she was teaching Eleanor to swim, Eleanor panicked and grabbed her around the neck. They both almost drowned. Once she got Eleanor safely to shore, she went back into the water and swam so that she wouldn't lose her nerve to swim in the future.

Martha and Gustave were hard workers and resourceful. They ran a boarding house in the upstairs rooms of their home. When Gustave was injured in 1928 and couldn't return to work, he opened and managed a store outside of their house. Martha was a designer and dressmaker for private clients late into her 70s when her eyesight got too poor. She continued to sew many of the dresses for her granddaughters.

Martha and Gustave watched their children grow into young adults. Eleanor married Arnold and Harold went into the U.S. Navy. Eleanor became a widow after being married only two years. Harold attended the University of Michigan after his three-year military service ended. Eleanor remarried in 1946. Martha married George E. Wood in 1947. One month later Harold married Pearl Wood Heller. Pearl was George's daughter and had two daughters, Joyce, and Sandra.

Martha and George continued to live in Toledo and see their new grandchildren. During an early morning in February, there was a break-in at their home by the paperboy. As he went upstairs toward the bedroom, Martha came out of her bedroom and was pushed down the stairs by him. She broke her hip and refused help initially. She was finally taken to the hospital where she then died.

ELEANOR RUTH GUTZMER married **WALTER ANDREW GILLEN** on November 23, 1946, in Toledo, Ohio. They had nine children together.

Peter and Margaretha Gillen 1898

Peter and Margaretha Gillen 1949

THE WALTER AND ELEANOR GILLEN STORY

August and Johanna Gutzmer
1919

Gustave and Martha Gutzmer
1938

Walter and Eleanor's Lineage

NOTES

1: Walter's Early Life

1.   Noreen Gillen Litchard, *Gillen Family History*. 04.14.2021

2.   622 67 77 GILLEN, Walter Andrew, *Notice of Separation from U.S. Naval Service*. 1/4/46.

2: Eleanor's Early Life

3.   Eleanor R. Bucklew, *Eleanor's Journal* March *19, 1946, to November 23, 1946, Our Wedding*. n.d.

4.   Catherine [Gillen Osborn], Heritage album, *Eleanor R. Gillen*. n.d.

5.   [Eleanor Ruth Gutzmer], *Our Family, A Historical Journal* for Virginia Ruth Gillen. n.d.

3: Farm Life in Ohio

6.   Noreen Litchard, *Gillen Family History*. 04.14.2021

7.   [Irene Gillen Snider], *Heritage Album in loving memory of Walter Andrew Gillen (Dad)*, n.d.

8. [Catherine "Cathy" Gillen Osborn], *Heritage album for Eleanor R. Gillen by Catherine.* n.d.

9. [*Eleanor* Ruth Gutzmer], *Our Family, A Historical Journal* for Virginia Ruth Gillen. n.d.

4: Growing up in Michigan

10. Noreen Litchard, *Gillen Family History.* 04.14.2021

11. [Irene Gillen Snider], *Heritage Album in loving memory of Walter Andrew Gillen (Dad)*, n.d.

5. Eleanor's Coffee Shop

12. Promissory Note August 14, 196,4 signed by Vincent Comstock, Walter Gillen, and Eleanor Gillen

13. Ledger pages: Monday – Aug. 17, 1964, Saturday – Aug. 29, 1964, and October 13 – Monday 1969

6. Home Life after Brooklyn

14. *Deed Time Line*, 7993 Springville Highway, Onsted, Michigan 49265, Cambridge Township, Lenawee County, Michigan, Section 35 NW 5S 2E. 1835 Land Grant to Sylvanus Kinney.

8. Cathy and Dave Osborn

15. whitmanarchive.org/published/LG/1891/poems/27, *Song of Myself.* (Leaves of Grass (1891-1892)) – The Walt Whitman Archive accessed 2023-01-14.

10. Ginger and Jim Poole

16. USS. (2023, January 13). In *Wikipedia*. https://en.wikipedia.org/wiki/USS_Iowa_(BB-61)

17. Britannica, T. Editors of Encyclopaedia. "Grace Hopper." *Encyclopedia Britannica*, January 1, 2023. https://www.britannica.com/biography/Grace-Hopper.

18. https://en.wikipedia.org/wiki/SeanO'Keefe

19. Britannica, T. Editors of Encyclopaedia. "Paul Wolfowitz." *Encyclopedia Britannica*, December 18, 2022. https://www.britannica.com/biography/Paul-Wolfowitz.

20. Nita Scoggan *Pentagon Review*, (Royalty Publishing Company). 1996.

21. Virginia Poole, "*Advanced Concept Technology Demonstration: Acquisition Transition Strategy Effectiveness and Resource Impact.*" SELC Research Project (OUSD (A&T)API/AR, June 1998).

22. United States Capitol Historical Society, *We, the People*. 12th ed., Library of Congress catalog number 81-52034 ISBN 0-9162-00-00-0

23. https://rickover.com

24. https://en.wikipedia.org/wiki/Wayne_E._Meyer

25. https://www.en.wikipedia.org/wiki/WashingtonNavyYard shooting

18. Walter and Eleanor's Lineage

26. [*Eleanor* Ruth Gutzmer], *Our Family, A Historical Journal* for Virginia Ruth Gillen. n.d.

27. Noreen Litchard, *Gillen Family History*. 04.14.2021

28. [Irene Gillen Snider], *Heritage Album in loving memory of Walter Andrew Gillen (Dad)*, n.d.

Printed in the USA
CPSIA information can be obtained
at www.ICGtesting.com
JSHW041957020823
45650JS00004B/7